THE IDEAS-INFORMED SOCIETY

THE IDEAS-INFORMED SOCIETY

Why We Need It and How to Make It Happen

EDITED BY

CHRIS BROWN
University of Warwick, UK

And

GRAHAM HANDSCOMB
University College London, UK

United Kingdom – North America – Japan
India – Malaysia – China

Emerald Publishing Limited
Howard House, Wagon Lane, Bingley BD16 1WA, UK

First edition 2023

Editorial matter and selection © 2023 Chris Brown and Graham Handscomb.
Foreword and the Individual chapters © 2023 The authors.
Published under exclusive licence by Emerald Publishing Limited.

Reprints and permissions service
Contact: permissions@emeraldinsight.com

British Library Cataloguing in Publication Data
A catalogue record for this book is available from the British Library

ISBN: 978-1-83753-013-7 (Print)
ISBN: 978-1-83753-010-6 (Online)
ISBN: 978-1-83753-012-0 (Epub)

INVESTOR IN PEOPLE

TABLE OF CONTENTS

ABOUT THE EDITORS

Chris Brown is Professor in Education and Director of Research at the University of Warwick's Department of Education Studies and Distinguished Visiting Professor, University of Tübingen. Chris has a long-standing interest in how people go about harnessing great ideas to improve the human condition. Traditionally Chris' work has focussed on the education system, but more recently Chris has turned his attention to the 'ideas-informed society' more generally, and how we can ensure ideas are available and used effectively to the benefit of everyone. Chris has written or edited some 21 books and nearly 100 journal articles in the broad sphere of research, evidence and ideas-use.

Graham Handscomb is Honorary Professor with University College London (UCL) and Visiting Professor at University of Bolton, and Durham University, UK. He was previously Professor of Education and Dean of The College of Teachers. He is a fellow of numerous organisations and universities, has written many books and articles over the last 30 years and is editor of a number of journals including *Professional Development Today*. Graham also runs a consultancy service where he provides interim management for medium to large organisations, including schools, local authorities and universities, to help implement complex business critical change in cost-effective, tight timescales. He pioneered the concept of the *Research Engaged School* which has become an internationally adopted practice and policy model.

ABOUT THE CONTRIBUTORS

John Baumber has enjoyed over 35 years of school leadership including being CEO of a Multi Academy Trust and an executive head in three Bolton High Schools before moving to lead schools with Kunskapsskolan in Sweden and the United States. John is at present Director of Education for Global Spirit Ed, facilitating an extensive international group of schools committed to creating high impact from student agency and personalisation. He is also a visiting Professor at Sunderland University. In addition, he leads the Global Research School Partnership encouraging action research by teachers to systematically enhance leadership, teaching and learning.

Vivienne Baumfield is Professor of Education at the University of Exeter where her research focuses on the role of universities in initial and continuing professional learning. In her previous post at the University of Glasgow she was Professor of Pedagogy and the International Dean for Eurasia and South Asia. Prior to taking up her first academic post, Vivienne was a secondary school teacher in the North East of England. Working in both schools and universities has confirmed the importance of valuing the knowledge of practitioners and of building partnerships to promote education in democracy.

Dr Belinda Board is the founding CEO and Chief Psychologist at Peoplewise. She is a Chartered Clinical Psychologist, with a PhD in leadership behaviours and workplace well-being, postgraduate degrees in Organisational and Forensic Psychology, and is a Fellow of the British Psychological Society (FBPsS). She is a visiting Lecturer at Hertfordshire University where she specialises in Leadership, Workplace Culture and Optimising organisational performance through people. Belinda is a world-renowned business psychologist and executive coach practitioner who is passionate about the power of psychology to transform people and organisations all over the world. She has particular interests in building change ready cultures, workplace behaviour transformation, leadership potential and development, high performance teams, psychometric design, positive resilience, strategic thinking and cultural and gender diversity. Her published papers on functional and dysfunctional leadership behaviours and workplace well-being can be found in the *Journal of Affective Disorders*, the *Journal of Psychology, Crime and Law* and the *American Journal of Industrial Medicine*.

Sabra Brock is Chair of the Business & Accounting Department at NYSCAS in Touro University, New York City. She received a PhD in Business Education from NYU in 2007, focusing on trans-formational learning. Dr Brock publishes widely in scholarly journals and with the Touro University Press. She is on the IdeaSpies Advisory Board. Prior to entering academia, Dr Brock held global leadership positions at Citicorp, Colgate-Palmolive, DuPont, Young & Rubicam.

The Revd. Canon Helen Cameron is a presbyter of the Methodist Church. She was ordained in 1991. She currently serves as Chair of the Northampton and the Nottingham & Derby Districts as well as being Moderator of the Free Churches Group and is the Free Church President of Churches Together in England. Helen trained originally as a physiotherapist and after ordination served two churches in Birmingham. She then began a career in theological education and served as Director of Methodist Formation in the Queens Foundation for Ecumenical Theological Formation in Birmingham. Helen wrote 'Living in the Gaze of God' (SCM, 2018) which explores ideas of human and ministerial flourishing. Helen is married to Iain, a retired GP and they have three adult children.

John Castling is an archaeologist, researcher and curator who works to make archaeology engaging and accessible. He's been a field archaeologist, museum curator and educator, and now looks after archaeology on The Auckland Project's estate in Bishop Auckland – including a mediaeval castle and a Roman fort. He's also a PhD student at Durham University exploring Roman and

Early Mediaeval North-East England. John is passionate about using archaeology's power to bring about positive change through people engaging in discovery and curiosity. He has a three-year-old daughter and four-year-old sheepdog, who regularly inspire and exhaust him with unrelenting, unbounded and uncontrollable curiosity!

Professor Sir Paul Collier is Professor of Economics and Public Policy at the Blavatnik School of Government, Oxford University; a Director of the International Growth Centre and a Distinguished Invited Professor at the Paris School of International Affairs, Sciences Po. In *The Future of Capitalism: Facing the New Anxieties* (2017), he attacked the misdirection of public policy and private business that has caused avoidable polarisation and the decline of Britain's regions. Having grown up in South Yorkshire, now the poorest region in England, he advises local and national government on practical ways of regional renewal.

Katherine Crisp is the Founder of Social Innovation for All, a social enterprise on a mission to unleash the creative potential of children and young people to address social challenges through programmes such as the Young Green Briton Challenge and Primary Pioneers. She was previously global lead for youth innovation at UNICEF, scaling UPSHIFT (UNICEF's flagship youth social innovation programme) from 6 countries to its current footprint of 45, alongside designing and delivering global youth social entrepreneurship challenges. Katherine initially qualified as an engineer before working as a strategy consultant. Her work spans sustainable livelihood development in India to new service development and new financing models for disabled children and young people. Katherine is a Fellow of the RSA and Chair of Governors at the Windmills Junior School.

Alastair Donald is Associate Director at Academy of Ideas and co-convenor of Battle of Ideas festival. For the charity Ideas Matter, he organises Living Freedom to allow younger generations to explore the meaning and ideals of freedom. Alastair has worked in the United Kingdom and internationally to develop festivals, exhibitions and curated programmes. He is author of *Letter on Liberty:*

The Scottish Question, co-editor of *The Lure of the City: From Slums to Suburbs* and *The Future of Community: Reports of a Death Greatly Exaggerated* and co-author of mantownhuman's *Manifesto: Towards a New Humanism in Architecture* which featured in *100 Artists' Manifestos* by Penguin Classics.

Professor Sir Les Ebdon CBE DL, after a distinguished career as an award-winning Professor of Analytical Chemistry and University Vice Chancellor, was a highly successful Director of Fair Access to Higher Education. Consequently, he is recognised by the media as one of the leading voices in this country promoting the benefits of higher education and social mobility. Three times he has been cited as one of the 100 'most influential' people in Britain by *Debrett's* and *The Sunday Times*. He received both his BSc and PhD from Imperial College London and has taught in universities in Uganda, Sheffield and Plymouth. He is regarded as having transformed the University of Bedfordshire during his time as Vice Chancellor. He was awarded a CBE in 2009, appointed Her Majesty's Deputy Lieutenant for Bedfordshire in 2011 and knighted in 2018. Currently he chairs the Board of Spurgeon's College, London, a Baptist theological college with degree awarding powers.

Dr Benjamin Freud is an educator, advisor, writer and podcaster. He is the founder of Coconut Thinking, a educational consultancy that creates spaces for emergent learning that contributes to the welfare of the bio-collective – every life form that has an interest in the healthfulness of the planet. He is also the Head of Upper School at Green School Bali and has held several leadership and teaching roles in some of the world's most innovative schools. Benjamin began his career in consulting, where he worked in Silicon Valley, Europe and Japan across different industry sectors.

Dr Sam Fowles is a barrister and author specialising in constitutional law. He is a member of Cornerstone Barristers, Director of the Institute for Constitutional and Democratic Research and a Lecturer at St Edmund Hall, University of Oxford. Sam has acted in many of the leading matters in modern English constitutional law, including *Miller v The Prime Minister* (concerning the unlawful prorogation of parliament in 2019), *Hamilton v Post Office* (the unlawful conviction of Post Office workers) and the parliamentary enquiry into the policing of the Clapham Common vigil for Sarah Everard. He is the author of *Overruled: Confronting Our Vanishing Democracy in 8 Cases* (Oneworld, 2022) and writes a regular column for *Perspective* magazine.

Stéphane Goldstein has been Executive Director of InformAll since 2015, which, through research, analysis and facilitation, promotes the relevance and importance of information literacy. He is the author of reports, articles and other material on the relevance and applicability of IL to a range of settings. As an advocate for IL, he brokers relationships between information professionals and other stakeholders, and facilitates joint projects. He is the coordinator of the Media and Information Literacy Alliance (MILA) and is a Fellow of the Royal Society of Arts (RSA). His prior roles included 10 years spent at the Research Information Network (RIN) with a focus on scholarly communications policy and practice. He previously worked in a range of science and research policy roles at the Medical Research Council and Research Councils, UK.

Charlotte Hankin is co-founder of Coconut Thinking and an international educator with over 23 years' experience in a variety of roles including teacher, leader, school-to-school consultant and education policy advisor for the UK government, working in the United Kingdom, Hong Kong, Saudi Arabia and Thailand. Currently, Charlotte is a homeroom teacher of mixed-aged students, relishing the creativity, technology and collaboration that this community of learners bring. Working at the nexus of theory and practice, Charlotte is also pursuing her PhD in Education with Bath University, exploring how schools frame children's relationships with nature and the natural world.

Valerie Hannon is a global thought leader, inspiring systems to re-think what 'success' will mean in the 21st century, and the implications for education. The co-founder of the Innovation Unit, Valerie is a radical voice for change, whilst grounded in a deep understanding of how education systems currently work. She now works independently to support change programmes across the world. She has advised governments and worked with systems, schools and leaders in education innovation on every continent. Valerie advised the OECD on its *Education 2030* project, and on is its current *High Performing Systems for Tomorrow* programme. She is a regular keynote speaker and facilitator at international conferences and workshops. Her best-selling book *THRIVE* has been highly influential. Valerie was the Australian Learning Lecturer for 2020 on the subject of *The Future School*. The resulting book *FutureSchool* is published by Routledge. In 2021 she received the Edufuturists' award for Outstanding Achievement in Education.

Anne-Lise Harding (she/her) is Senior Liaison Librarian at the House of Commons and Deputy Chair of the CILIP Information Literacy Group (ILG). After graduating with an MA in Librarianship in 2011, she held several roles in the education sector, making the transition to the government sector in 2020. Her role supports both the House of Commons Library and Select Committee Teams, focussing on Information Literacy training, liaison and outreach. She is leading on Information Literacy work to make research for scrutiny more diverse, inclusive and representative. Anne-Lise is currently working on developing the Media and Information Literacy Alliance's (MILA) framework with the support of ILG and the wider information professional community.

Jude Hillary is co-head of the UK Policy and Practice team, leading two of NFER's strategic portfolio areas, namely Systems and Structures, which incorporate school funding and accountability, and Optimal Pathways, which incorporates education to employment and social mobility. He is also the principal investigator of a large Nuffield funded research programme entitled 'The Skills Imperative 2035: Essential skills for tomorrow's workforce'. Jude has directed several quantitative research projects including: the evolving nature of the school system; University Technical Colleges; projects on free schools; and social selection in top comprehensives in England, Scotland and Wales. He was the principal investigator of a major quantitative research project on teacher retention and turnover, funded by the Nuffield Foundation. Recently, Jude has overseen work to develop new longer-term post 16 destination measures. Prior to joining NFER in 2016, Jude had worked as a statistician in the Government Statistical Service for over 25 years, including several years as head of statistics and data in the Department for Education.

Jilly Johnston is an artist, creative facilitator and transformative arts officer. She's been a teacher in primary, early years and higher education, and now works in the engagement and learning departments at The Auckland Project with a focus on the Spanish Art Gallery, Mining Art Gallery and artistic collections in the castle. She creates arts projects aimed at connecting people to art and creativity. Jilly loves using creative facilitation and creating engaging projects and programmes which address key barriers in the community of Bishop Auckland. She loves painting, drawing and encouraging others to find their creative spark!

Carolynn Kerr started teaching English in a secondary school in Wallsend almost 30 years ago, and has taught and led English departments in secondary schools in Northumberland and New-castle. At Valley Gardens Middle School, she took on responsibility for Project Based Learning, working with staff to develop and embed a creative, innovative and bespoke curriculum for children and harness the passion and interest of staff.

Iain King CBE is based in Baghdad as Director of NATO's Mission in Iraq. He spent four years working for the EU and UN in Kosovo just after the 1999 intervention, coordinated international civilian operations in Benghazi during the Libyan civil war of 2011, and has worked in more than 10 conflict-affected countries. He is the author of five books spanning international interventions, military history and philosophy.

Rafael Klein is an artist who grew up in Brooklyn and studied at the University of Chicago and the Art Students League of New York. His work has been exhibited extensively in the United States, the United Kingdom and Europe and is held in collections including the Tate, the British Library, MoMA and the Brooklyn Museum. Klein has created many public sculptures and his work has been featured in the press including the *Times*, the BBC and *la Repubblica*. Klein lives and works in London and Puglia.

He is married with two daughters. https://rafaelklein.com/.

David Leat is Professor of Curriculum Innovation at Newcastle University. His career has included classroom geography teaching, teacher training and working for the Department for Education. His research interests started with thinking skills and developed to embrace Learning2Learn, metacognition, formative assessment, widening participation, teacher coaching and professional learning. He was Executive Director of the Research Centre for Learning and Teaching at Newcastle for 12 years. His current projects revolve around Enquiry/Project Based Learning and Community Curriculum Making – supporting schools to collaborate with cultural venues, businesses, conservation bodies and Northumbria Police Violence Reduction Unit. He is a director on a local Multi Academy Trust board, with responsibility for Climate Change and Sustainability, an Associate Editor of the *Curriculum Journal*, and has many conservation interests including bird ringing, forestry and regenerative agriculture.

Paul Lindley OBE is Chancellor of the University of Reading and an award-winning British entrepreneur, social campaigner and author. Paul founded Ella's Kitchen. Built on a core social mission, it is now the UK's largest baby food brand. In 2017 his first book: *Little Wins: The Huge Power of Thinking like a Toddler* was published, and he second, *Raising the Nation* will be published in 2023. He is Chair of the Mayor of London's Child Obesity Taskforce and of Robert F Kennedy Human Rights UK and is a Trustee of Sesame Workshop, the creators of Sesame Street.

Anthony Mackay AM is immediate past CEO and current Co-Chair of the Washington DC -based National Center on Education & the Economy. He was inaugural Chair Australian Institute for Teaching & School Leadership; Inaugural Deputy Chair Australian Curriculum, Assessment & Reporting Authority; immediate past Chair Australian Council for Educational Research and immediate past Deputy Chair of the Education Council New Zealand. Anthony is Deputy Chancellor Swinburne University, Melbourne; Honorary Senior Fellow, Melbourne Graduate School of Education at the University of Melbourne; and Visiting Professor, International Center for Educational Enhancement, University of Bolton UK. He is CEO, Centre for Strategic Education, Melbourne, & Co-Chair of Learning Creates Australia.

Will Millard is an Associate Director at the policy and economic research consultancy, SQW. Will's expertise relates to the education and youth sectors, and he leads a wide range of research and evaluation projects for clients across national and local government, business and the third sector. A former school teacher and leader, Will writes and presents regularly, and is a trustee for the children's charity *I Can Be*.

Judith Mossman read Classics at Corpus Christi College Oxford. After a Junior Research Fellowship at Christ Church, Oxford, she taught at Trinity College, Dublin from 1991 until 2003, becoming a Senior Lecturer and a Fellow. She was Professor of Classics at Nottingham University until 2017, when she was appointed Pro-Vice-Chancellor for Arts and Humanities at Coventry University. She works on Greek tragedy, mostly Euripides, and Greek literature under the Roman Empire, mostly Plutarch. She believes strongly in the power of the arts and humanities to change lives for the better.

Lesley Saunders has worked all her life in education, as teacher, researcher, policy adviser and independent consultant. Her main posts were as Principal Research Officer and Head of the School Improvement Research Centre at the National Foundation for Educational Research; and subsequently as Senior Policy Adviser for Research, General Teaching Council for England. Lesley is a visiting professor at UCL Institute of Education and her professorial lecture, given in 2004, was called 'Grounding the Democratic Imagination: Developing the Relationship between Research and Policy in Education'. She is also a published poet, with seven full collections.

Sir Anthony Seldon is one of Britain's leading contemporary historians, educationalists, commentators and political authors. He was Vice Chancellor of The University of Buckingham from 2015 to 2020 after being a transformative head teacher for 20 years of Brighton College and then Wellington College. He is author and editor of over 45 books on contemporary history, including the inside view books on the last five Prime Ministers. Anthony's contribution to public life is extensive and wide ranging. This includes: the co-founder and first Director of the Institute of Contemporary British History; the co-founder of Action for Happiness; honorary historical adviser to 10 Downing Street for 10 years; the UK's Special Representative for Education to Saudi Arabia; Deputy Chair of The Times Education Commission; a member of the Government's First World War Culture Committee; Chair of the Comment Awards; Director of the Royal Shakespeare Company; President of the International Positive Education Network; Chair of the National Archives Trust; Patron & member of several charities; Founder of the Via Sacra Western Front Walk; and Executive Producer of the film *Journey's End*. Anthony appeared on Desert Island Discs in 2016. For the last 15 years he has given his money for writing and lecturing to charity. He has three children; his wife of 34 years, Joanna, died of cancer in December of 2016, and he married Sarah in 2022.

Tim Slack is the founder and co-director of Appreciating People. He has worked in youth work and community based regeneration for over 35 years, holding several senior posts in local government, community engagement and arts organisations. Tim is an experienced Appreciative Inquiry trainer and facilitator and author of a number of practical Appreciative Inquiry resources including 'How to be more Awesome', a journal and workbook co-designed with young people supporting resilience and well-being. He has been the AI adviser on the Appreciating Church programme and the co-author of Appreciating Church resource and workbook. Currently with NHS partners he is co-create Appreciating Health and Care an Appreciative Inquiry guide to the health (published in late 2023.

For more information www.appreciatingpeople.co.uk.

The Revd, Fiona Thomas background includes agricultural botany, community work in India, international development, adult learning, theological education and pastoral ministry. She values appreciative enquiry as an approach which draws together theory and practice from all of these areas. After co-authoring the book *Appreciating Church* in 2017 she co-founded the organisation of the same name as a self-supporting community of practice across churches and their communities. Fiona was Head of Education and Learning for the United Reformed Church. Alongside consultancy work she is currently offering transitional ministry with three small United Reformed Church congregations in South London.

Ulrike Thomas is a Research Associate in the School of Education, Newcastle University. Before embarking on a career in research she was a Primary School teacher for 9 years. Her interest in Community Curriculum making has developed as a result of her involvement in a range of research projects which have examined the impact of innovative pedagogy and curricular on students and teachers. She works with university academics, community partners and schools to develop project ideas and resources that will inspire teachers to adopt this approach to curriculum-making.

Neil Thompson is an independent writer and educator. He has held full or honorary professorships at five UK universities and is currently a visiting professor at the Open University. He is a well-published author, sought-after international conference speaker and highly respected developer of online learning. His recent books include *Anti-racism for Beginners* and *The Managing People Practice* manual. His website, with his acclaimed Manifesto for Making a Difference, is at www.NeilThompson.info.

Ruth Webb is a class teacher at Valley Gardens Middle School. She had 15 years of teaching experience and managerial experience with the John Lewis Partnership prior to this. Ruth has a passion for the environment, with a degree in Environmental Science, so in addition to teaching responsibilities, she coordinates the activities of the school's Eco Club, and her school was recently awarded the prestigious 'Green Flag Award'.

Alison Whelan was a former Modern Foreign Languages teacher who now combines her skills and experience in languages and classroom-based educational research in the role of an Associate Lecturer and Research Associate in the School of Education, Communication and Language Sciences (ECLS) at Newcastle University. Her main research interest is in collaborative curriculum innovation and she has worked with schools, FE colleges and heritage and arts organisations in supporting the creation and sustainable implementation of research-based, innovative approaches to learning.

Dr Raphael Wilkins started as a teacher before progressing to local authority educational administration, including 12 years at chief officer level. He had advisory and consultancy roles in Parliament and with the local authority associations, and other bodies, before joining the (then) University of London Institute of Education, as Pro Director (London), subsequently Pro Director (International Consultancy). He was President of the College of Teachers UK, in which capacity, with others, he enabled the creation of the Chartered College of Teaching. He has written five books and over 70 articles and book chapters, and is currently an independent scholar.

Lynn Wood is the Founder and Chief Idea Spy of IdeaSpies, an open innovation platform sharing ideas that do good. She has an MA (USYD) and an MBA (AGSM). Her executive career included senior marketing positions with American Express, Myer, Citicorp and Schroders. Lynn also has experience on many private, public and government boards, including as Chair. She was awarded a Centenary Medal in 2001.

FOREWORD: ARE IDEAS ENOUGH?

This startling and opportune volume shines a vivid light on a little-studied or understood aspect of modern Britain.

Ideas.

Without ideas, no progress can be made.

With the wrong ideas, no progress can be made.

But with the right ideas, at the right time, anything is possible.

Ideas can be portmanteau, like capitalism or communism, feminism or wokeism. Or they can be micro, as with ideas which affect just a particular area, like the idea of creating vaccines to combat coronavirus, or a new style in architecture, like art deco. Many Prime Ministers try to define their premierships by having big ideas, like 'Thatcherism'. But most fail to do so, whether John Major with his 'citizens' charter', Tony Blair with his 'Third Way', David Cameron with his 'big society' or Boris Johnson with 'levelling up'. Only rarely is it given to a prime minister to define their entire premiership with a wraparound idea. Most find it hard to deliver even micro ideas.

Why do ideas matter so much? And why are they never of themselves enough? This Foreword will explore both these questions.

Without ideas, sterility reigns. Without John Maynard Keynes, government economic policy would've remained rooted in the non-interventionist ideas of the early twentieth century. His advocacy of fiscal and monetary policy paved the way for governments managing aggregating demand, and mitigating the worst effects of economic depression. Without social reformer William Beveridge, the welfare state introduced by the Labour government of Clement Attlee from 1945, would not have emerged in the form it did. Ideas are equally important in the world of art, with perspective, impressionism, expressionism and abstract art ushering in successive revolutions in art forms.

Ideas matter because they break the hold of status quos. The status quo hates new ideas, and will try and discourage, disparage and snuff them out whenever they see them. They might succeed in the short term, but ideas will inevitably break through sooner or later. The absolutist monarchies of France and Russia were brought down by ideas of equality. The mighty coercive power of the Soviet Union was broken by the ideas of freedom. For each idea, a season. Millions of companies worldwide that flourished for years were brought down within a decade of the digital revolution arriving in their countries. High Streets are being revolutionised by the idea of online shopping.

Ideas matter because we live in a dynamic world. To stand still is to go backwards. Resisting ideas is as futile as baying at the rising sun snuffing out the despondent moon. Ideas embrace and enshrine new technologies, new mindsets and new frontiers. Humans cannot go anywhere but forward. Retro thinking is not about going backwards: it's about reimagining the past and serves it up nice and crisp in the modern era.

Finally, ideas matter because they refresh policy and politics. Britain has a partially broken democracy, a deeply flawed education and health system, and it has a culture which is heavily skewed towards the well-off. We still have to find solutions to combating climate change, the cost of social care, how to reduce inequality, have affordable green energy and address the concerns around artificial intelligence (AI). As the chapters in the book show, there are solutions on all these areas and many more.

No one argued more persuasively than the late Ken Robinson that creativity is as vital as it is undervalued. We have a school and university system which privileges regimentation and producing the 'right' answer over creativity. And we have an economy which has been historically weak at rewarding creative thinking and developing promising home-grown ideas into successful products in the market place.

So are ideas then our total salvation?

No. Ideas are necessary but not sufficient to securing future survival and flourishing.

Why aren't ideas then sufficient? First, as I argued in 'Ideas are not enough' [in the book I edited with David Marquand *The Ideas that Shaped Post-war Britain* (Fontana, 1996)], they are only effective if they are in a positive relationship with three other forces: individuals, interests and circumstances. Ideas need to be adopted and advocated by those in positions of power, with the finance, authority and the means to make them happen. Even then, they will be unsuccessful if there are powerful forces ranged against them: it could be the media, financial interests or popular opinion. Even if the ideas, interests and individuals are all positively aligned, it still requires the right circumstances for them to flourish. Disruptive change (e.g. war, economic downturn or natural disasters) has often been the friend to the blossoming of new ideas. World War I thus allowed nascent ideas, including popular democracy, the vote for women and scientific and medical advance to fructify, while World War II changed notions of the role of government and the size and responsibilities of the state.

Some ideas are bad. Eugenics is one such. Aryanism and Nazism equally ideas all reasonable people would find repugnant. Other ideas are more subjective. In the west, we celebrate democracy: most of the world lives in regimes that are autocratic. The idea that the Iraqis en masse would welcome the invasion of Iraq in 2003 and want to embrace democracy proved not to be the case. The majority of the world lives in states that refuse to condemn Russia's invasion of Ukraine.

Ideas can provide the solution when so many are diametrically opposed to each other. The rights of the unborn child versus the woman's right to choose, for example. The right of each individual to choose their gender versus the rights of others, including some parents, female athletes and women's groups, to argue that gender is not a choice. The European Union is an idea, but so is Brexit. Fervent supporters on both sides believe that the evidence supports their own case.

Ideas can easily be exaggerated in importance. Many of the most significant changes in history have been brought on by developments, which have nothing to do with ideas, including epidemics, natural disasters and the changing climate. Elevating ideas to being all important can distort human agency.

Often people don't want governments with highfalutin ideas: they just want the potholes filled and for the trains to run on time.

Finally, we can elevate the importance of ideas forgetting that we have still to develop applicable ideas to save humankind from the biggest risks to its future, including weapons of mass destruction, rogue states with aggressive ambitions and AI out of control.

Relying on AI to solve the biggest problems we face might just be the most stupid idea of them all.

This volume is clever precisely because it elevates ideas while recognising their limitations.

Sir Anthony Seldon

PART 1

THE CONCEPT OF AN
IDEAS-INFORMED SOCIETY

1

POTENT IDEAS, ENGAGED CITIZENS, HEALTHY SOCIETIES

Chris Brown and Graham Handscomb

SPARKS OF INSPIRATION

Let's start with what we know. Ideas always have and always will change the world, whether this happens via gradual shifts in understanding or behaviour, or from the introduction of revolutionary new ways of knowing and being.[1,2] When these ideas are good (and naturally how we judge 'goodness' is very much steeped in our norms and values), we all benefit as a result. This is expressed well by television presenter, archaeologist and historian Neil Oliver,[3] who suggests that when life-enhancing, life-changing ideas have occurred during humankind's history, sparks of inspiration have become flames and these flames have served to positively light up the world.

But, as you will have noticed, Western society is actually in a bit of a fix right now. Smack bang in the midst of environmental emergency and an obesity crisis, we are also faced with growing disparities between the haves and have nots, and a danger that hard won moves towards equity and rights might be lost. We have also seen, in more recent times, many individuals beginning to turn their back on what science and what traditional politics have to offer, with a concomitant growth in reactionary populism and forms of social media that are rapidly becoming the Wild West when it comes to veracity and honesty. So it would seem that now – more than ever – it's timely to consider how to support citizens to become both willing and able to engage with and evaluate ideas.

THE BENEFITS OF AN IDEAS-INFORMED SOCIETY

With this context in mind, we see the notion of the ideas-informed society as a desirable situation. One in which (1) our citizens see value in being well-informed through staying up to date and (2) citizens regularly keep themselves up to date by actively engaging with new ideas, doing so both openly and critically.[4] But ushering in an ideas-informed society is not simply a desirable intellectual exercise; research indicates a range of benefits materialise from citizens actively engaging with ideas. These include (3) citizens becoming more knowledgeable and (4) citizens finding themselves better positioned to make beneficial decisions and achieve personal fulfilment. For instance, being ideas-informed is linked to better health and other measures of wellness, since the key to personal fitness – as well as tackling many illnesses, such as diabetes – is information and education. Likewise, within the overall umbrella of the coronavirus (COVID-19) pandemic, the spread of the Omicron variant (which occurred after the mass availability of vaccinations and booster jabs) highlighted how those less well informed were more likely to end up in intensive care units as a result.

Being ideas-informed can also, amongst many other things, ensure that people (1) maintain a broad understanding of scientific and technological advances and, where relevant, how these can be harnessed to improve our own lives as well as that of society more generally[5]; (2) demonstrate a general awareness of artistic, literary or cultural developments – with cultural capital linked to a range of positive outcomes, from success at school to future levels of income[6,7]; and (3) are cognizant of political events.[8] This final point leading to strengthened democratic processes, with politicians and local community leaders being held to account.

A further benefit of ideas engagement is that citizens can align their perspectives with desirable societal values.[9,10] By this we mean values that are progressive in nature: i.e., values that tend towards fairness, equality and social and environmental justice. This tendency is evident in recent studies which show that the vast majority of the UK population (80% of those surveyed, based on a poll of 2,244 UK citizens) now believe it important to be attentive to issues of racial inequality and social justice.[11] Likewise, progressive norms present themselves in terms of increased concern about the current environmental emergency and attitudes regarding how it might be tackled, including the now widespread acceptance of veganism.[12] The totality of these benefits also positively impacts society when they result in a population that is generally more happy, healthy, inclusive and empathetic, and where there is more social, cultural, scientific and political engagement, as well as educational and economic productivity. While in an ideas-informed society, these types of outcomes may not always materialise, nor always result in behaviours that are commensurate with under-standing, the more citizens engage with ideas, the more likely this will be the case over the longer term.[13]

Finally, we also believe that more ideas-engagement has significant and positive implications for the whole area of leadership and decision-making in society. As more citizens engage with ideas, and become more critically informed, then the momentum towards collaboration and participation, not just in the democratic process, but also in collaborative social leadership more generally, becomes increasingly compelling. As such, we see more genuine ideas-engagement fostering a 'density' of leadership and social participation throughout society.[14] Given its potential positives, it is our aspiration, therefore, that the ideas-informed society is available to all and can be enjoyed by everyone.

CAVEATS AND CHALLENGES

It's also worth that we briefly pause to introduce some pragmatism into our argument. Having made the case for the promotion and fostering of ideas-engagement and the hugely positive dividends this can bring to society, we are not so naive that we cannot also see that there are some potentially problematic considerations with our position. Certainly, we are not labouring under the simplistic assumption that all ideas that 'take off' (or take root) will be 'good', 'positive' or actively contribute to human flourishing. Indeed, as a number of our contributors argue, although we may like to believe that good arguments will always defeat bad ones, with the truth winning out, this is often evidentially not the case when ideas battle themselves out.[15] In fact quite the opposite situation can occur when toxic ideas or fake news gain momentum to overwhelm and corrupt society.[16]

The other caveat also explored in this book is that the promotion of a society which encourages ideas-engagement may be met by considerable organisational, cultural and even psychological resistance – often by the very people and sections of society that would gain most from this.[17] Nonetheless, as indicated earlier, we believe our aspiration is well worth pursuing, with potential benefits far outweighing such concerns – if these concerns can be adequately addressed – and its development best achieved by drawing from a range of sectors.

Given our goal, we note with interest, but also concern, that there are some who neither engage with ideas, nor make attempts to do so; an issue, because the presence of these attitudes and behaviours serves to limit the extent to which the types of beneficial outcomes we detail above can be achieved.[18] Of particular worry are the findings of previous studies which indicate that, amongst the population generally, there are substantive numbers of people who are 'ideas refusers': i.e. members of the public who see little value in engaging with ideas. For instance, findings from a representative survey of some 1,000 voting age citizens in England, show that, in response to the question: 'How important is it to you to keep up to date with news, current affairs and new developments (such as political, economic and scientific developments)?', 13% of respondents indicated that this was 'unimportant' to them, with 16% seemingly ambivalent (responding that it was 'neither important or unimportant').[19]

Analysing this data further reveals that 'ideas refusers' are more likely to be from low education backgrounds, reside in communities where friends, family and colleagues also possess low levels of education, and will predominantly be in low skilled employment. An additional insight of interest is the reluctance by 'ideas refusers' to discuss new ideas with friends, family or work colleagues. This places 'ideas refusers' in a diametrically opposed position to those who are 'ideas engagers'. What's more, as well as ascribing low value to ideas-engagement, ideas refusers are also less likely to see value in the types of progressive ideals we see as vital. For instance, the same survey asked respondents to consider the importance to them of a range of topics, including the importance of inclusion and tolerance; the importance of business practices that are both ethical and sustainable; and the importance of supporting one's own and other's physical and mental health. Again, a sizable proportion (ranging from 15% to 24% depending on the statement) considered these items to be of no or of indeterminant value. Interestingly, these findings mirror those of other recent studies.[20,21] At the same time, such individuals (as well as the wider communities within which they live) stand much to gain from becoming increasingly knowledgeable, in a better position to make good decisions and from being more responsive to progressive beliefs and norms. So, as we see it, there is a clear need to know more about how to close the gap between the ideal (i.e. the actualisation of the ideas-informed society) and the real (i.e. the current situation). But how to achieve this is the part we don't yet know: hence the need for this book.

OUR AUTHORS – WIDE EXPERIENCE AND DEEP INSIGHTS

It is our belief that, if the benefits we outline above are to be realised and concerns successfully mitigated, a collective endeavour is required. Naturally, therefore, in order to pull together this work we reached out to the great and the good: those with vast experience and even vaster minds, to see what they thought was required in understanding the nature of an ideas-informed society and how to make it happen. We also wanted our contributors to outline the challenges and pitfalls that might potentially hinder what we would like to see realised, or that might even threaten to corrupt our aspirations into something undesirable. And we are more than delighted with the result.

What you have in your hands represents the wisdom of 35 respected, authors, thinkers and practical players in the field of ideas. Our contributors hail from a diverse range of fields and include leading lawyers and entrepreneurs, as well as artists, archaeologists, church ministers and educationalists – with a number of leading academics thrown in for good measure. Individually, they have been working in the broad field of ideas-engagement in very different ways. So, just to give a few examples: Dr Sam Fowles, as a barrister focused on public and constitutional law, is concerned with truth telling and holding our leaders and democratic system to account (even successfully taking former Prime Minister Boris Johnson to court for illegally proroguing Parliament); Sir Paul Collier is a leading campaigner tackling what he argues is a starkly unequal, polarized society in the UK; Katherine Crisp is Founder of Social Innovation for All, a social enterprise on a mission to unleash the creative potential of young people to address social challenges; Paul Lindley is an award-winning British entrepreneur and Chair of the Mayor of London's Child Obesity Taskforce; Sir Les Ebdon is a champion of fair access to higher education for the marginalised; The Revd Canon Helen Cameron of the Methodist Church, meanwhile, has, for some time, been concerned with the idea of human flourishing. Some have also been directly involved in ideas-related initiatives. For example, see the IdeasSpies website discussed in the chapter by Lynn Wood and Sabra Brock; the 'Battle of Ideas' festival that is co-convened by Alastair Donald from the Academy of Ideas; or Stéphane Goldstein's 'InformAll' initiative, which promotes the relevance and importance of information literacy.

THE SECTIONS OF THE BOOK

To corral all our contributions effectively, we have arranged them into the following sections:

1. The Concept of an Ideas-Informed Society;

2. Truth-telling, Democracy and Community;

3. Creativity, Arts and the Environment; and

4. Education and Empowering Young People.

The first of these sections explores what it means for a society to be ideas-informed. As well as explore what ideas 'are', chapters in this section cover the whole gamut of tensions that exist when we consider how to bring to fruition a society that is ideas-informed. For instance, whether or not there are issues that should be considered undebatable and the extent to which speakers and audiences should be free to challenge all orthodoxies. Likewise, the tension between the paradigms of scientific and legal 'truths': here, while the first aims to reach truth through testing hypothesis and drawing on evidence, the second seeks to find the truth through argument, and so depends not on the facts, per se, but on the oratorical skills and credibility of advocates. This legal approach to truth is beloved of politicians, and is more attractive to audiences, but in the age of social media, where people curate their own news and exclusively select opinions which support their own prejudices, this reliance on the legal paradigm has serious consequences – as witnessed in the rise of 'alternative facts' and in challenges to verifiable scientific evidence (e.g. with regards to climate change and COVID-19 vaccination).

Our second section, *Truth-Telling, Democracy and Community*, explores the role of truth in democratic societies. Intriguingly, the first chapter in this section lays down a gauntlet to challenge the notion of 'the battle of ideas'; something explored and advocated for in the ultimate chapter of section one. Promoting such a battle for truth, this contributor suggests, is 'naïve'; since we don't all have access to the same platforms from which to promote our ideas. In other words, those with the most access to the mainstream media, or that have the most followers on social media are likely to see their ideas adopted, irrespective of their worth – the battle, therefore, is hardly a fair one. As such, an ideas-informed society can only flourish when we attend both to the ability of everyone to represent their ideas and the ground rules we put in place to judge the *quality* of ideas. Other chapters in this section continue along a similar theme. They include the crucial contribution of information literacy, as well as the embracing of diverse sources of knowledge, to a truly flourishing democracy and society; how 'Appreciative Inquiry' can provide a framework for community ideas and creativity to flow; and the desperate need for new 'big' ideas if we are serious about helping our children, and nation, thrive. This section also details why the ideas-informed society needs people to be willing and have confidence to engage in public debate, as well as provide – in the powerful analysis of the tragedy of the former Yugoslavia – a chilling reminder of the consequences for societies when demagogues suppress ideas through a combination of fiery rhetoric and a distortion of the facts.

In our third section, *Creativity, Arts and the Environment*, readers will find the creative theme reflected in the style of the chapters as well as in the content. In particular, the chapter entitled 'The Power of Visual Ideas', contains and details nine pieces of original art by artist Rafael Klein as he explores the role art can make to the ideas-informed society and charts his own journey to becoming an artist. Other chapters include detail on an innovative project in Bishop Auckland (County Durham, UK) designed to bring about community regeneration through ideas-informed cultural engagement. This contribution provides a detailed account of how fixed negative mindsets about the value of Bishop Auckland and attitudes towards galleries and cultural spaces were tackled through a creative approach, using the disciplines of art and archaeology. Contributors also discuss the need to make ideas widely available, mindsets which most effectively help in the engagement with ideas, as well as the need to defend ideas from judgements based solely on usefulness or utility: especially when it comes to the flourishing of ideas originating from the arts.

Finally, in our fourth section, *Education and Empowering Young People*, our contributors, including a number of expert academics from the field of education, explore how education systems can support young people to become equipped to engage with a range of ideas. In particular chapters detail the need for future citizens to develop the capacity to collaboratively and critically evaluate competing ideas, as well as the need for us all to apply a set of values to ideas that tend towards justice: environmental, societal and racial, and personal.

Overall our authors suggest an ideas-informed society can be possible and, subject to the caveats they raise, should be welcomed. We agree and we hope that your takeaways from the book include a newfound, or perhaps even a reinforced, commitment to becoming ideas-informed. Our hope is that readers will find the book stimulating and engaging in a number of ways. The range of diverse contributions from authors open out a world of ideas across many sectors of society. Reading these discussions may, in turn, encourage your own reflection on the merits of an ideas-informed society and indeed might perhaps be the catalyst for considering your own engagement and contribution. What emerges from this book is reaffirmation about the potency of ideas and how the positive engagement of citizens with them makes for a healthier society. We are excited about the possibilities that emerge from the book and to taking the next steps in making the ideas-informed society a reality!!

REFERENCES

1. Brown, C., Groß Ophoff, J., Chadwick, K. and Parkinson, S. (2022) Achieving the 'ideas-informed' society: results from a Structural Equation Model using survey data from England, *Emerald Open Research*. https://doi.org/10.35241/emeraldo penres.14487.1.

2. Hochschild, J. (2010) If Democracies Need Informed Voters, How Can They Thrive While Expanding Enfranchisement? *Election Law Journal: Rules, Politics, and Policy*, 9, 2, pp. 111–123.

3. Oliver, N. (2021) *The world in 100 moments* (London, Penguin Random House).

4. Brown, C., Luzmore, R. and Groß Ophoff, J. (2022) Facilitating the Ideas-informed Society: A systematic review, *Emerald Open Research*, 4, 25. https://doi.org/10.35241/ emeraldopenres.14729.1.

5. Pinker, S. (2018) *Enlightenment Now The Case for Reason, Science, Humanism, and Progress* (London, Penguin).

6. Brown, C. (2021) *The Amazing Power of Networks. A [research-informed] choose your own destiny book*, (Woodbridge, John Catt).

7. DiMaggio, P. (1982) Cultural capital and school success: The impact of status culture participation on the grades of U.S.

high school students. *American Sociological Review*, 47, pp. 189–201.

8. Lamb, S., Huo, S., Walstab, A., Wade, A., Maire, Q., Doecke, E., Jackson, J. & Endekov, Z. (2020), *Educational opportunity in Australia 2020: who succeeds and who misses out*, Centre for International Research on Education Systems, Victoria University, for the Mitchell Institute, Melbourne: Mitchell Institute.

9. Brown, C., Groß Ophoff, J., Chadwick, K. and Parkinson, S. (2022) Achieving the 'ideas-informed' society: results from a Structural Equation Model using survey data from England, *Emerald Open Research*. https://doi.org/10.35241/emeraldo penres.14487.1.

10. Hochschild, J. (2010) If Democracies Need Informed Voters, How Can They Thrive While Expanding Enfranchisement? *Election Law Journal: Rules, Politics, and Policy*, 9, 2, pp. 111–123.

11. Anjeh, R. and Doraisamy, I. (2022) The Centre holds, available at: https://ourglobalfuture.com/wp-content/uploads/2022/04/GF_TheCentreHolds_Report_10.pdf, accessed on 2 May 2022.

12. Quinn, B. and Henley, J. (2019) Yellow vests: protesters fight for ideological ownership, available at: https://www.the-guardian.com/world/2019/jan/13/yellow-vests-protesters-fight-for-ideological-ownership, accessed on 19 November 2022.

13. Brown, C., Luzmore, R. and Groß Ophoff, J. (2022) Anomie in the UK? Can cultural malaise threaten the fruition of the ideas-informed society? *Emerald Open Research*, 4, 28.

14. Handscomb, G. (2011) Fostering Resilience Through School Leadership in *Beyond Survival: Teachers and Resilience* in Day C.; Edwards A.; Griffiths A.; and Gu Q. (Eds). ESRC; University of Nottingham and University of Oxford, available at: https://www.nottingham.ac.uk/research/groups/crelm/documents/teachers-resilience/teachers-resilience.pdf.

Dabell, J. (2018) *Leadership Density or Density of Leadership*. Blog to be accessed at: https://johndabell.com/2018/12/16/leadership-density/.

Handscomb, G. (2022) *Everyone's a leader*. Reform, June 2022. pp. 24–25.

15. Fowles, S. (2023) Battle of Ideas: Weaponising Miltonian Fallacy in Brown, C. and Handscomb, G. (2023) The Ideas-Informed Society: Why we need it and how to make it happen. Emerald Publishing.

16. King, I. (2023) When ideas fail. in Brown, C. and Handscomb, G. (2023) The Ideas-Informed Society: Why we need it and how to make it happen. Emerald Publishing.

17. Saunders, S. (2023) A little Conceptual Housekeeping: Ideas and their contexts. in Brown, C. and Handscomb, G. (2023) The Ideas-Informed Society: Why we need it and how to make it happen. Emerald Publishing.

18. Brown, C., Luzmore, R. and Groß Ophoff, J. (2022) Anomie in the UK? Can cultural malaise threaten the fruition of the ideas-informed society? *Emerald Open Research*, 4, 28.

19. Brown, C., Groß Ophoff, J., Chadwick, K. and Parkinson, S. (2022) Achieving the 'ideas-informed' society: results from a Structural Equation Model using survey data from England, *Emerald Open Research*. https://doi.org/10.35241/emeraldo penres.14487.1.

20. Anjeh, R. and Doraisamy, I. (2022) The Centre holds, available at: https://ourglobalfuture.com/wp-content/uploads/2022/04/GF_TheCentreHolds_Report_10.pdf, accessed on 2 May 2022.

21. Brown, C., Groß Ophoff, J., Chadwick, K. and Parkinson, S. (2022) Achieving the 'ideas-informed' society: results from a Structural Equation Model using survey data from England, *Emerald Open Research*. https://doi.org/10.35241/emeraldo penres.14487.1.

2

THE VALUE OF UNCERTAINTY AND THE TYRANNY OF THE CLOSED MIND

Sir Les Ebdon CBE

CONFLICTING PARADIGMS

In 1959 C. P. Snow caused considerable controversy by describing British society as being divided into two cultures:[1] the sciences and humanities. He postulated that each had been poorly educated in the disciplines of the other and, as a consequence, each had little understanding of the other. I want to suggest that there is a greater division in our society today between two contemporary paradigms for searching for the truth.

The scientific paradigm, with which I am most familiar as a chemist, aims to reach the truth by testing a hypothesis. No specific test ever completely proves the hypothesis, as there may be another explanation, possibly one not yet conceived. As the experimental evidence mounts, however, the confidence that the hypothesis is true grows. So, infuriatingly for nonscientists, no scientist will ever claim to be 100% certain of any hypothesis. There are dangers to having a closed mind. The history of science has clearly shown this. A little bit of doubt both demonstrates integrity and stimulates further progress.

The other paradigm, which I shall call the legal paradigm, seeks to find the truth by the opposition of two, fundamentally opposed views. While this may be effective in a court of law, it does depend

not on experiment, but in large part on the oratorical skills and
credibility of the advocates. It is also beloved by politicians who,
while they may lack credibility, glory in their formidable debating
skills as a way of seeking the truth. It is particularly problematic in
complex matters and in novel situations where evidence has not yet
been gathered. In such circumstances, we often see opposing ideas
rapidly consolidated into two opposing camps which exhibit closed
minds to any evidence that is subsequently discovered.

Unfortunately, the media have decided that the legal paradigm
attracts bigger audiences. So, for years, we have seen the big ideas
and issues in our society treated as a matter of opinion, to be
debated between those selected, not because of their knowledge or
understanding of the evidence, but because of their entrenched
views. This has led to the pitting together of the expert scientist,
willing to admit the level of uncertainty, with rhetorically skilled
charlatans, prepared to advocate unevidenced ideas with complete
certainty. It may have led to good entertainment, but it has poorly
served the advancement of the truth, and has promoted the tyranny
of the closed mind.

In the age of social media, where people curate their own news
and exclusively select opinions which support their own prejudices,
this reliance on the legal paradigm has serious consequences. We
now live in a society where blatant untruths abound and conspir-
acies are to be found everywhere. There is an urgent need to return
to evidence led debate, honest doubt and the testing of ideas before
more damage is caused to our society. Let us look at some recent
examples.

ALTERNATIVE FACTS

One of the most surprising, dare I say ridiculous, developments of
recent years is the concept that 'you can have your facts and I can
have my facts'. Perhaps this idea of alternative facts is consistent
with an age where one can live both in the real world and the
virtual world.

Alex Jones is an American broadcaster, often described as 'a
far-right conspiracy theorist'. He has for years maintained that the

mass school shooting at Sandy Hook was not real but a hoax, part of a left-wing conspiracy to discredit the gun lobby in the USA. This has caused enormous distress to the parents of children lost in this atrocity and he was eventually sued by one of them. The Judge's comments in the case, make interesting reading: 'You believe everything you say is true, but it isn't. Your beliefs do not make something true... Just because you claim to think something is true does not make it true'. It is tempting to see this case as the beginning of an era where truth finally defeats alternative facts. It is, however, unlikely that the battle is over, not least because those trading in alternative facts can achieve electoral success and lucrative careers (Jones had been making up to $800,000 a day from his website online store).

Andrew Tate is a former kickboxing world champion and reality TV show star, who was recently detained in Romania on charges of alleged sexual assault and exploitation. More significantly Tate is an 'influencer' who had 4.7 million Instagram followers before he was banned by Meta for violating its policies on dangerous organisations and individuals. His social media posts were extremely misogynistic, including videos of him saying women are a man's property, rape victims are to blame for their own assaults, talking about hitting and choking women, trashing their belongings and stopping them from going out. There is understandably great concern about Tate's influence on millions of young men but how could such views have become so widely accepted? His content on TikTok has been viewed more than 12.7 billion times. Perhaps because these were views that his followers wanted to believe were true.

Recent research[2] has shown that only 4% of participants in a study could correctly identify bogus stories, so-called 'fake news', presented to them. It seems that virtually all of us are vulnerable to being misled because of our tendency to accept information consistent with our core beliefs and, on the other hand, tend to reject that which is inconsistent with our beliefs. This is termed 'confirmation bias'. The author of this study has warned that there is growing evidence that our inability to filter out fake news is undermining democracy and putting many lives at risk. Wild conspiracy stories such as 'stolen elections' or 'secret microchips in vaccines' flourish. Sophisticated manipulation strategies are used to fool people into believing the unbelievable. If only we had grown up in a society where ideas are debated as hypotheses and supporting evidence is sought, as opposed to a society where fortunes can be made from being an outrageous liar.

The media has a long history of not letting the facts get in the way of a good story and this is not confined to fringe publications. For example, *The Times* recently ran a front-page story with the banner headline 'Censorship on campus'. Unfortunately, the evidence didn't quite live up to the headline. The hypothesis was that books are being removed from undergraduate syllabi in English universities because of their content. The evidence from the 300 Freedom of Information Act requests to 140 providers of higher education was that there were only two examples of text removal. Neither of these were demonstrably examples of censorship. Again, a society more used to conducting debate through the evaluation of evidence might be better equipped to call out such fantasies.

Professor Peter Vickers of the University of Durham has proposed in his recent book[3] that we need a way to assess scientific opinion on a large scale and internationally, so that the challenging question of what can be confidently called a scientific fact can be resolved. Vickers uses the example of the idea that smoking causes cancer which was accepted as an established fact by scientists sometime in the twentieth century. That is to say of the many environmental causes that might have led to lung and throat cancer, for most scientists, the level of uncertainty on the hypothesis that smoking was a significant cause of cancer, had in the minds of the vast majority of scientists researching in the area reduced to the level that it became an accepted scientific fact by the 1960s. This idea was strongly resisted by tobacco firms, of course, who sought out scientists and influencers who had yet to be persuaded with the consequence that many thousands of individuals continued to smoke, hoping that there was no danger. Vickers postulates that people think on many issues that scientists are split 50–50, where the actual ratio might be 80–20. Again, this is probably the effect of the predominance of the legal paradigm over the scientific paradigm. Peter Vickers proposes that by accessing scientific opinion on the large-scale and internationally, it might be easier to convince people of what he calls scientific facts. In the world of the Internet and social media, opinion and beliefs are prevalent, evidence is rarer, and admitted uncertainty, even scarcer.

CLIMATE CHANGE

No current area of debate better illustrates the frustration that many scientists feel about the way the media treats scientific evidence, than the controversy about the extent and cause of climate change. I can recall lecturing to students in the 1970s about the potential for anthropogenically induced climate change. At that time, there was not enough evidence, either of global warming, or of the impact of the burning of fossil fuels to conclude with any certainty that the planet would experience significant warming. Over the years, I have watched with interest as the evidence mounted concerning a warming planet and our measurements of carbon dioxide levels in the atmosphere, and that of other gases which contribute to the so-called greenhouse effect, have improved. So that the degree of uncertainty has decreased and a scientific consensus has emerged that not only is global warming happening but that it is caused in large part by human activity, particularly by the burning of fossil fuels. We also have strong evidence that other climate changes are the result of human activity. If there is a controversy remaining, it is amongst politicians and lobbyists for fossil fuel producers. That these antagonists have been able to sow doubt on the scientific consensus is in large part because of the adoption of the legal paradigm in the media.

Even the reputable British Broadcasting Corporation (BBC) has been responsible for pitting eminent and knowledgeable scientists against politicians and lobbyists with no scientific credentials for being in a debate about meteorology. The defence has been that there is a need to have a balance in news reporting, but how can you have a balance between evidence and fantasy? It is noticeable that lately several eminent presenters have left the BBC citing the use of so-called impartiality or balance to 'shut down' journalists.

The subtle balance of our atmosphere, and its interaction with the climate and ecosystems of the planet, is an excellent example of the need to be trained in the ability to analyse critically information to establish evidence and to differentiate fact from fiction. Scientists do this by open debate, experiments to collect more evidence for the debate and hypothesis testing. At all times, keeping an open mind until the uncertainty is resolved. Evidence is tested by publishing in peer-reviewed journals. Rhetoric and closed minds have no place in such complex debates.

COVID-19

The mainstream media seem to have played a more responsible role during the COVID-19 pandemic, at least from the middle of 2020–2022. From the start of the lockdown in the UK, in late March 2020, until the lifting of restrictions, following widespread vaccination, both the government and the media seem to be unusually responsive to the evidence presented by scientists. It was left to the wilder fringes of the Internet and social media to promote lockdown-scepticism and anti-vaxxer views. So prevalent is the view that there is always another side to an argument there are people who are open to the wildest of speculation on the Internet and to fantastic conspiracy theories on social media. Some experts were attacked outrageously on social media and indeed, one leading expert was physically attacked in London. Professor Devi Sridhar of the University of Edinburgh, who was one of the earliest scientists to sound the alarm on COVID-19 in mid-January, still receives a daily torrent of vitriol and criticism from lockdown-sceptics, anti-vaxxers and those who accuse her of meddling in politics. For a Professor of Global Public Health this is extraordinary and has led her to speculate in her latest book[4] whether University experts will be quite as willing to enter the debate in the event of another pandemic.

The European response to the pandemic was quite rightly a scientifically based approach. An approach that is not based on the counterpoint of two opposed narratives, but on the accumulation of evidence to support or to question a hypothesis. In any new situation evidence will always take time to acquire, there will therefore be considerable uncertainty as to the correct approach to take. This is when the scientist will argue that we must take the precautionary principle, a cautious approach until the level of uncertainty has been reduced as more evidence accumulates and clarity emerges. Those familiar with the scientific paradigm found such caution, until a more authoritative plan of action could be justified, an essential feature of the response to the COVID-19 pandemic. It was important to keep an open mind and to recognise that uncertainty is not a sign of weakness but an indication of the need for more research to produce more evidence.

THE CHALLENGE

In recent years, many people have noted that the tone of public debate has become increasingly strident and the battle of ideas increasingly polarised. I have attempted to show how this can be traced back to the triumph of the legal paradigm over the scientific paradigm in media debate. This has conditioned the public to believe that in every debate there are two sides and that the correct way to identify truth is to listen to both sides, rather than to accept discovering the truth is a matter of searching for evidence. This challenge to society has become even more acute in the age of social media. We no longer have to listen to both sides of the argument nor search for evidence. We can create our own news, select our own evidence, choose our own facts and follow policy-based evidence rather than evidence-based policy. It is imperative that those who have learnt the value of keeping an open mind, of being prepared to challenge accepted ideas and present evidence for their views speak up. We should not be afraid to be open about the uncertainty we honestly have but value uncertainty and denounce the tyranny of the closed mind.

The utilitarian philosopher, John Stuart Mill, in 1867, delivered an inaugural address at the University of Saint Andrews and famously said 'Bad men need nothing more to compass their ends, than that good men should look on and do nothing'.[5] The same is true of bad ideas and unchallenged by evidence, and not tempered by uncertainty, they can do much damage. Indeed, the consequences can be fatal. The closed mind of anti-vaxxers, for example, has led to many deaths. That this should be happening over 300 years after the dawn of the age of scientific enlightenment is all the more remarkable.

REFERENCES

1. Snow, C. P. (1959) The Two Cultures. Cambridge University Press.
2. van der Linden, S. (2023) Foolproof: How We Fall for Misinformation and How to Build Immunity. 4th Estate.
3. Vickers, P. (2022) Identifying Future-Proof Science. Oxford University Press.
4. Sridhar, D. (2022) Preventable: How a Pandemic Changed the World and How to Stop the Next One. Penguin.
5. Mill, J. S. (1867) Inaugural Address Delivered to the University of St. Andrews, 2/1/1867.

3

A LITTLE CONCEPTUAL HOUSEKEEPING: IDEAS AND THEIR CONTEXTS

Lesley Saunders

. . . what threatens democracy is not erroneous beliefs or fake news but a social and economic crisis that political elites are incapable or unwilling to address.

–Nicolas Guilhot[1]

. . . intuitively, for most people, any uplifting myth is as good as any other.

–Professor Steven Pinker[2]

WHAT ARE IDEAS AND WHOSE IDEAS COUNT?

For over two decades, the editors of this book, Chris Brown and Graham Handscomb, have each made impressive and influential contributions to what has become known as the 'evidence-based' or 'research-informed' agenda in education. Their work in academia and, probably even more valuably, in partnership with schools and local education systems has changed the way many teachers and other educators think about and practise inquiry-led teaching and evidence-led decision-making. Their publications encompass books,[3] articles, webinars and – in Graham's case – the editorship of *Professional Development Today*, a journal for teachers which emphasises the role of inquiry and research. Consequently, I assume that this latest book is a next step in the evolution of the agenda, an ambitious effort to extend those rationalist principles to society as a whole, and to encompass intellectual endeavour more generally, beyond the confines of academic research.

However, 'research' and 'evidence' are relatively bounded concepts compared with 'ideas'; they tend largely to be expressed and communicated in textual and/or numeric modes, and for that reason are rendered capable of being publicly assessed on quality criteria and disseminated via explicit protocols for publication, such as peer review. Notwithstanding the many disagreements about such criteria and protocols (which in the educational research world became known as the 'paradigm wars'), I suggest that there is a broad consensus about what is within and outwith the scope of 'research' and 'evidence'. The same cannot be said of 'ideas'.

So this brief chapter offers some preliminary conceptual housekeeping intended to assist with how we grapple with the following overarching questions:

- What are 'ideas' and what do they typically purport to contain and to do?

- How do we decide – and justify to others – which ideas matter and whose ideas count?

SEARCHING FOR CLARITY ABOUT MEANING

Let me start at the beginning, with the coinage of the word 'idea' by Plato in the fourth century BCE The Greek 'ἰδέα' is cognate with 'οἶδα', 'I know', and in the Platonic sense means something like 'that which is real and true', as distinct from what is merely perceived through our fallible senses. 'Ideas' exist in the 'ideal' universe of immaterial unchanging forms rather than in the world of mutable and unreliable sense-impressions and personal opinion. Our modern everyday uses of the word retain a little of this abstract connotation, in that ideas reside only in the mind, are created by our minds. However, the word has accrued various other connotations, as the following non-exhaustive list indicates. These days, the term 'idea' can be used to mean:

- A concept or conceptualisation ('Hobbes' idea of human nature')

- An opinion ('my idea of social justice is quite different from yours')

- A possible course of action ('the idea of performance-related pay was not universally popular')

- An aim ('he arrived with the idea of resolving things')

- An approximation ('please give me an idea of how long it will take')

- Not the reality ('she liked the idea of going abroad')

- An impression ('I got the idea she was hiding something')

- A notion or a sense of something ('I've no idea what to do')

- Imaginative thinking ('let's have some ideas, guys').

The last example is an interesting one: 'ideas' in the plural is a term that seems to attract adjectives like 'fresh', 'new', 'big', as if we require ideas to be in a state of permanent excitation. In an opinion piece[4] columnist James Marriott described "ideas" (in quotation marks) as *that sought-after cultural commodity*. What is it that we seek from 'ideas', what do we want ideas to do for us? For instance, to make sense of an uncertain and bewildering world? To describe and explain a dire set of circumstances in such a way as to suggest a potential resolution, intellectually and/or practically? And are we sufficiently clear about how an idea differs from a theory, an argument, a belief, a worldview?

POSING SOME FUNDAMENTAL QUESTIONS

Perhaps above all we want grand concepts that can be translated into coherent policy programmes or, more abstractly, an intellectual consensus on (political) theories of change, as distinct from ideologies, policies or mere slogans. Well, whatever work we want ideas to do for us and for society, it seems to me that there are some underlying epistemological and ethical ambiguities which we need to tease out, in the form of some questions for further discussion. To that end, I offer the following:

- As an overarching question, to what extent can or should we situate the proposition of an 'ideas-informed society' within a contemporary Enlightenment framework? By that I mean – putting it very simply – a conviction that human beings are rational creatures, and a belief that human progress is made through the free, tolerant and cooperative exercise of reason. Even if enlightenment thinking has been partially discredited for its associations with positivism, colonialism and so on, we can still discern traces of it in, for example, the Nolan Principles of public life: selflessness, integrity, objectivity, accountability, openness, honesty and leadership.

- If these kinds of enlightenment principles are central, or at least pertinent, to the book's theme, other questions follow. Are we, the contributors, articulating a plea for governance and/or public opinion to be driven by rationality, as the philosopher Professor Steven Pinker (see below) believes both desirable and possible? If so, how is this to be achieved, given all the other factors that press upon on policymaking and opinion-forming? What might be the role of think tanks (whether conservative, liberal-progressive or socialist) in this as distinct from research organisations?

- Furthermore, the ideas we seek and support must presumably be 'good ideas'. In the context of so-called culture wars and the TwitterNet, therefore, what might be the *necessary and sufficient conditions* for good ideas to gain circulation and cogency? Such conditions might include the critical exploration of the underpinning *evidence and values* of any given idea, since we call it 'ideology' when ideas are untempered by evidence or logic.

- To unpack this a little, there is no paucity of ideas circulating within groups and communities on- and offline, as the book's introduction makes clear; we have, perhaps as never before, a strongly ideas-imbued society. The issue is not the existence, accessibility and proliferation of ideas, but rather their *quality, provenance, significance* and *ethical implications*.

- And who is in a position, who possesses the requisite influence and credibility, to assess circulating ideas against such criteria and to judge them legitimate, 'good'? Gloria Origgi writes about the 'reputational path' of a claim,[5] a kind of audit trail which can be followed and critiqued online, and therefore presumably by anyone with access to the internet. This would go some way to addressing the potential democratic deficit of ideas being judged as acceptable or otherwise by a perceived social-intellectual élite.

- A different sort of question is, *what kind and scale of ideas* are we, as commentators, interested in? 'Big' ideas about how to address the socio-economic challenges of climate crisis, for instance, or about how artificial intelligence affects democratic engagement? Or somewhat less grand but still interesting ideas such as the role of the arts in public health, or the modern family as a foundation of civil society?

- A related issue then would be, what are the standards by which we choose the ideas we deem worthy to be engaged with? Such assumptions need to be made explicit from the outset, as one person's 'must-have' may be another person's 'whatever'; one person's rationality may be another's self-serving self-interest; one person's conspiracy-theory may be another's insightful sense-making. This is because ideas never arise or gain credence independently of cultural contexts, personal beliefs and lived experience; we need understand, interrogate and, at least to some extent, empathise with how ideas *interact in complex ways* with specific circumstances, times and places – for example, ideas about nationalism and national identity or gender, ethnic and language differences, which are inherently contestable.

- Consequently, we have to interrogate who 'we' are, and where our own ideas come from: problems of *implicit bias* (in terms of class, ethnicity, gender) needs to be aired with care and candour, including which community/ies the contributors can honestly be said to speak for, and how to reformulate our *idées reçues* as debatable questions.

- Finally, there is an inherent paradox in producing an academic book on democratic engagement; so the most likely *audience* for the book – say, school and college educators, and education policymakers – needs to be kept very firmly in mind; the people 'we' may most want to reach out to will most likely not even come across, let alone read, the kind of book we are writing.

WHERE MIGHT WE GO FROM HERE?

As I write, the shameful spectacle in 2022 of the UK Conservative government's mishandling of their financial and political strategy has culminated in the resignation of Prime Minister Liz Truss. This was a strategy driven, it has to be said, first and foremost by strong ideas. William Davies made an attempt, in an article of the time,[6] to trace the provenance of these ideas to what he calls 'the tradition of Austrian economics identified with [Friedrich von] Hayek, Joseph Schumpeter and Ludwig von Mises'. He goes on, 'Especially in its more libertarian forms, this school understands capitalism as an evolutionary system that is constantly remade by entrepreneurs and risk-takers, but which must periodically suffer periods of great crisis as a form of systemic cleansing, through which inefficient firms, outmoded technologies and bad investments are exposed and abandoned'.

So it would be a serious mistake to believe that the main problem with the policies adopted by the then Prime Minister Liz Truss and the then Chancellor of the Exchequer Kwasi Kwarteng is that they lacked ideas. This is, of course, only one – if particularly egregious – example of the ubiquitous influence of ideas and ideology on public life: my general point is that, if we want to engage with people's views and visions, we must look to something more, or other, than the mere presence or absence of 'ideas' to express and justify our agreement or opposition.

We might, for example, want to turn to the prophylactic of 'rationality' as promulgated by the modern enlightenment philosopher and arch-rationalist Professor Steven Pinker.[7] For Pinker, rationality is the cultivation and practice of healthy intellectual habits; he argues that skills like media literacy and critical thinking should form part of all educational provision, and not taught as discrete 'subjects' but suffused throughout the whole curriculum. Such '*everyday etiquette*', Pinker argued (in an interview on a BBC Radio 4 programme[8]), should include being able to make the strongest counterargument, to use probabilities, not to generalise from anecdote, and not to fall prey to fallacies like arguing from stereotypes or ignoring statistical base rates. In the same interview, he also admitted that such educative provision – including his own seminars – may have little impact on people's mindsets in the long run because humans tend to cling on to the 'myths' or morality-tales that offer meaning and purpose, which have at least as psychological valency as appeals to 'evidence'.

In any case, in a chapter in another book[9] I have argued that the notion of hard-and-fast evidence is itself suspect, given the epistemological and systemic problems associated with framing, collecting, analysing and publishing research data even in relatively uncontentious fields.

So I believe that to mount a powerful defence of our own ideas we need not only to demonstrate that we can think rationally and critically about them in terms of logicality and evidence, but also to espouse and articulate a set of values and ethical principles that our ideas serve. For people with a left-leaning perspective, these might include, let's say, 'equality', 'solidarity' and 'pluralism' in addition to 'freedom'. To express and develop these values properly, we would need to resist thinking in clichés about them. We would need to understand – and critique – their historical origin, to understand the mutual contradictions and trade-offs involved, and to take good account of what is now called 'intersectionality': the multiple and differential ways in which disadvantage and discrimination interact to affect different groups in society. We would need to be prepared to re-think, even abandon, some of our deeply-held positions as a consequence.

Even if we think we are equal to the task, this still leaves the major problem of how our own intellectual and ethical activity could counteract the massive over-simplifications, unhelpful polarities and downright mad conspiracy theories that seem now to occupy many public intellectual spaces. We could, for example, ask that social and other media sites and platforms are even more actively managed and held even more punitively accountable for hosting or posting misinformation; we could suggest that search engines carry health warnings about any content accessed thereby; we could call for more independent public bodies analogous to the UK's Office for Budget Responsibility to be established with authoritative oversight for the soundness of all public policy pro-posals; and so forth. But is this ultimately the direction we think is appropriate for an ideas-informed society to go in, or does it sound too much like George Orwell's 'Thinkpol' (the thought police in his novel *1984*)?

The challenge remains that the people we may believe are most in need of the affordances of rationality, defensible values, nuanced argument and open-minded dialogue are those least likely to be able to access them, or – if and when they do – to be amenable to the immense psychological work entailed in holding up their cherished world-views and narratives to forensic critique, those very ideas that shore up their souls against the uncertainty and unpredict-ability of being alive. And when I say 'they', I mean 'we', of course.

REFERENCES

1. Guilhot, N. 'How not to save democracy', *London Review of Books* blog, 22 December 2022.
2. Pinker, S. 'Interviewed on BBC Radio 4', *Today* programme, 12 October 2022.
3. For example, *Leading the Use of Research and Evidence in Schools* (2015); *An Ecosystem for Research-Engaged Schools: Reforming Education Through Research* (2019); *The*

research-informed teaching revolution: A handbook for the 21st century teacher (2020).

4. Marriott, J. 'I'm getting bored of octopus wisdom', *The Times*, 5 August 2022.

5. Origgi, G. https://www.edge.org/conversation/gloria_origgi-what-is-reputation.

6. Davies, W. 'Madman economics', *London Review of Books*, 20 October 2022, pp 3–5.

7. Pinker, S. 2021. *Rationality: What It Is, Why It Seems Scarce, Why It Matters*. London: Penguin.

8. Pinker, S. 'Interviewed on BBC Radio 4', *Today* programme, 12 October 2022.

9. Saunders, L. 2015. '"Evidence" and teaching: A question of trust?' In: Brown, C. (ed). *Leading Evidence Use for Schools*. London: Institute of Education Press.

4

BATTLE OF IDEAS: SHAPING THE FUTURE THROUGH DEBATE

Alastair Donald

THINKING BEYOND CONTEMPORARY ORTHODOXIES

The middle weekend in October 2022 was to prove significant. The then month-old Conservative Government, led by Prime Minister Liz Truss, was crumbling as scheming grandees and grey-suited upstarts prepared to impose a new leader.[1] In the days that followed, for the second time in as many months, a new Prime Minister was installed without recourse to the views of the electorate.[2] Instead, the British public had been cast as bystanders, expected to watch from the sidelines.

That same weekend, a crowd of nearly 3,000 people descended on London's Westminster, for centuries the focal point of British democracy and political life. The crowd was marked out by its refusal to accept the status of onlookers, keen instead to stake a claim as participants in shaping the political future. They were there to attend the Battle of Ideas festival, the flagship annual event convened by Academy of Ideas (AoI). Since the turn of the millennium, AoI has organised public debates where people from all walks of life come together to engage in intelligent discussion, often on challenging and controversial topics.

Ranging from knowledge-hungry school pupils to seasoned politicians, the crowd included students and professionals happily rubbing shoulders with campaigners and trade unionists, think tankers, academics and critics. The topics were wide-ranging, including the cost-of-living crisis, the return of war in Europe, the Culture Wars, the energy crisis and religious freedom, to name but a few. The debates provided both food for thought and a focus for constructive dialogue amongst an audience spanning political divides from left to liberal to conservative, and beyond. Notably, in an age of political tribes and intellectual silos, debate thrived on the presence of people prepared to think beyond the confines of contemporary orthodoxies and who embraced freedom of expression to argue a wide variety of views and positions. This was a space for ideas to be scrutinised and argued over, for the future to be shaped through *public* debate.

Today, ideas are widely celebrated, but they also occupy an ambiguous status in public life. This chapter explores the context for the Battle of Ideas festival and its ambition to make ideas central to shaping the future once more.

THE AMBIGUOUS STATUS OF IDEAS

Just over a century ago, in 'The Outline of History', his story of man from the origins of the earth through to the Great War, H.G. Wells asserted that 'human history is in essence a history of ideas'.[3] Writing in the aftermath of the turbulent destruction of the First World War, Wells asserted that moving beyond destructive national rivalries required common historical ideas and a common knowledge of ideas. 'Men and women, in every country', he said, are 'studying, thinking, writing, and teaching, getting together, correcting false impressions, and trying to find out and tell the truth'.

A century on, the conference 'Ideas, Intellectuals and The Public',[4] organised in 2003 by Academy of Ideas [then Institute of Ideas], noted an important shift in public life and argued that there is now 'ambiguity about the role of ideas'.[5] On the one hand, we live in a so-called 'knowledge society' where modern technologies ensure information at a click of a button. More young people than ever before go to university, and we have Substack and BookTok, popular historians and cultural pundits, museums, ideas hubs and literary festivals aplenty. On the other hand, the university, the pre-eminent space for ideas, is mired in controversy[i] over the freedom to explore ideas and pursue new knowledge.[6] Elsewhere, many worry over the dumbing down of culture, the declining status of intellectuals and a rise in conspiratorial thinking and 'post-truth' societies. In our soundbite society, Wells's paean to the essence of ideas is a slogan printed on fridge magnets.

Whatever the claims today that 'ideas no longer matter',[7] the problem is not that ideas no longer matter per se. Rather, when post-modern relativism creates an anything-goes world or intellectual inquiry is dictated by particularist, identity-driven perspectives that erode common standards and universal truths, then intellectual life, knowledge and ideas become devalued. And when society is less convinced ideas will make a significant difference, those who do insist on undertaking a journey of intellectual discovery become defensive, fearing being labelled elitist or irrelevant.[8]

POLITICS WITHOUT IDEAS

In the political sphere, the possibility of cohering society around a set of ideals has long co-existed with apprehension that mass society will be influenced by ideas. Take the liberal economist J.M. Keynes, who, like his contemporary H.G. Wells, wrote about the role of ideas in history. But writing during the interwar years marked by radical ideologies such as communism and fascism, Keynes also worried about the way ideas *shape* history and that what he termed 'illogical and dull doctrines' can exercise so 'powerful and enduring an influence over the minds of men and, through them, the events of history'.[9]

A century on, ideas are much diminished as the guiding force of politics. The age of ideologies proved short-lived, as ideas-oriented future visions unravelled in the post-war era.[10] When the End of

---

[i]Williams details how academic freedom to pursue knowledge and explore ideas is being distorted by marketisation, targets, diktats on relevance, academic activism, devaluation of knowledge in the face of multiple challenges including political and commercial agendas or imposed by Governments or corporate funders.

History[11] was declared at the conclusion of the Cold War, many drew the conclusion that the capacity for ideas to positively shape the course of history no longer existed. Instead, the claim that 'ideology is dead: it's competence we need now'[12] makes a virtue of avoiding future visions. Politicians now promise to run governments like businesses, based on 'results', not big ideas. An obsession with 'delivery' prevails amidst calls to follow the 'evidence' or 'The Science', with deference to experts replacing ideological vision.

But the rise of political managerialism co-exists today with a palpable sense of loss. 'There's a gaping hole at the centre of British politics where ideas used to be', declared one newspaper columnist bemoaning that 'where ideas once animated politics, now our political class is rudderless at a time of crisis'.[13] This sense of loss spans the political spectrum. For the Conservative Party-supporting *Spectator*, 'There is currently no theory in conservative politics' and 'the party no longer understands why or to what end they wield such power'.[14] Meanwhile the left-leaning *New Statesman* asks 'Where are Labour's big ideas?' and worries that: 'In an age of permanent crisis, a party that stands only for managerialism will be washed away'.[15]

POLITICS WITHOUT A PUBLIC

Those lamenting the absence of ideas were right to worry. The transition away from a contest over political ideals to the new expert-led, evidence-based managerial forms of politics leaves little capacity to inspire or engage the public. The result has been steeply declining political party membership and voter turnout at elections alongside a sense of political and moral disconnection between politicians and those they are meant to represent.

It's a problem exacerbated by new institutional and constitutional arrangements that place political debate largely beyond genuine democratic engagement. Where mass political parties, trade unions and numerous formal institutions and informal networks once provided arenas where the interests of civic society were worked out, political managerialism leaves little space for the public. Big decisions become the domain of global institutions, while elected governments develop policy via interacting with member states in various distant councils of the European Union.[16] It's a form of decision-making largely insulated from public opinion. At a local level, it takes the form of devolved executives and regional assemblies, who take their lead from NGOs and the third sector, and then give their decisions a formal gloss of democratic input via bloodless 'public consultation' exercises. The result is a 'void',[17] the hollowing of democracy such that new Prime Ministers can be installed beyond the say-so of electorates.

NEW CHALLENGES TO ADDRESS NEW INCURSIONS ON FREEDOM

The necessity is to revitalise ideas-based politics shaped by open public debate. But events of recent years demonstrate the scale of the challenge. Take the democratic demand for a voice claimed by millions of people who feel that the political system no longer takes them seriously. This informed the global rise of populist movements and, in the UK, a vote to leave the European Union. It is true that the referendum campaigns and accompanying media discussion betrayed failure to place ideas at the centre of debate. Important issues, such as the meaning of national sovereignty or why borders matter, were downplayed in lieu of soundbites and the politics of fear. But the re-engagement of sections of society long alienated from the political process could have been seen as a positive, while at the same time making the case for improved, ideas-informed debate. Instead the opposite conclusion was drawn. Disillusion with the referendum outcome led to questions over the capacity of electorates to grapple with important issues and the advisability of involving them in such decisions.[18] In today's ideology-lite times where many still fear the volatility of public opinion, some declared 'democracy works better when there is less of it'.[19]

The COVID-19 pandemic has served to boost the authority of technocratic decision-making. Whatever view one takes on lockdowns, vaccine mandates or other pandemic controversies, the alleged imperative of following the evidence and *The Science* effectively sidelined important political and moral questions – such as freedom of assembly or bodily autonomy – from public life.

Equally concerning are attempts to ring-fence issues judged acceptable for debate and define what constitutes acceptable views. The TwitterFiles investigations published in late 2022 revealed concerted efforts by the media, institutions and the state to limit information and ideas placed in the public arena. New or proposed legislation on protests, hate speech, misinformation and online safety places further constraints on public debate. Beyond state prohibition, a new problem is conformist social pressure exerted by our peers, meaning that exploring ideas is sacrificed to a perceived need to self-censor what we say. The trend for 'compelled' speech that shot to prominence in 2020, when 'Silence is Violence' became the slogan of Black Lives Matters, goes further, demanding we speak out in support of new racial justice etiquette or other iden-titarian[ii] causes because to do otherwise is judged to be complicit in discriminatory behaviour.

Some say that such attacks on freedom of conscience are a price worth paying for trying to live in a more equal society. What is wrong, they say, with changing social and cultural linguistic norms to rid ourselves of offensive or discriminatory views? In reality, expanding boundaries of what constitutes unacceptable opinion mean this new conformism serves to undermine debate on wider issues. Those keen to critically explore the politically driven ethos of multiculturalism or critical race theory, for example, may refrain from doing so if dismissed as racism-deniers or benefiting from white privilege.

The succumbing of universities to new orthodoxies has been much debated but remains largely misunderstood as simply an issue of 'no platforming' speakers. The bigger problem is the plethora of measures from trigger warnings to creating safe spaces that help embed a mindset suggesting that criticism, debate and encounters with controversial ideas are so discomfiting as to require chaper-ones and constraints. Notably, whereas in the past the notion that

---

[ii]Left-wing historian David Swift notes an identitarian outlook centred on four 'identity myths' – class, race, sex and generation – each of which has been essentialised and endowed with moral authority that makes them difficult to challenge. Swift makes the case for a return to recognising complexity, common causes and universalism. (David Swift, 'The Identity Myth', Constable, 2022).

ideas were potentially dangerous mainly emanated from conservatives, today such sentiments are embraced across society, but most forcibly expressed by the left and illiberal liberals.[20]

A significant problem for those organising new festivals of political and cultural debate is that the 'safe space' ethos of the university now permeates wider society. Notoriously, in 2018, the *New Yorker* rescinded an invitation to Steve Bannon, former chief strategist in the administration of US president Donald Trump, to speak at its literary festival, caving in to demands of some fellow speakers and a Twitter mob.[21] Meanwhile in London, admirably, *The Economist* resisted similar pressure to de-platform speakers at its Open Future Festival. Sadly, this merely prompted some panellists to withdraw in protest: 'I will not debate you', boasted one.[22] Preventing 'institutional recognition' for those who hold different opinions has become a cause that trumps the quest for truth through a collision of ideas.

Of course, platforming controversial figures is in some instances a shallow attempt to gain publicity. But in the intellectual arena, the existence of 'controversial' ideas might once have been understood as symbolic of the clash of views necessary for thriving pluralist democracies. Today, too often, 'controversial' ideas are simply condemned for causing offence or challenging received wisdom. They become a means to justify constraints on what can be said in the name of preventing encounters with views that cause intellectual discomfort.

WHY THE BATTLE OF IDEAS FESTIVAL?

If vibrant public life depends on open discussion of ideas and constructive dialogue, then society needs new spaces where ideas, beliefs and political positions can be scrutinised and freely debated.

It is this space that the Battle of Ideas festival set out to create. The convenors of the inaugural event in 2005 noted the aim was to attract those committed to going behind the headlines and engaging in open and robust debate: 'Taking ideas seriously means they must be interrogated, argued for and fought over', they argued. As an alternative to the minutiae of everyday policy, the festival

unashamedly aimed to initiate open-ended discussions on important social, political, scientific, academic and cultural issues,
regardless of demands for immediate practical outcomes. Instead of
rehearsing their latest book or policy paper to an audience of
experts in the field, speakers are asked to 'apply their insights to
broad questions of intellectual importance' and challenged to
interact with a *public* audience and engage with their ideas, all with
the aim of fostering 'an atmosphere of intellectual freedom and
open-ended exploration of new ideas'.[23]

DEBATING FIRST PRINCIPLES

As a starting point, no issue is considered beyond debate and speakers
and audience alike must be free to challenge orthodoxies and examine
first principles. Take for example the issue of environmentalism,
where new orthodoxies of climate change mean that debate is now
often limited to what measures should be deemed necessary to achieve
'sustainable' outcomes. But if the outcome is determined then all that
remains to discuss is expert technical prescriptions devised to get there.
Left untouched in this scenario are bigger questions raised by the
embrace of the environmental worldview, including a shift in
long-established understanding of humanity's relationship to nature,
questions of human-centred progress and of why the environmental
outlook itself has recently gained unquestioned moral authority.

Consequently, while it is certainly necessary to explore solutions to
climate change, we must also be free to debate the bigger issues such as
the apocalyptic worldview associated with the 'climate emergency', as
it is now called. Why is climate change now viewed as an 'existential
threat' rather than a practical challenge? Does the rise of 'eco-anxiety'
risk a paralysing impact on young people and wider society?

SEARCHING FOR A COMMON LANGUAGE

One challenge today is to find commonly agreed meaning and
language with which to debate issues. Concepts that we thought we
knew the meaning of – like class, community or racism – have

changed markedly in recent years. Ask 30 different women what feminism means to them and you might well get 30 different answers. Even well-established political categories such as 'liberal' and 'conservative' are widely interpreted and can feel outdated and lacking in meaning. Indeed, when epithets such as 'neo-fascist' and 'cultural Marxist' are hurled at presumed opponents, such labels often seem grounded in assumed group identity rather than political reality, leading those on different sides of a debate to talk past each other rather than engaging in constructive discussion.

With language itself now a politicised battlefield, a common vocabulary cannot be determined by dictionary guardians but must be worked out through discussion and debate. This is difficult when the Culture Wars leaves people divided within identity-based silos, closed to alternative points of view. But while debate on a wide range of political and cultural issues can be ill-tempered – some would say 'toxic' – the solution is to open debate up, not shut it down. Whatever the appearance of the Culture Wars as engrained individual antagonisms, it is actually rooted in contested political ideals such as the preservation (or not) of traditional cultural and social norms. The task of the festival in all topics is to locate such conflicting ideas and provide the space to productively grapple with new developments to better understand our complex world.

FREE THINKERS WELCOME

To do so, the freedom to raise difficult questions and express unfashionable opinions is essential. That's why the festival mottos – 'free speech allowed' and 'free thinkers welcome' – are not just slogans but statements of intent. Critics decry such commitment to free speech as simply enabling bigotry and facilitating privileged individuals to 'punch down', for example, against women or people of colour. But while posed as a progressive concern, in reality such views reveal critics' own diminished view of minorities who are now cast as lacking the capacity to engage equally in open discussion. Not only does this reveal disenchantment with open democratic debate, it also can operate as a form of moral coercion used to exert control over what is to be judged a legitimate matter of debate and to prevent airing what are intuited to be 'bad' ideas. In reality, it is far better if contentious views are stated and then confronted and debated, rather than remaining unspoken and therefore unchallenged and left to fester.

However, a commitment to free expression does not mean that we should accept that 'everyone has their own truth' and all opinions are deemed to be equally valid. But just as an 'anything goes' outlook points to the grip of post-modern relativism, at the same time others believe that people are overly 'judgemental' and that to judge is a form of cultural imperialism. Regardless of whether one thinks there is a deficit or a surfeit of judgement, in reality objective standards of right and wrong are our main defence against bad ideas and if we lose those standards we are in trouble.[24] Therefore, it is even more important than ever to uphold the importance of considered judgement and our capacity to be critical as a means to seek clarity. All festival attendees are urged to be both tolerant and open to listening to all views, but equally, to be prepared to express opinions and to judge what is right. Whatever your own views, truly creative discussion comes about only when we accept there can always be another side to the story, that others hold opposing views in good faith and they may well have a point. But as the words that we use become more heavily scrutinised, policing language is seen as a way of changing behaviour and evading tough issues. More than ever, we need freethinkers rather than 'correct' ways of thinking.

EMPOWERING ROBUST EXCHANGE OF IDEAS

Without freely and openly debating ideas, the notion of an ideas-informed society can only ever be superficial. Hearteningly, there is an audience out there willing to freely question the ideas of others but also put their own ideas to the test. Indeed, this is the factor often missed in our fatalistic times where a new paternalistic outlook embodies the view that people are too fragile to engage with difficult and potentially upsetting ideas. Actually, many people are more than willing to grasp that opportunity. They resist flouncing off at the first sign of a view they disagree with and instead rise to the challenge of what has been said, and argue back. Even where they still end up disagreeing, they do so from a more informed standpoint, better equipped to support their own views.

The Battle of Ideas festival aims to create an intellectual journey, with many different routes to take. It is not simply about listening to academics and commentators telling you what *they* think. Instead, the *audience* is the festival, and they are actively encouraged to have their say.

At the end of the day, a society informed by ideas cannot be magicked up through reading a book or attending a lecture, commendable as each may be. Nor is taking a course on critical thinking a substitute for engaging with and arguing over ideas with peers as a means to recreate the public square. For those looking to achieve that – and for answers to the big questions thrown up by contemporary politics and culture – the Battle of Ideas festival is the place to be.

NOTES

1. Ellen O'Dwyer, Can Liz Truss be ousted as Prime Minister? How a potential Rishi Sunak and Penny Mordaunt coup might work, *i*, 14 October 2022 https://inews.co.uk/news/liz-truss-prime-minister-can-ousted-rishi-sunak-penny-mordaunt-coup-explained-1911088.
2. Ben Quinn, Calls grow for general election after Rishi Sunak becomes Tory leader, *The Guardian*, 24 October 2022 https://www.theguardian.com/politics/2022/oct/24/calls-grow-for-general-election-after-rishi-sunak-becomes-tory-leader.
3. H. G. Wells, The Outline of History, *The Project Gutenberg EBook*, 2014 [1920] https://www.gutenberg.org/files/45368/45368-h/45368-h.htm.
4. Institute of Ideas, Ideas, Intellectuals and the Public, conference programme, 2003.
5. Dolan Cummings, Introduction: Ideas, Intellectuals and the Public, *Critical Review of International Social and Political Philosophy*, p. 1, Vol. 6, No. 4, Winter 2003.

6. Joanna Williams, Chapter 4, Disciplines under attack, in Academic Freedom in an Age of Conformity: Confronting the Fear of Knowledge, Palgrave Macmillan, 2016.

7. Terry Eagleton, Today Ideas Don't Matter, *The Guardian*, 23 March 2004 https://www.theguardian.com/books/2004/mar/23/immigrationpolicy.politics.

8. Frank Furedi, Where Have All the Intellectuals Gone?, *Continuum*, 2005.

9. J. M. Keynes, The End of Laissez-faire, Hogarth Press, 1926. Republished https://eclass.uoa.gr/modules/document/file.php/ECON246/John%20Maynard%20Keynes%20Laissez%20faire%201926.pdf.

10. Daniel Bell, The End of Ideology: On the Exhaustion of Political Ideas in the Fifties, 1960.

11. Francis Fukuyama, The End of History? The National Interest No. 16 (Summer 1989), Center for the National Interest, pp. 3–18.

12. William Hague, Ideology Is Dead: It's Competence We Need Now, *The Times*, 17 October 2022 https://www.thetimes.co.uk/article/ideology-is-dead-its-competence-we-need-now-9tjlxl07r.

13. William Davies, There's a Gaping Hole at the Centre of British Politics Where Ideas Used to be, *The Guardian*, 13 August 2022 https://www.theguardian.com/commentisfree/2022/aug/13/gaping-hole-british-politics-ideas-liz-truss-rishi-sunak-keri-starmer.

14. John Oxley, The Crisis at the Heart of the Conservative Party https://www.spectator.co.uk/article/the-crisis-at-the-heart-of-the-modern-conservative-party/.

15. Neal Lawson, Where Are Labour's Big Ideas? https://www.newstatesman.com/comment/2022/05/where-are-labours-big-ideas?.

16. George Hoare, Behind Boris's Failure, *Compact*, 8 June 2022.

17. Peter Mair, Ruling the Void: The Hollowing of Western Democracy, Verso 2023 [2013].

18. Jared Diamond, Brexit Too Complicated for Referendum, Says Jared Diamond, *The Guardian*, 1 June 2019.

19. Janan Ganesh, Democracy Works Better When There Is Less of It, *Financial Times*, 9 September 2020 https://www.ft.com/content/f68c13a4-1130-49d5-b3c6-2270711d819e.

20. Claire Fox, The Dangers of Illiberal Liberalism, *The Economist*, 17 August 2018 https://www.economist.com/open-future/2018/08/17/the-dangers-of-illiberal-liberalism.

21. Justin Charity, Steve Bannon, The New Yorker, and the Merits of Deplatforming, *The Ringer*, 4 September 2018 https://www.theringer.com/2018/9/4/17821274/steve-bannon-the-new-yorker-festival-deplatforming.

22. Laurie Penny, No, I Will Not Debate You, *Longreads*, 18 September 2018 https://longreads.com/2018/09/18/no-i-will-not-debate-you/.

23. Battle of Ideas festival programme, 2005.

24. Maarten Boudry, Why Relativism is the Worst Idea Ever, The Official Blog of the American Philosophical Association, 29 July 2021.

PART 2

TRUTH-TELLING, DEMOCRACY AND COMMUNITY

5

'BATTLE OF IDEAS': WEAPONISING THE FREE SPEECH FALLACY

Sam Fowles

THE FALLACY OF THE 'BATTLE OF IDEAS'

An ideas-led society presumes inputs of ideas. Some suggest that all ideas should be treated as equal, allowed to fight it out in a 'battle of ideas' – a Hobbesian 'war of all against all'.[1] This idea is at best naive and at worst oppressive. It ignores the structural imbalances of power which make it impossible for all ideas to begin on a level playing-field. Approaching public discourse as a pure 'battle of ideas' thus, in practice, serves to exclude, rather than embrace, original thinking. A meaningful public discourse requires grappling with these inequalities.

A SALUTARY TALE!

Let's begin with a story. Rod and Tim met working for Labour MPs in the 1980s. They went on to work together at the BBC. Rod rose to become editor of the Today programme. Tim edited the Scotsman (for four months). Turning to academia, he eventually became Principal of South College at Durham University.[2] Rod left the BBC after breaking its allegedly neutrality rules.[3] He embarked on a lucrative career as a contrarian columnist, writing for the *Sun*, the *Sunday Times* and the *Spectator*.[4] Rod's work included producing a documentary featuring an uncritical interview with the leader of the British National Party,[5] suggested he should be free to look at child pornography (because he is a journalist),[6] wrote a piece jeopardising the trial of Stephen Lawrence's killers[7] and pushed various racist myths.[8] He also made headlines after accepting a caution for punching his pregnant girlfriend.[9]

Tim, however, was stuck by his friend. In December 2021, he invited Rod to speak at the South College Christmas Formal, a dinner for students. Rod opened by expressing his disappointment that there were no prostitutes present. He went on to mock transgender students, then spent some time defending British colonialism. Students present objected. Some exclaimed 'racist' and 'disgusting'. Many walked out. This enraged Tim. He shouted at his students, calling them 'pathetic'.[10] His wife called them a 'bunch of inadequates [sic]'.[11]

Tim claimed his reaction reflected his 'commitment to freedom of speech'.[12] But he seemed more committed to his mate's privilege. Tim commanded a powerful platform: a captive audience of some of the country's brightest students. He could have given that platform to anyone (including the many interesting speakers who have never been accused of endangering a conviction for murder, spreading racist myths, or assaulting their partners). But Tim chose to give that platform to Rob. He certainly wasn't committed to his students free speech – indeed, he appears to have been offended by it. It seems that, for Tim, his friend was entitled to air his views but those who disagreed were not.

Tim was asked to step back from public appearances for a few weeks. He was allowed to keep his position, his salary and his benefits.[13] In response, in articles, television spots and radio interviews across the country, Rod and Tim's former colleagues in the media came to their defence. The *Daily Mail* named and shamed Durham professors who had offered pastoral support for the students.[14] Columnists in national newspapers waxed lyrical about 'cancel culture'.[15] Meanwhile, Rod (in the name of 'freedom of speech') demanded the students apologise for protesting against his views and criticising his friend.[16] None of Rod's critics were offered a similar platform.

THE HYPOCRISY OF PSEUDO-FREE SPEECH

The story of Rod Liddle and Tim Luckhurst is just one of many battles being fought over 'cancel culture'. Complainants often turn out to be no more than entitled individuals who don't like being subject to criticism. Harrow-educated Laurence Fox claimed that 'our culture [of free speech] is under attack like never before'[17] after fellow actors criticised him for attacking the Black Lives Matter movement.[18] He was given multiple spreads in The Times[19] and interviewed on almost every major television channel. Peter Tatchell claimed to have been 'no platformed' after a National Union of Students officer declined an invitation to speak with him at an event. He was given an interview on the Guardian to talk at length about his restricted freedom of speech[20] (the NUS officer was given no such platform).[i] Matthew Goodwin, a senior figure at the Legatum Institute think tank (and regular television guest), claimed his freedom of speech was under threat because, *inter alia*, a colleague described his work as 'problematic'.[21]

The hypocrisy of pseudo-free speech advocates is well documented, but their arguments flow from a deeper intellectual fallacy – that public discourse can be organised as a 'battle of ideas'. This takes literally the Miltonian exhortation to 'let Truth and falsehood grapple; who ever knew Truth to be put to the worse in a free and open encounter?' It is certainly superficially attractive. We would all like to believe that good arguments will always defeat bad ones and the truth will always be out. But the 'battle of ideas' thesis fails on first contact with reality. It presumes a level playing field for discourse that does not exist in the real world.

---

[i]To be clear, Tatchell was still invited to speak at the event, the only person who lost their right to speak was the NUS officer themselves.

SOME CLARITY ABOUT 'SPEECH' AND 'PLATFORM'

First, the 'battle of ideas' theory fails to account for the fact that not all ideas can receive a platform. This flows from the 'cancel culture' myth that conflates 'platform' with 'speech'. Proponents claim that any failure to provide someone (almost always someone with whom they agree) with a platform represents an attack on 'free speech'. A report by the Adam Smith Institute, for example, accused various students' unions of 'undermining freedom of association and expression'. It exclusively cited examples in which speakers (generally prompting perspectives with which the ASI agrees) were either not offered an invitation to speak or had such an invitation withdrawn.[22]

But 'platform' and 'speech' are not the same. Speech is a right. It is recognised in law and as an essential component of democratic society, and has been for centuries. Platform is a resource. There are a finite number of opportunities to present ideas to an audience. Not everyone can be on a television show, write a column or appear on a panel.

Student unions have a platform. They have people willing to organise events, venues and (in many cases) a substantial audience willing to attend. But none of these are infinite. Student unions are private organisations (their legal status is roughly akin to private members clubs). It is up to the members and leadership to decide who gets to use their platform. They are should be entitled to invite who they want and, should they choose to do so, disinvite who they want as well. Whether one agrees with students' decisions is irrelevant. The freedom of speech of the invitees is not impacted by whether or not they are given access to a platform.[23] The same is true, for most television providers, newspapers, magazines and every other platform. Although it might be argued that those with a public function (like national media) have a moral duty to platform a diverse range of ideas.

To be given a platform, therefore, is a privilege. Seen through this lens the 'battle of ideas' takes on a very different shape. We must ask ourselves who is being given a platform and why. The burden lies, not with the platform holder (to justify why it has been denied to a certain individual), but with the person seeking a

platform (to explain why they, rather than others, should be entitled to that privilege). Moreover, it means that public discourse
must also be analysed in the context of existing privileges and
power structures. If a functional public discourse requires a diverse
range of inputs, then the focus should arguably be on platforming
the perspectives of those who are historically or structurally
excluded or oppressed.

TREATING THE TRUTH AS IRRELEVANT

Second, in treating all perspectives as prima facie equal, the 'battle
of ideas' theory fails to account for the prevalence of 'bullshit' in
public discourse. 'Bullshit' describes a statement which aims to
convince without regard for the truth. Princeton's Harry Frankfurt
distinguishes a 'liar' from a 'bullshitter'. The former implicitly
acknowledges the truth by subverting it. The latter treats the truth
as irrelevant.[24]

Bullshit increasingly dominates public discourse in the West. In
the UK, our understanding of many issues is often almost entirely
divorced from reality. This is exemplified by the debate around
immigration. Between 1990 and 2020, the tabloid media produced
an average of four stories per day about immigration. The majority
portrayed immigrants in a negative light and had, at best, a
tangential relationship with the truth. By 2020, opposition to
immigration correlated negatively with actual experience of immigrants. In other words, the belief that immigration was problematic
was more likely to be held by those with no experience of
immigrants in real life.[25]

This phenomenon persists across public discourse. Ipsos MORI
regularly polls public perceptions about the factual context for
policy issues. These consistently show our perceptions to be
divorced from reality.[26] As the *Independent*'s headline put it,
reporting on one such survey, 'British public wrong about nearly
everything'.[27]

Many supposed instances of 'cancel culture' turn out to be
bullshit. In September 2020, Matthew Goodwin tweeted:

> *David Hume, the Enlightenment titan, gets cancelled...*
> *[sic] in Scotland. If the plan is to cancel everybody who*
> *had unsavoury views or social circles more than 250*
> *years ago then I fear for colleagues in political theory –*
> *they will soon have nothing to teach.*[28]

In fact, all that had happened was the University of Edinburgh had changed the name of a building on one of its campuses. No change had been made to any syllabi, nor at any of the 14 other universities in Scotland. In 2017, the Telegraph ran the headline 'Student Forces Cambridge to Drop White Authors'. This was entirely fictitious. A group of students at Cambridge had written a letter to the post-colonial literature faculty requesting that more minoritised authors be added to the curriculum. No white author had been dropped and no student had requested that the university do so.[29]

Truth is inherently democratic. Anyone can tell the truth. When public discourse is anchored in reality, arguments are convincing to the extent they are based on facts and evidence. But when discourse is bullshitised, success in public debate is determined by the number of people who can be reached with the lie. Liz Truss, for example, based her populist appeal in the 2022 conservative party leadership election around the claim to have gone to a failing comprehensive school. Several newspapers quickly discovered that she actually attended a highly rated school in a wealthy suburb.[30] But Truss was able to repeat her bullshit backstory from influential and privileged platforms and so, for many, it became part of her public image. The fact that it was never true simply didn't matter. Truss was able to convey the populist image, drawing a distinction with her rival (the patrician Rishi Sunak), which secured her the Conservative leadership and the job of Prime Minister. In a Miltonian 'battle of ideas', one would expect Truss' dishonesty to count against her. Once exposed it would suggest she was untrustworthy and damaged her credibility. But it did the opposite, helping to deliver political success for Truss. Truth and falsehood grappled but truth was undoubtedly 'put to the worse'.

STRUCTURAL INEQUALITY

Third, the 'battle of ideas' theory fails to account for structural inequality. We do not all start with the same advantages and so cannot all engage in public discourse to the same effect. It is not, and has never been, 'a free and open encounter'. There is no need to repeat the wealth of research[31] on structural inequality here. Suffice it to say that members of certain groups, particularly racialised communities and the poor, face significant disadvantages compared to members of more privileged groups. These disadvantages are not transient or specified to the individual but baked into the structure of society.[32]

Guy Standing identifies those disadvantaged by structural inequality generally as a distinct class: 'the precariat'. Members of the precariat are not simply disadvantaged in economic or political terms but are less able to play a full and active role in society than more privileged citizens.[33] They are, consequently, less able to contribute to public discourse – to take up arms in any 'battle of ideas'. Members of the precariat are, for example, less likely to be given a platform. Indeed the (so-called) 'Battle of Ideas Festival' event on 'populism', which purported to discuss ideas about how to 'take back control' from the mainstream media, comprised a panel made up predominately of commentators from the *Telegraph*, *Spectator* and *Spiked*. All three publications were owned or funded (whether entirely or partially) by non-domiciled billionaires. The *Telegraph* and *Spectator* were both owned by Frederick Barclay, one of the 'big six' media barons who control around 75% of the UK media market.[34] Not a single member of the precariat was on the panel.

The precariat are also excluded in less direct ways. Those struggling to survive economically tend to work longer hours, cannot afford childcare and spend significant portions of their lives dealing with labyrinthine government bureaucracy (such as the benefits and social housing systems) and so have less capacity to educate themselves and engage in public discourse. Children growing up in the precariat are not offered the same opportunities to learn the skills necessary to engage in a battle of ideas (like public speaking and debating). Humanities subjects, which teach the 'soft skills' necessary to engage in public discourse, have been defunded or eliminated in state schools by successive governments.[35]

The 'battle of ideas' theory ignores these three factors, pretending that all ideas start off on a level playing field. It is thus, in its own way, a form of bullshit: a wilful denial of reality. A 'battle of ideas' on such terms inevitably narrows, rather than broadens the range if inputs into an ideas led society. Those with the greatest privilege are able to dominate the available platforms, confining public discourse to the narrow set of shibboleths promoted by a privileged class.

BUILDING AN IDEAS-LED SOCIETY

How, then, to achieve an 'ideas led society' without a 'battle of ideas'? In a perfect world we would address the broader social and political problems that make a meaningful 'battle of ideas' impossible. But, frustratingly, it is not clear how we can address those problems without an effective public discourse.

The answer to this Catch-22 lies in the allocation of platform. Proponents of 'battle of ideas' and cancel culture myths fixate on the denial of platform to those like them or with whom they agree. Given that (ironically) they often dominate high profile media platforms themselves, public debate around denial of platform tends to focus on the circumstances in which already powerful individuals are not provided with the further platform to which they consider themselves entitled. This obscures the genuine problems around the distribution of platform – the exclusion of marginalised communities and the platforming of bullshitters.

Building an ideas-led society requires tackling the structural imbalances of power addressed above. In the absence of wholesale social reform, it must begin with the distribution of platform. This applies across the spectrum of platforms, from national media to the most minor speaking or writing opportunity. The platform resource should be used to enhance public discourse rather than diminish it. I therefore propose two criteria by which platform should be allocated: representation and quality.

The representation criterion addresses the problem of structural inequality. It means ensuring that those who are often excluded from full participation in society have an equivalent level of platform-opportunity as the traditionally privileged.

The 'quality' criterion addresses the problem of bullshit and seeks to enhance the standard of inputs into public discourse. It means assessing the likely quality of a candidate for platform's proposed contribution by prioritising *inter alia*, genuine expertise and/or experience, rejection of bullshit, avoiding conflicts of interest, and arguments which are demonstrably evidence-based and internally coherent.

These two criteria will sometimes pull in different directions. That is inevitable when applying subjective concepts. Whatever approach to public discourse is adopted, however, platform will inevitably be conferred based on subjective criteria. The only debate is about what criteria are adopted. Under the status quo 'battle of ideas', platform is often awarded based on perceived entitlement or embrace of controversial views. If we are to ensure that an ideas-led society is driven by ideas that are both diverse and well founded, then the dual criteria of representation and quality are preferable.

FINAL REFLECTION ON IMPROVING PUBLIC DISCOURSE

Policy is only effective insofar as it is rooted in the real world. Perhaps the greatest challenge to the achievement of an ideas led society is that the language of 'free speech' is consistently adopted to legitimise and buttress existing privilege (ironically – or perhaps intentionally – with the effect of chilling the speech of those with genuinely innovative or alternative perspectives). I have sought to address that challenge by tacking the intellectual fallacy underlying the 'battle of ideas' thesis. It is a view of public discourse which conflates platform with speech, bullshit with truth and structural inequality with lack of deference to the powerful. It is, in essence, a bullshit conceit, based on wilful ignorance of reality. Little more than a pseudo-intellectual justification for maintaining the privilege of the powerful.

An ideas led society requires an effective public discourse. In an imperfect world, I suggest our discourse can be improved by allocating platform based on two criteria: Representation (i.e., seeking to counteract structural inequalities which exclude minoritized people from public debate), and quality (preferring good arguments to 'controversy for its own sake'). These principles can set us on the road towards achieving a genuine marketplace of diverse and high-quality ideas (even if it upsets Rod and Tim…).

REFERENCES

1. Hobbes, T., (1642), *De Cive*, (re-printed by CreateSpace 2017).
2. https://www.theguardian.com/education/2021/dec/09/durham-head-steps-back-after-calling-students-pathetic-at-rod-liddle-event.
3. According to the BBC's own investigation into the matter. https://www.theguardian.com/media/2002/sep/28/pressandpublishing.broadcasting2.
4. https://www.theguardian.com/media/greenslade/2010/jan/11/theindependent-simon-kelner; https://www.celebsagewiki.com/rod-liddle.
5. https://www.thetimes.co.uk/article/liddles-argument-blows-up-in-his-face-jc509k6c6bx.
6. https://www.theguardian.com/society/2003/jan/14/childprotection.rodliddle.
7. https://www.theguardian.com/media/2012/may/09/spectator-magazine-charge-lawrence-trial.
8. https://www.standard.co.uk/hp/front/rod-liddle-censured-over-racist-blog-on-black-crime-6777153.html.
9. https://www.thetimes.co.uk/article/liddle-gets-caution-for-row-with-girlfriend-2fvkhxsbpn5.

10. https://www.theguardian.com/education/2021/dec/09/
    durham-head-steps-back-after-calling-students-pathetic-at-
    rod-liddle-event.

11. https://www.dailymail.co.uk/news/article-10288183/Rod-
    Liddle-demands-grovelling-apology-Durham-University.html.

12. https://www.theguardian.com/education/2021/dec/09/
    durham-head-steps-back-after-calling-students-pathetic-at-
    rod-liddle-event.

13. https://www.theguardian.com/education/2021/dec/09/
    durham-head-steps-back-after-calling-students-pathetic-at-
    rod-liddle-event.

14. https://www.dailymail.co.uk/news/article-10300045/Durham-
    University-lecturers-accused-stoking-left-wing-students-
    campus-free-speech-furore.html.

15. https://www.thetimes.co.uk/article/the-compulsion-to-cancel-
    is-out-of-control-0kmzscfv3.

16. https://www.dailymail.co.uk/news/article-10288183/Rod-
    Liddle-demands-grovelling-apology-Durham-University.html.

17. https://www.express.co.uk/comment/expresscomment/
    1397423/Lawrence-Fox-The-Reclaim-Party-mission-state-
    ment-freedom-of-speech-latest.

18. https://metro.co.uk/2020/09/10/laurence-fox-claims-rebecca-
    front-has-cancelled-him-after-lewis-co-star-blocks-him-due-to-
    all-lives-matter-claims-13251372/.

19. https://www.google.com/search?q=laurence+fox+interview
    +the+times&client=safari&rls=en&sxsrf=APq-WBtAxYiD
    cl6CNEMnTG98Pw029xKRxw%3A1644246413541&ei=
    jTUBYsK8IJmX8gKjurOABQ&ved=0ahUKEwiCt5ub7-31A
    hWZi1wKHSPdDFAQ4dUDCA0&uact=5&oq=laurence+
    fox+interview+the+times&gs_lcp=Cgdnd3Mtd2l6EAM6B
    AgAEEc6BQgAEIAEOgYIABAWEB46CAghEBYQHRAeSgQ
    IQRgASgQIRhgAUP8EWJoMYOoMaABwAngAgAFYiAHv
    BZIBATmYAQCgAQHIAQjAAQE&sclient=gws-wiz.

20. https://www.theguardian.com/uk-news/2016/feb/13/peter-
    tatchell-snubbed-students-free-speech-veteran-gay-rights-
    activist.

21. https://www.politics.co.uk/comment/2021/01/25/the-invented-
    free-speech-crisis/.

22. Young, M., and Dube, L., 'State of the Unions: How to restore free association and expression, combat extremism and make student unions effective', ASI, (20 September 2020).

23. The exception to this may be where it could be proved that a union deliberately refused access to its platform on the basis of a protected characteristic recognised by the Equality Act 2010. It is worth noting however that 'holding offensive views' is not a protected characteristic.

24. Frankfurt, H., *On Bullshit*, (Princeton; Princeton University Press, 2005).

25. Fowles, S., *Overruled: Confronting Our Vanishing Democracy in 8 Cases*, (London; Oneworld, 2022), pp. 159–160.

26. Ipsos MORI, 'The Perils of Perception' (2018), (6 December 2018), available at https://www.ipsos.com/ipsos-mori/en-uk/perils-perception-2018 (last accessed 18 September 2020).

27. Paige, J., 'British public wrong about nearly everything, survey shows', The Independent, (17 February 2014), available at https://www.independent.co.uk/news/uk/home-news/british-public-wrong-about-nearly-everything-survey-shows-8697821.html (last accessed 10 November 2020).

28. https://twitter.com/goodwinmj/status/1305407204082823170?s=12.

29. Malik, N., *We Need New Stories: Challenging the Toxic Myths Behind Our Age of Discontent*, (Kindle Ed.), (London; Widenfield & Nicolson, 2019), l. 759.

30. https://metro.co.uk/2022/07/26/what-did-liz-truss-say-about-her-school-roundhay-comments-reaction-17068449/.

31. See, for example, George, A. S., 'Structural determinants of gender inequality: why they matter for adolescent girls' sexual and reproductive health', [2020] BMJ 368; Dressler, W., Oths, K., and Gravlee, C., 'Race and Ethnicity in Public Health Research: Models to Explain Health Disparaties', 34 Annu. Rev. Anthropol. 231; UNESCO, 'Structural inequality impedes geneder equality in education', Global Education Monitoring Report, (2019), available at https://gem-report-2019.unesco.org/gender-report/structural_inequality/.

32. See, for example, Royce, R., (2008), *Poverty and Power: The Problem of Structural Inequality*, (Lanham; Rowman & Littlefield, 2008).

33. Standing, G., *The Precariat: A New and Dangerous Class*, (London; Bloomsbury, 2011).

34. Fowles, S., *Overruled: Confronting Our Vanishing Democracy in 8 Cases*, (London; Oneworld, 2022), p. 140.

35. https://www.politics.co.uk/comment/2022/02/17/nadhim-zahawi-is-wrong-our-education-system-needs-less-balance/.

6

REVERSING POLARISATION: HOW CHALLENGING IDEAS CAN HELP PEOPLE FIND COMMON PURPOSE[i]

Sir Paul Collier

BRITAIN'S EMBARRASSINGLY UNEQUAL LIFE-CHANCES

Life-chances, more fancily termed *inter-generational mobility*, describe the likelihood that someone born into the poorest 40% of households will, during their adult life rise into the highest 40%. It is an important concept, in many respects more important than the more familiar concept of inequality in current incomes. Although high inequality in current income is socially problematic in many respects, deep differences in life-chances are more crushing. They are the graveyard of hopes of self-improvement. If someone currently poor knows that they and their children are condemned by circumstances over which they have no control to remain poor for the rest of their lives, they are likely to respond with either anger or despair.

Although it has been little-noticed, Britain has the lowest inter-generational mobility in the whole of the OECD. This is an

---

[i]This article summarises some of the themes in my forthcoming book, *The Future of the Left-Behind* (Allen Lane, 2024). Some were first sketched in my earlier book, *The Future of Capitalism: Facing the New Anxieties* (Allen Lane, 2018).

astounding and disgraceful failure of national public policy. Since it has persisted for at least the past four decades, it has spanned phases in which both the main political parties have controlled government, and included two during which the Liberal Party was in alliance, once with the Labour, and once with the Conservatives. If we look at differences in life-chances – the levels of intergenerational social inequality, Britain has the highest level of inequality of any country for which we have useable data, with the sole exception of Peru. Denmark has the lowest degree of intergenerational inequality in the modern world. And the difference between Denmark and Britain is staggering. How do we get from Britain to Denmark? How do we escape such extreme differences in opportunities?

Nor does Britain's extreme inequality in life-chances reflect a trade-off between them and average prosperity. There are many countries in the OECD which have achieved both more equal life-chances and higher average income than Britain: Denmark itself, Norway, Sweden, the Netherlands, Ireland, France, Belgium, Germany, Japan, Canada and even the USA. This suggests that as a nation we have a lot to learn from other countries, yet to date neither our political parties nor our civil service has shown any interest in doing so. This unwarranted arrogance is in some respects even more astounding than the facts themselves.

Within Britain, I will focus on England because unlike the other three component countries of the United Kingdom which have recently benefited from some degree of devolution, England has been run from London. Indeed, England is[ii] exceptional in the degree to which power is centralised in its capital city. Not only is government exceptionally concentrated in London, but so are the courts, the media, finance and the nation's transport infrastructure. While England is run from national government in London, London itself is an exception: considerable powers have been

---

[ii]Britain has 90 universities of which 18 are ranked in the global top 100 for their research. But within them there is a striking hierarchy of status, reflected in funding and applications. Oxbridge has unique prestige; while Imperial and UCL are top-ranked in their flagship departments. Awareness of status is reflected in the creation of the 'Russell Group', is a self-appointed brand used for marketing by 20 universities to distinguish themselves from former Polytechnics.

devolved to it from central government: it has a mayor, a large administration and its own transport authority. It has also been favoured by Whitehall with far higher public spending on virtually everything.

The gross inequalities in life-chances are related to this exceptional centralisation because the key determinants of English life-chances are strongly related to geography. Again, this is exceptional: in most other OECD countries, differences in life-chances might be due predominantly to characteristics like disability, race, language or the gender of the household head. In England, all such characteristics are overwhelmed by two other influences. One is the region where you are born: the rule is simple, be born in the South-East. Failing that, be born as near to it as possible: the further North or West your birthplace, the worse are your life-chances. The other is to be born to parents at least one of whom has been to one of the top four universities (Oxbridge, Imperial or UCL). Failing that, have a parent who has been to a university that is as highly ranked as possible. If you tick both boxes – you were born in the South-East, and your parents went to a 'top four', you are in the best country in the world. Even if you are stupid and lazy, your chances of remaining in the highest-income (40% of households) are very high indeed. I think of such young people as 'camouflaged clots'. If you are born in London itself, even if your parents did not go to university, you should not be too dismayed. As part of the sizeable London-bias in public spending, far more will have been spent on your schooling than if you had grown up elsewhere in England, so you are far more likely to gain entry to a good university.

If, however, you are at the other end of the spectrum, born far from the South-East, with parents who had little education, your life-chances are wretched. Quoting the advice of her uneducated father about their home-region of the North-East, which was 'there's nothing for you here', Fiona Hill, who took his advice and left for America, has now turned his words into a brilliant book.[1] Paradoxically, by leaving the North-East, she has just been elected Chancellor of Durham, its most prestigious university; had she stayed, her chances of attaining such a position would have been far lower.

I will draw on the experience of Sheffield, my hometown. It is now the poorest city in the whole of England, and South Yorkshire, the region of which it is the core city, is also the poorest region in England.[2] South Yorkshire voted heavily for Brexit. Indeed, the Brexit vote can be predicted by how well a region has done since the mid-1970s. Those regions like South Yorkshire, which were once prosperous but collapsed and have not subsequently recovered, all seized the opportunity of the Brexit vote to mutiny against their political and civil service masters in London. Given the way they have been treated, this mutiny is all too understandable.

The government has recently done research on what societal purposes people agree on around Britain: what their common ground might be. It reveals that as a society, Britain has become bitterly polarized between Labour and Conservative, between Brexit and Remain, between social classes, and between rich and poor. Yet despite these divisions, there is one – and only one – objective on which everybody agrees. An overwhelming majority agree that reducing intergenerational inequalities in life-chances is a worthwhile purpose: We can unite on this as our common purpose.

Yet the research also reveals a second overwhelming consensus: despite its stated intentions, people think that the government will not be able to achieve this goal. I share these doubts. Although Boris Johnson ostensibly made 'Levelling Up' his flagship policy, he clearly lacked the seriousness-of-purpose needed to craft and sustain a credible strategy. During the fleeting, chaotic and unethical leadership of Liz Truss, the goal itself was publicly abandoned. Under the current leadership of Rishi Sunak and Finance Minister Jeremy Hunt, the goal has been reiterated, but not matched by any finance for it.

COMMUNITIES AND POLITIES

In order to understand communities, we need to take a brief look at the latest research on evolutionary biology. One of the current leaders in this field is Joseph Henrich, head of the department of evolutionary biology at Harvard.[3] His essential argument is that unfortunately humans have evolved to be less than saints. We're a mammal, and most mammals are greedy, selfish and lazy. Never-theless, we are a very unusual mammal. For a start, we have evolved over the last 200,000 years to be remarkably prosocial. We work in groups, and there's a very good reason for that. When we came down from the trees onto the African Savanna, we didn't have fur, armour-plating or scales unlike other animals, nor did we have big claws. We were trying to stand upright to see above the grass, but we weren't very good at it because we were designed to move on four legs not two. We weren't very fast either. Yet we found ourselves in a desperately scary environment populated by mam-moths and lions. The only way we could survive was to cooperate in big groups. These groups of around 150 individuals taught us mutuality. We learned to work together for common purposes and to trust each other. 150 people is thought to be the maximum number of people that one can know.[4] By means of gossip within such a community, individuals can gradually build a reputation for being reliable or unreliable. And with that incentive, one can build a reputation for being trustworthy. That's the evolutionary process which made humans unusually prosocial, leading to communities that trust each other and cooperate for common purposes.

In addition to that, we turned out to be remarkably imaginative and creative. This is another feature in which we're a very unique mammal. Take squirrels for comparison. Squirrels are very clever; they think ahead and save nuts for when it's cold and there's no food. But what squirrels don't seem to have done at any stage in their evolution is to imagine whether there is a better way of life than being a squirrel. If you want to understand the life of a squirrel 100,000 years ago, you just need look at one today. Their genetics and behaviour remain unchanged. If on the other hand we want to understand the behaviour of people 100,000 years ago, it's completely useless to look at people today.

How have we got from where we were 100,000 years ago, terrified to be gored by a mammal or chased by a lion, to today? We managed to face this common challenge by being social, imagina-tive, and creative. That has driven us to ever more ambitious goals and purposes. Human beings can imagine things that are better than the situation we're in. Our tragedy is that it's much easier to imagine better things than to achieve them. That is the unique feature of the human condition, and it plunges us into a state known as *radical uncertainty*: we're always trying to achieve goals that we don't know how to achieve.[5]

In modernity, we live in big organisations, in communities of work and of place. Modernity is a world that goes beyond communities. It's a world of political entities and states: *polities*. Polities have a very different dynamics from communities. As mentioned above, communities can comprise up to 150 individuals. They can't grow much beyond that because we can't know and trust everybody. Polities, however, can be big. Polities have emerged from scale economies and violence. They are militarised hierarchies in which a leader used his military power to build a polity. The big advantage of polities over communities is scale. Every economist will agree that scale is very useful. I spent much of my life working with the 'bottom billion': left-behind countries or regions within countries which are struggling to catch-up with the rest of mankind. In recent years, many of them have been losing that struggle because although people work hard, they are desperately short of firms: the organisations which would enable them to reap economies of scale.

Polities are therefore useful because they enable the scale necessary to escape mass poverty. Communities on the other hand produce mutuality and trust. What we need is a combination of these features of community and polity. However, combining the two is very difficult. Almost every place in the world has both polities and communities, but few have managed to fuse them to their advantage. Most places I work on have instead fused the worst features of polities and communities. These are societies doomed to mass poverty because they can't achieve economies of scale in production, and their communities are fragmented with oppositional identities. Nor does their political leader benefit from enough trust to pull fractious groups of people together.

ESCAPING POLARIZATION

How do we escape this situation? How can we transition away from a polarized society to one that comes together? I will suggest three principles supported by practical examples.

The first is that we need to *fuse two very different sorts of knowledge*. One is the generic knowledge of academics like myself. If you are looking for an informed strategy to guide a society, it's not a bad idea to listen to a specialist. But we should never leave these specialists in charge because academics often have little lived experience. Although a polarized society needs to draw on their generic knowledge, agency must lie with the people that have the necessary contextual knowledge of lived experience. For example, in my home region of Sheffield in South Yorkshire, during 2022, an initiative by the region's mayor and chief executive brought people together around a new common purpose: all agreed that they wanted South Yorkshire to be a more prosperous place for their children. But to achieve that it is vital that local people have the agency, not the politicians or civil servants in Whitehall. Nobody based in London can save Sheffield because they know too little about the city. Agency must be localised in society, but there is no sign of any serious appetite for devolution of powers and resources in any of the political parties, and most crucially, in Britain's Treasury, where power has been increasingly concentrated. Without it, the crucial fusion of generic and contextual knowledge is infeasible.

This brings us to the second principle: *subsidiarity*. Subsidiarity is about who exactly should have agency for achieving a goal. The answer is the lowest level at which that goal is feasible to be achieved. A few goals can only be achieved with global cooperation. Peace in Europe has to be achieved by the whole of Europe coming together. Many other goals can be achieved at the level of the city.

The final principle is *rapid learning*. Given that we are faced with humanity's existential problem of trying to achieve goals that we don't know how to achieve, what should we do? We must learn rapidly, both from others around the OECD, and from experiments. To experiment means to try different things and to track what is working. For example, Britain should have known that COVID-19 was coming. After all, it had already happened in Italy. The British Civil Service, however, has a belief that it is the finest civil service in the world and so doesn't need to look at anything else. If it looks anywhere, it looks at America and congratulates itself on being better.

BOTTOM-UP PROCESSES OF RENEWAL

There are bottom-up processes and top-down processes. The great student of the bottom-up processes is the Harvard sociologist Robert Putnam, his *magnum opus* being *The Upswing* (2021). Bottom-up processes work in both directions. Unfortunately, some build hatreds: we need to look no further than social media, which has produced teenagers obsessing about their curated selves. Girls in particular are terrified that their online selves are not sufficiently attractive. Suicide and depression rates amongst teenagers have increased. This is a tragedy that is entirely[6] avoidable.

There are yet more damaging instances. In 1992, Ethiopia was an extremely poor society, which for the next 20 years grew very fast, leading to great successes in reducing poverty and bringing society together. Then it fell into civil war: what helped to ignite that conflict? Facebook (now rebranded as Meta) developed algorithms designed by the most brilliant people in the world, whose purpose is to keep people on the platform: this is because Facebook's revenue source is ads. Frances Haugen, a senior Facebook official turned whistleblower, testified under oath in the British Parliament that Facebook's algorithms were intentionally designed to feed people's extreme views. Across the US, there were many Ethiopian migrants from different ethnic groups, for example the Oromo, the Amhara and the Tigrayans. These groups wanted to stoke grievance against other groups living in their home regions. Even before Ethiopia got into civil war, appalling violence broke out as the majority ethnic group in each region, incited by emigrants in America, advocated ethnic cleansing. The ensuing violence displaced three million people within Ethiopia, all driven by Facebook algorithms. The devastating evidence is that Facebook knew this was happening but allowed it to continue because it was profitable. This is an example of a bottom-up process building hatreds.

Fortunately, there are also bottom-up processes of kindness. Robert Putnam's wonderful book tells the story of the formation of the Rotary Club, which was founded by Paul Harris. Harris was from a small town in Iowa with a strong sense of community. When he migrated to boom-town Chicago, he got a good job and was doing well, but he was lonely because he missed that sense of community. In Chicago, he could only find a lot of successful individualists like himself. He thus decided to put out an advert in the paper, asking for others like him, those who are successful but lonely, to get together. 200 people showed up for the first meeting. There they all agreed that this new society's purpose would not be to discuss business deals, but to further community action in Chicago. Thus was born the Rotary Club, with the purpose of helping the less fortunate people of Chicago as its guiding principle. 10 years later, the club was so successful that it branched out to other towns in America. Today, the Rotary Club is an international organisation with millions of people. Of course, the people of the Rotary Club are not saints. But they are much better than the greedy, lazy, selfish individualists who libertarians such as Liz Truss and Ayn Rand celebrate.[iii]

Let me give you one other example of kindness. Because my grandfather lived in a little village near Stuttgart, I'm often invited back to Stuttgart to speak. The business community in Stuttgart has come together impressively by establishing a norm to train the city's next generation of young people. Not just the clever people who are going to become lawyers, but the people who just want a skilled job. I noticed that in Germany and in Switzerland firms don't brag about how many people they are training. If one firm chose to save money by not training the next generation of local youth, its executives would feel ashamed about it. In Britain on the other hand, the training of young people has completely collapsed since the apprentice-system was dismantled. This is a major reason for the lack of social mobility in the UK. You either go to university and become a lawyer or some other lucrative profession, or your opportunities collapse. There is no middle ground of skill left in Britain. Trying to rebuild that is enormously difficult. Individual firms don't want to train because the cost is too high. That's the trap into which Britain has fallen.

[iii] *Atlas Shrugged*, by Ayn Rand, was a celebration of individual success, and a denial that those who achieved success had any obligations to those less fortunate then themselves. Unsurprisingly, it is popular among the sociopathic super-rich.

TOP-DOWN PROCESSES OF RENEWAL

What about the top-down processes? Top-down processes are interesting because there are two styles of leadership that are both evolutionarily stable and unique to humanity. In the animal world, there is only one stable form of leadership: the alpha male. There are many examples of modern political leaders who exhibit this alpha male type of leadership by dominance. Until recently, one such leader was president of the United States of America. Today, we are all too conscious of another such leader in Russia. This dominance of a leader is characterised by bragging, and exaggerated self-confidence. I have already suggested that humanity's radical uncertainty requires us to embrace rapid learning. Putin does not follow the principle of rapid learning! He has made the fundamental mistake of every dictator before him by surrounding himself by people who dare not tell him even the basic realities. In comparison, Ukraine's president Volodymyr Zelenskyy is a very different type of leader. This difference shows itself in their respective backgrounds. President Putin's background is the military intelligence and hierarchy from his time in the KGB. Zelenskyy's background, on the other hand, is comedy and entertainment, which makes him very good at communicating.

Along these lines, I distinguish two types of leaders: *commanders in chief* and *communicators in chief*. When Putin invaded the Ukraine, Ukraine desperately needed a communicator in chief like Zelenskyy who could speak to people and say: 'Things have changed. We're going to have to learn rapidly'. He established trustworthiness by a statement of self-sacrifice: 'I am going to stay in Kyiv even though I'm target number one. I am willing to die in Kyiv because I believe in this country'. After establishing credibility, he suggested a strategy: 'If we fight against Putin, I can talk to leaders of other countries and shame their respective communities into helping us. But you must show solidarity of purpose. If you're a male of fighting age, I ask you to stay in Ukraine and fight. But I cannot tell you exactly what you need to do. I'm a comedian, not a soldier. Therefore, I'm going to devolve agency to local fighting groups. Join your militia in your town and work out yourselves how best to resist'. That's a strategy of devolved agency, and it began to work. Zelenskyy is a brilliant communicator. Country after country, he appealed directly to the people of other nations to shame their leaders into action, leading to significant change. Zelenskyy is an example of the type of leaders we need for the twenty-first century. Zelenskyy brought Ukraine together under a common identity, uniting both Russian speakers and Ukrainian speakers to say 'We're all Ukrainians'.

CONCLUSION: LEADERSHIP FOR RENEWAL

President Zelenskyy has shown us that a leader with good ideas can transform a situation that appeared to be disastrous. Conversely, that Britain now has such disgracefully unequal life-chances is the responsibility of bad ideas that British politicians and senior civil servants adopted as an orthodoxy and clung to for the past four decades.

It is time that Britain learnt from the abundant evidence from elsewhere in Europe that such extreme divergences in life-chances are avoidable, and where they are not avoided – as in East Germany during the Communist era – they are reversible. But for it to happen, Britain will need a new breed of politicians and senior civil servants with the moral decency to bring people together around a socially worthwhile purpose. They will need the communication skills to set that purpose as a common goal. And they will need the modestly to devolve agency to local people who can then harness their key advantage, which is that they understand the context of their own community.

Will it happen? I am a human scientist, not a clairvoyant, but all of us have some degree of voice and agency. During the current times of hardship, those of us who are fortunate have an especial responsibility to use these powers responsibly. Do we compound polarization by self-promotion, the denigration of the left-behind, and support for the politics of the extreme? Or do behave modestly, emulate Paul Harris in bringing people together, and support political leaders like President Zelenskyy? It is our individual choice, but it will set our collective fate.

NOTES

1. F. Hill, (2022) *There's Nothing for You Here*, Allen Lane.
2. This and other regional statistics are well-documented in the government's massive Levelling Up Whitepaper of 2022.
3. See J. Heinrich, *The Weirdest People in the World*, (2020), and Cecilia Hayes, *Cognitive Gadgets*, (2018).
4. R. Dunbar, (1998) The social brain hypothesis. *Evolutionary Anthropology*, 6, pp. 178–190.
5. See J. Kay and M. King, (2020) *Radical Uncertainty*.
6. See R. D. Putnam and S. R. Garrett, (2021) *The Upswing: How America Came Together*.

7

WHEN IDEAS FAIL

Iain King CBE

Some things we only notice when they're gone; when societies are deprived of the free-flow of ideas, they can descend into truly terrible places. This chapter will show how, in Yugoslavia and elsewhere, demagogues were able to brutalise the national conversation, and plunge their countries into civil conflict. Calamity came quickly and easily; it was always far closer than many imagined. Recovery has proven to be far more difficult, and it may be impossible for a society to heal completely from ethnicity-based bloodletting. But history shows there are some steps which help survivors and their communities start to flourish again...

FALSE MYTHS AND THE YUGOSLAVIA TRAGEDY

On the 24th of April 1987, on the orders of his patron, Serbia's then President, Ivan Stambolic, the new President of the Communist party was dispatched to an autonomous province. Visiting a suburb of Pristina, the administrative centre of Kosovo and Metohija, the man's task was to listen to aggrieved Serbs, who alleged they had been harassed and bullied. To increase the political temperature, the communist leader from Belgrade arranged for stones to be thrown at local police; the stones came from a truck parked just out of sight of television news crews, some of which accompanied him on the trip. After a meeting with the protestors, the future supremo of Yugoslavia, and primary instigator of wars in Bosnia, Croatia and

Kosovo, talked straight into the TV cameras. 'No one should dare to beat you', he declared. The man was Slobodan Milosevic.

Until that day, Milosevic had been a communist apparatchik – some regarded him as a policy wonk, to others a Machiavellian politician; he was certainly not a firebrand. But from that visit to Kosovo Polje onwards, he became a Serb nationalist. Milosevic promoted fear, and abandoned the national policy which had aimed to unite the disparate ethnic groups of Yugoslavia. Civic ideas were displaced by base emotions. Amnity gave way to enmity. Milosevic defined a semi-mythical narrative about a historic struggle, exploited any example he could find of Serb victimhood, and championed exaggerated claims for his ethnic group at the expense of other communities. Milosevic would soon replace Stambolic, and he remained national leader for the next 11 years.

The result for Yugoslavia was catastrophic. Before Milosevic, the country had been the most prosperous and permissive in the socialist world, a leading member of the non-aligned movement in the Cold War, host to the acclaimed 1984 winter Olympics, and a much-loved holiday destination for people from all over Europe. But Milosevic's rule ripped the country apart. The two-thirds of Yugoslav citizens who were not Serbs were revolted by his incendiary rhetoric and divisive policies. Slovenia, the western-most of the six republics which made up the country, voted for independence in 1990, and after a 10-day war in summer 1991, became free. Bosnia, Croatia and Macedonia followed, but with much more protracted conflict and suffering. Soldiers who had served together sometimes just months earlier fought each other over confused battle-lines, and purged territory of civilians from other ethnicities. The death toll ran into six figures, many millions lost their homes, the economy crashed, and Yugoslavia's infrastructure was scarred for decades. Milosevic himself was eventually deposed in 2000, although he made sure to have his predecessor as President, and one-time patron, Ivan Stambolic assassinated during his last year in power.

DEMAGOGUES AND THE SUPPRESSION OF IDEAS

Societies which spark and flourish on the ingenuity of ideas should never take their freedom and diversity for granted. Demagogues, rabble-rousers and autocrats around the world still evoke a mythical 'other' as the source of all problems – problems they promise to fix, on condition that they are granted untrammelled power to fix them. And when they have that power, especially over local media, they can infuse fear into a population, and eventually stoke it into a 'hatred of the other'. They suffocate and then toxify the public space in which ideas are nurtured.

It is an old tactic. The most familiar twentieth-century case is, of course, Adolf Hitler. Through fiery rhetoric and by distorting facts, he crafted a story of victimhood which he used to take power in Germany, steal land outside the country, and plunge the world into war. But there are many other examples. Some leaders of the US confederacy used similar tactics in the mid-nineteenth century. There are instances of demagoguery in different parts of Europe during the Thirty Years' War. And there is literature on rhetoric from classical figures in ancient Rome and Greece which spark a similar tone to Milosevic's. Beyond the Anglo-European tradition, there are examples in Africa and Asia, too, of low-minded leaders resurrecting traditional hatreds of people from other groups. It is almost always an excuse for power, generating widespread misery in the process, and shutting down free-thinking and ideas.

FRACTURING HISTORY

The tragedy of these cases is not just in the immediate impact of their actions – the many tens of thousands of lives cut short because of Milosevic's reign as the Premier of Serbia, or the economic devastation of the US civil war, for example. The true impact is incalculable, because they make history swerve; the might-have-beens and almost-happened will never be known, once life has been forced to take the grimmer trajectory. Demagogues like Milosevic twist societies until they buckle and break. Progress gives way to polarisation, ideas to enmity.

It might be imagined that only a few societies are susceptible to the lure of ethnic victimhood stories, like those of Milosevic. Certainly, the messages get more traction in some places than others. But we do well to remember that most demagogues who rose to power by exploiting ethic fears did so against a large mass of people against them. Most Germans in the early 1930s had a higher view of human nature than Hitler, and many tried to stop him – the lawyer Hans Litten, the journalist Fritz Gerlich, the student-activist Sophie Scholl, and the priest Alfred Delp. It isn't just brave individuals, either: in 1991, some half-a-million protestors took to the streets of Milosevic's home city of Belgrade to oppose his dangerously antagonistic leadership, and to save Yugoslavia from war. Sadly, they failed.

HOW TO RESIST THE RISE OF MALIGN FORCES

Perceived Economic Grievance

There is evidence that certain characteristics can inoculate a society, and protect against a spiral into savagery. The first is the absence or removal of economic grievances. Grievances can arise from expectations being unmet, or from a sense of unfairness – often something which suggests power is being misused, and so should be used differently. Being poor does not, itself, create a grievance; a fact highlighted by the tendency of terrorists to come from middle-income groups (failed suicide-bombers most often cite humiliation and desperation, not poverty, as the reason for their efforts). Hostilities are not generated by an economic downturn, but by the perceived explanation of why some people are poorer than expected. It is when they provide a simple, plausible narrative for this perceived injustice that demagogues get a route in.

Education and Critical Thinking Skills

The second factor is the degree to which ideas are assessed rather than just accepted by people as they are transmitted within a society. Education which produces critical thinking skills – generally developed in secondary and higher education – can make it much harder for malign ideas to spread; whereas primary education alone, the common standard throughout Europe in the run up to the First World War, will often just unify language within national borders. It can make simple ideas appeal and leave a society vulnerable to jingoism.

Flourishing Media

Linked to this is media diversity, and whether inflammatory ideas on current issues are challenged, or allowed to spread unchecked. It is no coincidence that media in the totalitarian regimes of the 1930s allowed the transmitters in Berlin, Moscow and Rome to broadcast just a single, extreme worldview. Radio – more than television, newspapers and the town-criers of old – has perhaps the darkest history here. Of the different varieties of one-way mass communication, radio allows reality to be distorted most convincingly, a fact exploited for mischief by Orson Welles in 1938, and for mass murder in Rwanda in 1994. When the algorithms of social media present their audiences with an unchallenged and incendiary worldview in contemporary times, they can propagate peril.

Reaching Across the Political Divide

Demogogues in some countries have exploited flaws in the political process. Milosevic, for example, had few votes to win from non-Serbs. If there had been a different electoral arrangement, he would have been forced to spur more cross-community appeals, and a sense of compromise; perhaps he would never have become the Supremo of so many bloody Balkan wars. Recognising this risk, The Good Friday Agreement of 1998, for example, made sure to create incentives for politicians to win support from across the divide. It has delivered peace in Northern Ireland ever since.

THE ROAD TO RECOVERY

The High Cost

Recovering from the lethal tribalism of Milosevic and his ilk is incredibly difficult. The wars in the Balkans throughout the 1990s sparked tremendous sympathy around the world. In a bid to stop the killing, there were hard-edged military interventions in both Bosnia and Kosovo. Western troops stayed to enforce the peace, and their governments' donor agencies tried to repair the war damage. Tens of billions in reconstruction aid have been poured into the region in the last quarter-century, much of it invested in physical repairs: restoring the schools, roads, and civic buildings which had been destroyed across the former republics of Yugoslavia. Sarajevo airport, which took on totemic significance during the Bosnian war, now welcomes almost 20 flights a day.

Tackling Segregation

Much harder to repair was the social damage wrought by Milosevic. By enflaming identities based on immutable ethnic or national characteristics, the Serb leader forced people to take sides. Even people who opposed Milosevic's divisive approach found themselves categorised according to something they could never change: their ethnicity. Middle-aged professors who used to teach students from all communities, sports team managers with fans across a whole city, and health workers who had treated everyone, regardless of their background: they were all forced to accept a label they did not want, and an identity divide they had worked hard to reject.

Dividing people in a society according to a characteristic they can't change, like their ethnicity, removes their agency. Unlike political systems where people are free to choose between different sets of ideas which empower people, when society becomes segregated according to a so-called 'given characteristic', the fear inevitably grows that are skewed to serve another group more than one's own. That fear becomes stronger when war makes everyone poorer – who else is there to blame, but members of the 'other'?

Investment and Employment

Money can help heal these divisions, but it can exacerbate them, too. There is some research which shows that, in South Asia, the most divided communities became even more polarised when new funds were invested in the area, because each group assumed a rival community has got more. And if the new cash is brought in too quickly, it will just cause prices to rise, again stirring instability. Money can only salve social wounds when it comes in certain ways. Ideally, it should be targeted on programmes which bring communities together, and used to encourage long-term investment.

Slightly better is the notion of boosting employment in post conflict societies, especially if care is taken to even out the benefits across the ethnic divide. Too often, in the Balkans and elsewhere, the newest jobs after conflict were working for outside aid agencies and international organisations. This haemorrhaged skilled workers from the professions which are essential to rebuilding a society – teachers, health workers and mid-level government officials.

Where job creation has worked best in post-conflict societies, it has tended to mark a clear departure from pre-war business patterns. In Iraq, for example, there is an emerging computer-based sector, led by dynamic young people who have lived abroad. It is a world away from the mass employment monoliths of old. In post-war Kosovo, heavy industries and manufacturing have given way to trade and commerce.

Reconnecting Citizens and Trust in Leaders

Most fundamental of all in restoring a post-conflict society is reconnecting citizens with their state institutions in the right way. People who have been through sectarian war need to know they can trust their leaders to govern again. Typically, this will be mean a clear prospectus from the government – what they promise to do, and how they will do it. In several countries, it has meant a multi-point list of progress indicators, from inclusive arrangements in the civil service, to better links with countries overseas and, of course, credible steps to reduce violence against targeted groups.

When conflict has become endemic, a local war economy can emerge. Spivs and gang-leaders find their niche trading small arms, or evading sanctions, often to make profits on a scale they would never make in peacetime. To overcome the incentives which encourage violence to persist requires a political arrangement which pulls a society together. Occasionally, a magnanimous leader can deliver this. More usually it involves an inclusive political settlement, where the elite can represent the most potent elements from each community, and channel their interests to be resolved in a non-violent forum. In modern Iraq, for example, there is an understanding that the most powerful 25 state positions are shared out between the different communities of the country in a certain way. It is an arrangement which has quelled a murderous civil war, and saved many thousands of lives.

Ideally, an inclusive political settlement will evolve into a structure which is capable, accountable and responsive to people's needs. But a history of violence inevitably slows this transformation: if a ruling elite bridges a fractured society to deliver peace, it will need to be unaccountable, at least temporarily, to those who seek to cause harm. Recovering from violence takes time – usually several turns of the political cycle, often generations. Once a demagogue has uprooted people's trust in each other, communities must come to terms with the bloody soil before they can recover, and so that a society's ideas can grow and flourish again.

Of course, by far the better path is to avoid the tragedy endured by Yugoslavia, and the other countries which have fallen into civil conflict. This safer track requires not just vigilance, against demagogues and their tactics, but also a genuine appreciation of what is at stake: the imperfect beauty of a society in which ideas flow freely, and where citizens work through bad notions before they realise their mistakes and steer towards better ones.

There is always a reason to complain – for everyone, everywhere, even for those who have been lucky, because they could always have been luckier. But it is important that those complaints are bounded in some way, to stop them cascading into catastrophe. Having an ideas-informed society may be the best safeguard for this, so that the different claims and injustices can be assessed in a reasonable and fair way. The ultimate protective measure to ensure ideas can still flow freely in the future is for ideas to flow freely now.

THE SCARS OF HISTORY

Milosevic died of a heart attack in 2006, while on trial for war crimes at The Hague. Sadly, his opportunistic abuse of latent inter-ethnic fear lives on. Large parts of the former Yugoslavia, neighbourhoods are still segmented by ethnicity, even though a generation has passed since the last of his wars.

In and around Kosovo Polje, the suburb he visited on that fateful spring day in 1987, streets and villages are split between those occupied by Serbs, and those where others live. There is still no mixing. Although the societies Milosevic ruined are starting to recover, people are still held back from the scars of that terrible history.

> *Iain King CBE is Director of NATO's Mission in Iraq. He coordinated international civilian operations in Benghazi during the Libyan civil war of 2011, spent four years working for the EU and UN in Kosovo, and is the author of five books spanning international interventions, military history and philosophy.*

8

BEARING THE TRUTH AND
BUILDING TRUTH TELLING
COMMUNITIES

Helen Cameron

FACING 'WHAT IS'

James Baldwin, the American writer, poet and social critic, spoke of
the need to build a nation capable of bearing the truth and of the
need to build truth telling communities in his unfinished book
Remember This House,[1] which reflects on race in America by
tracing the lives and assassinations of his three friends Malcolm X,
Medgar Evers and Martin Luther King Jr. In this work Baldwin
asserted,

> *Not everything that is faced can be changed. But
> nothing can be changed until it is faced.*

I would want to assert that the beginnings of forming a truth
bearing community who can witness to 'what is' requires a willingness to face those things which discomfort us, challenge us and
even de-stabilise what we have, in our privilege, become accus-
tomed to. Faith communities in particular need to be encouraged to
engage with those parts of their tradition which encourage bearing
witness to what is and to develop the capacity to discern, nurture
and encourage truth bearing as communities who gather around
shared values, practices and beliefs. Facing 'what is' rather than
living an illusion is vital – and is a fundamental feature of an

ideas-informed society The consequences of failing to deal with the truth, with facts, objectivities and evidence are significant and we have seen signs of what it means to present 'alternative truths', to construct a post-truth narrative, to take refuge in conspiracy theories, and to construct our own truths which fly in the face of the valid experience of others. Such modes of being lead to a more divided and polarised existence.

In the Hebrew Scriptures in Isaiah 1:18 we find the phrase

Come, now, let us reason together.

This portion of the Hebrew scriptures, a text both Jewish and Christian faith communities regard as influential, describes God inviting the people of Israel, through the prophet Isaiah into a conversation about right living. This conversation is one based on reason, honesty, transparency and truth. The prophet says to Israel, using the legal vocabulary of judges and the courts, that God wants the people to 'argue it out' with God, to enter into the kind of discourse as a community that results in the disclosure of the truth. The truth which the prophet is seeking to share with the people is that change is possible in the lives of women and men. Changes in people, in their practices, their values and behaviours can be so complete and thorough that for the prophet the change can be expressed in terms of *the change of something red* (the colour of the blood of sacrificed animals) *into something white* (the colour of snow). This language seeks to signify to the reader an image which accounts for change from a colour connected to death and decay to a colour which signifies promise of new life and hope. Snow, is after all, moisture and in a desert context (that of the people of Israel) water means life can be sustained.

In Christian scriptures we can read the account of the ruler Pilate's examination of the itinerant preacher Jesus after his arrest. Pilate asks Jesus, 'What is truth'?[2] Jesus does not answer. Christian faith communities believe and trust that there is an objective truth revealed in the person of Jesus Christ. For many others truth claims cannot be viewed as objective but only subjective and deeply contextual. Some wish to live in a post-truth society where nothing can be objectively asserted and we are offered instead, alternative truths to choose between. Such a world of complete subjectivity

potentially denies the reality of lived experience and material existence of those outside our group, tribe and country. To construct
the world in this way is to polarise and make those who think
differently to us, 'other'.

PROACTIVE TRUTH TELLING

In 2015, the Methodist Conference published a report entitled,
'Courage, Cost and Hope on the Past Cases Review of 2013–2015'.
This review of its historic safeguarding cases aimed to review all
safeguarding cases documented or known about since 1950. The
objective of the Review was to identify the Church's historical
response in each case to ensure that responses were safe, compliant
with legislation and policy for the state and the Church and to
review that responses made were pastorally appropriate. If remedial
action was required this was implemented and the Review was keen
that lessons learned about any necessary changes to practice or
developments were made in order to ensure that safeguarding work
within the Methodist Church was of the highest possible standard.
What is significant about this review is that it was put in place
voluntarily and proactively rather than in response to high profile
cases or poor public reputation. It was a moment of proactive truth
telling and because at that point record keeping was poor and
patchy, the review process relied on ministers, lay employees and
church members exploring their memories of events and sharing
those with others. It was a considered response, rather than a
reaction, which sought to identify action points which would result
in culture change and in its 23 recommendations identified changes
in practice which would bring this about. Such a worked example
can potentially lead us to an important discernment of how we
might become those who can tell the truth, bear witness to truth for
others, be those who can look critically at an organisation they are
part of, belong to, find their identity in and step back and say Who
are we? How are we experienced by others? Where does privilege
and power reside in this organisation and who are the quieter voices
and how do we enable their being heard? Evaluation and reflection
are therefore two key responses which can lead to change by

organisations and groups facing 'what is' experienced by others in their engagement with us.

FACING FRAILTIES AND FEARS

Those who identify as Christian want to believe that human beings are made for goodness, that people grow best and flourish most in the provision of truth-filled, stable, positive learning environments and from the encouragement and trust of others. But faith believers also know that human beings learn, are shaped and formed by separation, loss, failure, conflict and contestation. It is too easy to say that such challenging or painful experiences automatically enable flourishing – sometimes they just lead to sadness and sorrow. Human growth and development, transformation, and even flourishing is possible in the face of sorrow and grief if evaluation of, and reflection on the demanding experience is part of the response to the pain. The wound of the loss and sorrow will always remain in the soul but the landscape of the new world in which the wound still exists can be shaped and enlarged around the wound so that its dominance and prevailing influence is diminished. Resilience can be found and borne in the face of considerable adversity if attention is paid to what we find difficult and if frailties and fears are faced and acknowledged, and if there is reflection and self-reflexivity about the experiences faced. Resilience in our communities becomes possible when people have a developed and inner life resourced by a vision of a future which is better and different. Truth telling and bearing witness to what 'is' rather than what 'we might wish it was' is vital in forming human communities which can bear truth even when unpalatable, respond to it, be changed by it and through that change the world.

TRUTH TELLING, TRUTH FORMING, TRUTH
BEARING COMMUNITIES
Experiments in Witness to Truth

In asserting the importance of truth telling for faith communities, it is just as vital for the development of society based on and formed by ideas and creativity. It is important to acknowledge how often faith communities fail in their witness to 'what is' and on occasion, are very poor witnesses to truth. Such failures are often the direct result of a failure of imagination, independent critical analysis and a failure to let go of an ideal or mythical view of those in leadership resulting in a loss of challenge to the status quo even when that clearly is unjust or harmful. The pervading culture of faith communities can be a hierarchical, clerical, defensive, opaque and unsafe one for the weak and vulnerable. Those giving evidence to the Independent Inquiry into Child Sexual Abuse (IICSA) on behalf of the Church were clear that this was the case in some places and contexts but not always and not in every situation. The Church of England and the Methodist Church, for example, have both been clear that culture change was necessary regarding its safeguarding practice. Public statements from both churches have been clear that culture change is required, as is humility and a willingness to address unsafe practices and provide an accountable ministry of the ordained and lay.

It is important to acknowledge then that the faith community's life of witness and truth bearing cannot be a static thing. Rather, this life is found in constantly changing local experiments in witness to truth, in each challenging and changing location and context in which the faith community finds itself and, in each generation, and dominant cultural context. Such renewal of thinking and ideas and creativity is integral to health and well-being of individuals and communities.

Witness Is Local and Particular

The witness to truth of a faith community therefore is always local (even if the media of communication available to us now

increasingly stretches our understandings of locality or community). It always involves a specific group of people, and is found
authentically in their distinct patterns of action and speech and
relationship. Witness always takes place at a specific moment of
time. It is always particular; it is always concrete. It is always
changing. It is constantly being reformed, one might say, just as the
Church, or any other faith community, is. Witness is something that
particular people at particular times and in particular places try –
and sometimes fail at, and try again. There can be, if we are relaxed
and not anxious, a playful and creative aspect to the trying out of
different approaches and strategies. It would help us as faith communities to ask: What is the difference between an experiment and a
failure when we are seeking to communicate with others about our
ideas, plans, our hopes and our openness to all that the future might
hold?

Truthful witness might be said to consist of constantly changing
experiments in witness to the divine life in each location in response
to the insights of previous experience and knowledge of the context.
Peter Mandelson always denied mistaking mushy peas for guaca-
mole in a Fish and Chip shop in Hartlepool during an election
campaign, but as a story about dislocation of the 'metropolitan
elite' visiting the North-East during an election campaign, it is
treasured as a story by northerners who are used to being marginal
and so were amused by the discomfort of those who found it hard
to interpret a context and culture that they were less familiar with.

Witness as Improvisation

A kind of experimentation or improvisation might be called for in
which one discovers what works and what does not work primarily
by doing it: by trying it out, carrying on, and falling over, and
picking oneself up, and trying again. It is playful improvisation
when play means meaningful and purposeful thought and behaviour that has patterns to it but no prescribed or pre-determined
outcomes. Play permits not-knowing; a safe uncertainty where 'yet
to be' is a position which can be held with integrity.

For faith communities witness to the truth in every age is a matter of improvisation: of trying things or ideas out, risking failure, seeing what can be done with the resources that are actually to hand rather than in some ideal world where we could have whatever resources we needed. It is the kind of experimentation where whatever is borrowed from elsewhere has to be adapted to local circumstances, so that there's no guarantee that the results will be the same here as they were elsewhere. It is the kind of experimentation where the particular strengths and weaknesses of the people involved make all the difference.

Loveday Alexander, Mike Higton[3] and others including Samuel Wells[4] have all reminded us that the witness of the truth bearing community is also witness that is called to show in this particular place we are located at this time, the same truth, the same love, the same divine life. It is not simply a matter of improvisation for the sake of improvisation, but of faithful improvisation – of finding out how to say the same thing or exploring the same idea in a different language, in a different context, to different people. It is about speaking of faith in and through loving actions that are credible, compelling and attractive not in order to draw others in but rather to ease our ability to live and move and bear witness wherever we go. Such a way of living espoused by a faith community might be expressed as witness 'as we go' rather than the imperative 'go and witness' which the Christian faith tradition has identified as, 'The Great Commission'.

Deep Learning

All these local experiments in witness and truth bearing, our faithful improvisations, live by our capacity for learning new ideas. Improvising is something we can learn to do, and then learn to do better. Because we are called to *faithful* improvisation to witness that truthfully shows people the divine life we are called to, we are each called to learn to know God more deeply. We believe that we have to learn the heart of our faith *more* deeply because we are called to improvise witness to it than we would do if we were simply called to repeat it. Repetition can be sustained by rote learning, or by the kind of learning that simply hoovers up text, song, ideas and then regurgitates.

Higton suggests that improvisation, on the other hand, requires deep learning.[5] It requires the kind of learning where one becomes viscerally familiar with the way one's faith articulates what is connected to what, what depends on what, what can be bent without being broken, and what is brittle. It demands that we learn what we can and can't get away with, what we must cling to and what can be discarded as unhelpful accretion. There is, I believe, nothing frivolous or careless about trying things out playfully, not being discouraged by failure, being willing to try things out. However, learning for the sake of being equipped for improvisation is deeper learning than learning for the sake of business as usual. The wells of ideas deep enough to resource and sustain a truth bearing community need to be dug deeply and thoroughly. We go on unlearning and learning, being broken and remade, doing and being undone, dying and rising continuously. This is our vocation as truth bearers and receivers – to be learners.

Attending to Other Witnesses to Truth

The learning that effective truth telling witness demands of us therefore also involves deep attention to the great cloud of witnesses alongside and among whom we now witness. We learn truth from those who have witnessed to that truth before us and around us. In fact, we can only understand truth through the individual witnesses and communities of witness to it that we encounter.

We have to learn how to embody truthful witness to the same reality ourselves. There is no manual to download but there is history, reason, experience and tradition treasured by and interpreted by a diverse set of witnesses.

So, we are invited to study together in community, to learn in each other's company to read contexts, people, events together. We are inspired to truthful witness, enabled to imagine witness, and disciplined in our witness, in our encounters with the witnesses who speak to us in literature, history and the tradition. We need therefore to be those who are in love with literature and text, history, reason and tradition, critically engaged with these, familiar and literate with them, able to interrogate as well as learn from what has gone before.

Building communities capable of bearing the truth and acting on it cannot be a static thing. Rather, life and truth are found in constantly changing local experiments in witness and truth bearing, in each challenging and changing location and context, and in each generation and dominant cultural context. Privilege shifts and must be critically engaged with, again and again.

WITNESS IN ACTION

It is all very well to talk in grand terms about faith communities as truth bearing communities, as if this witness to truth were something obvious and visible when one takes the whole community in view, and looks at its life as a single fact. But the witness of the faith community is always the witness of specific people in specific locations, working out how to be witnesses here and now: how to live here and now, as people called to be holy, as people called to witness to truth in particular ways with particular people, using particular language and carrying out particular acts.

A powerful example of witnessing to truth though particular acts and language was an encounter I had in 2011 when I was fortunate to visit Sri Lanka. In the weeks before the Conference I was due to attend I visited the north of Sri Lanka. The normalisation of a country after a bitter and tragic civil war was beginning but the signs of the military activity of the Civil War were still present everywhere in the form of roadblocks, the continued presence of shells, and restrictions on travel. One young Christian minister who was in his early twenties took me along with him when he visited the local police station (formerly an army camp). He had developed a pattern of calling in each week and sharing a meal with the station cook. The young minister was Tamil and the cook Sinhalese. I was invited to sit under the shade of a tree and share food with them both – only for three jeeps to coming roaring into the compound and for the local police/army senior officers to emerge. My presence was causing some concern.

We continued to share the delicious food and discuss the situation in Sri Lanka. I listened carefully and when the meal was concluded I left after sharing my thanks in the few words of Sinhala I had. I was deeply impressed by the brave and courageous act of this young minister – many similar aged young men would have been rounded up and killed in the previous years before by people wearing very similar uniforms to the men we had shared the meal with. He used his language skills in Sinhala to build relationships over food and so increased understanding and communication.

We learn from past generations, from their history of experiments in embodied witness to God's gracious love in a whole series of contexts. Their experiments, as ours are, were always fallible, sometimes terrible, occasionally glorious, most often something of a mixture, but they were always experiments in embodied witness to the divine life, and we are able to learn what our witness might become by sitting at their feet rather than dismissing their contribution.

FAITH COMMUNITIES AND CULTURAL APPROPRIATION

We sometimes say that we stand on the shoulder of giants in order to express that sense of discovering truth by building on previous discoveries. We need to be those who, as well as attentive to text and tradition, experience and reason, can be attentive to the truth bearing witness of earlier generations, attentive in a way which is willing to gaze on what went before, to honour the core values and be willing to critique, re-visit, dismiss and adapt as necessary. So we need to honour the tradition, the rock from which we were hewn but not be too deferential to it. Faith communities, if they are bold enough to look unflinchingly at their legacy will see faith sharing globally as inextricably linked with colonialism.

Attitudes inherited unquestionably from positions of privilege are passed on with faith sharing as though faith and cultural attitudes are indivisible. Examples of such unholy alliances between faith sharing and cultural appropriation can be seen in many locations of British colonial domination. The roots of such an alliance are to be seen in the treatment of Indigenous Aboriginal people over many decades and continue in the present. On 13 February 2008 at Parliament House in Canberra, the Prime Minister of Australia Kevin Rudd made a historic statement acknowledging the truth and reality of the experience of many Indigenous Australian Aboriginal and Torres Strait Islander people as belonging to the 'the stolen generation'. The moment of truth telling concerned many indigenous Australian children who had been forcibly removed from their families and placed into 'out of home care'. Their names were changed, their identity lost and their culture and heritage denied.

The moment of Rudd's apology in 2008 was hailed as a moment of truth telling by the Australian government along with an apology, he offered for the role played by the government which laid the foundation for healing to take place. The Aboriginal and Torres Islander social justice commissioner in 2008, Tom Calma called on the Australian government to partner with Indigenous people to deal with that 'unfinished business'. Sadly 15 years later, much of that business of providing an indigenous voice on key policy areas remains unfinished. The number of indigenous children removed and placed in 'out of home care' has doubled since the apology was made in 2008 and is 10 times the rate of non-indigenous children.[6]

FACING UP TO DISCRIMINATION

The direct links between this case and those of the UK government's betrayal in reneging on promises made to the Windrush generation are clear.

We will, if we are able, learn from those around us now, who are experimenting in witness for themselves, if we can remain open and not dismissive if their witness does not look like ours. We need to learn how to witness along with them, especially when it applied to insights our faith communities have forgotten, or never learnt to articulate or have failed so far to realise how important those aspects might be for us and for the world we inhabit. The Church in the UK, for example, has been revived and transformed by Christians from the global majority. However, it is yet to listen with humility or work in transformative ways to include these Christians in the structures of the organisation and in senior leadership and we have no credible account to give of why this is so. Further, our interests and pursuits and indeed the Christian Church's insistence on focussing on issues of sex and sexuality, have meant other issues which should excite us, appall us, energise and drive our faith communities to action, change and transformation are ignored and neglected.

For example, a neglected truth in our society is that maternity survival rates in the UK differ depending on ethnicity. Most people would assume that maternal deaths in the UK are, although tragic and comparatively rare, a risk faced equally by all mothers. Sadly, research has shown that this is not the case. There appears to be a relationship between maternal death and ethnicity.

The link was highlighted by researchers at Oxford University's 'Mothers and Babies: Reducing Risk Through Audits and Confidential Enquiries' (MBRRACE) unit. MBRRACE investigated outcomes from a range of births during 2016-18 and found that maternal death was five times more likely in black women than it was in white women.

MBRRACE's report raised the spectre that, despite decades of progress, racism remains an institutional problem, and not something limited to the far right or ignorant chants on football terraces. The report,[7] using data from England, found that except for Chinese mothers, black mothers had worse maternity outcomes than white women. Death rates during or within 6 weeks of pregnancy were just eight per 100,000 for white women (and only five per 100,000 for Chinese women). Asian women had a death rate of 15 per 100,000, close to the rate for mixed-race women of 16 per 100,000. However, the rate for black women was, by a wide margin, the largest, at 40 per 100,000. This meant black women were not just five times more likely to die than white women, but also two-and-a-half more likely to die than any other ethnic minority.

Here is a clear example of the danger of the consequences of not facing up to 'what is' in order to make the future safer for black women. To overcome such discrimination demands that white men and women are honest in their accounting of their own privilege as prospective parents. Maternal safety for all women should be standard as a concept and as a lived reality but it isn't. The colour of a woman's skin in the UK determines what kind of maternal health and outcome they can have during and after a pregnancy.

Such a truth regarding maternal health and ethnicity should be one we all know and challenge, training for all ante-natal personnel should address this discrimination and change it in order to build a just and equal society.

TRUTHFUL PEOPLE AND TRUTH-TELLING COMMUNITIES

What is within us, our privilege and power (or lack of it) shapes and forms what we offer as our humanity and in service of others. We must pay attention to the inner landscape of our lives. Our hearts must be reachable and breakable. We must be truthful people who can form and sustain truth telling communities, if we cannot do this, then we become less than we were intended to be.

NOTES

1. James Baldwin *Remember this House*, Unfinished and unreleased manuscript. Material from this manuscript was used in the film re/member.
2. Gospel of John Chapter 18: 38.
3. Loveday Alexander and Mike Higton (eds), 2016, *Faithful Improvisation? Theological Reflections on Church Leadership*, London: Church House Publishing.
4. Samuel Wells, 2004, *Improvisation: The Drama of Christian Ethics*, Ada Michigan: Brazos Press.
5. Mike Higton, 2012, *A Theology of Higher Education*, Oxford: OUP.
6. Calla Wahlquist Rudd's apology, 10 years on: The elusive hope of a 'breakthrough moment', The Guardian, February 2018.
7. MMBBRACE Report *Saving Lives; Improving Mothers Care*, December 2020.

9

INFORMED SOCIETY AND REPRESENTATIVE DEMOCRACY – THE ROLE OF PARLIAMENTS

Stéphane Goldstein and Anne-Lise Harding

THE CONCEPT OF INFORMATION LITERACY

Information literacy (IL) makes a crucial contribution to democracy and society. Its relevance to democratic participation is increasingly recognised, particularly in the context of both the opportunities and the risks presented by information-saturated online environments. The UK's professional body for librarians and information professionals (CILIP) – frames IL as a means of empowering people to reach and express informed views and to engage fully with society.[1] The definition goes on to suggest that IL fits into five broad lifelong contexts, one of which is citizenship, where IL helps to acquire abilities and understanding that underpin civic engagement. The CILIP definition reflects the position of UNESCO, which aligns IL with media literacy to form the composite concept of media and information literacy (MIL) as a means of developing the critical thinking abilities of citizens.[2] IL may even be seen as an essential component of education for citizenship, in both formal education and lifelong learning.[3,4,5,6] And, even more broadly, in the consensual view of a panel of experts from multiple professional backgrounds, IL is a basic literacy for the digital world and an essential component of modern life.[7]

INFORMATION LITERACY AND DEMOCRACY

Implications for the Classroom

Much literature charts the contribution that IL makes to democracy, particularly regarding the role that education plays in fostering democratic engagement. Trust between citizens and information sources is fundamental to the functioning of democracy, and there is a relationship between MIL education, the building of trust and the democratising principle of civic agency.[8] Political literacy and IL may be seen as compatible concepts that are inextricably linked and should therefore be taught and stressed simultaneously to students in the classroom – with beneficial effects on their academic performance and their ability to become better informed citizens.[9]

Education and pedagogy need to reflect the relationship between IL and other disciplines too, and the multidisciplinary implications of situating IL within school curricula, as part of multi-literacy, in the shape of computer literacy, political literacy as well as IL.[10] Critical literacy should form part of the mix, to enable young people of secondary school age increase their political agency through nurturing their critical abilities - thereby addressing some of the limitations of IL theories.[11] This could include the notion of critical digital literacy, which incorporates having knowledge about the digital environments where information circulates, and about how the internet operates socio-economically.[12] In the face of the rise of authoritarian populism, and the disinformation that comes with it, traditional IL practices do not adequately engage with theory that examines the broader link between information and democracy. Hence, the imperative to develop democratic citizenship education and pedagogic practices at the intersection between information science, political science and critical pedagogy.[13]

The Contribution of Libraries

Relevant education should not just be limited to the formal school environment or narrow IL programmes, and in this respect, the lifelong educational role of libraries is often stressed.[14] Libraries

have historically played a role in the maintenance of democratic
norms through offering access to knowledge. The ubiquity of the
internet and hugely increased access to information enhances the
importance of this role.[15] By enriching society and the public
sphere, libraries can support the capacity of democracy to keep
pace with the challenge of confronting disinformation.[16] They have
a role as 'arsenals of lifelong IL', through helping users to navigate
political and current events characterised by streams of misinformation.[17] They may also be well-suited to addressing the IL needs
of those less privileged in society.[18] But libraries' educational
practices should also be able to adjust to changing informational
circumstances. It has been argued that traditional assumptions
about the role of libraries and information and democracy are
outdated; and that meeting the challenge of post-truth discourse is
not primarily about an information or knowledge deficit. Libraries
must therefore correspondingly adapt their response.[19]

Citizens' Engagement With Parliament

There is thus a complex mix, where IL and associated literacies,
whether enabled through formal education or through the lifelong
informational role of libraries, contributes to democratic engagement. But more specifically, how does IL contribute to enrich one
important aspect of democracy, namely the relationship between
citizens and the parliaments that they elect? This is a pertinent
question in the light of a tentative trend, since the beginning of the
century, for parliaments across the world to engage with citizens
and encourage citizen participation over and above the act of
casting a vote at elections. IL features explicitly in some research
about what governments do (and could do) to achieve openness and
accessibility of their online services and publications[20]; and
conversely about the failure of governments to meet user expectations in information provision.[21] But it is not present to any extent
in scholarship relating to the work of parliaments. And yet it could
be argued that parliaments benefit from an information literate
public and as such have a role in educating the public to
information.

We focus particularly on the work of the UK Parliament and the House of Commons and their role in building in fostering an informed society of information literate citizens through the dual role of the UK Parliament as users and producers of information and enablers of democratic participation.

PARLIAMENTS AS INFORMATION USERS AND DISTRIBUTORS

Reliable, trusted information is at the core a healthy, functioning democracy[22] as the last 20 years and the rise of the internet age and social media have proven. The impact of misinformation and disinformation on society and consequentially politics have been far-reaching and extensively documented.

Post-truth politics, a concept defined as 'relating to or denoting circumstances in which objective facts are less influential in shaping public opinion than appeals to emotion and personal belief'[23] [Oxford Languages, 2016] and its meteoric rise in the public consciousness in the last 10 years only serves to show the critical need for IL to permeate every aspect of society and Parliament.

Information Users

The UK Parliament strives to eschew from false information and to produce and distribute factually correct and critically appraised information.

Through their research and scoping work, the policy, research and analysis community in the House of Commons operate at the intersection of two contextualisations of IL: workplace and citizenship. They use information 'to help achieve organisational aims, and to add value to organizational activities'[24] with the mission of questioning and furthering democracy.

Being information literate is a critical element for the parliamentary policy, research and analysis community and underpins all internal research processes. All researchers have high-level qualifications or significant experience in policy areas and usually use this knowledge to support the work of parliamentary libraries or select committees.

To support the work of the UK Parliament, the policy, research, and analysis community relies on finding, analysing and recontextualising information to make it relevant for their audience and their business needs.

There is a wide range of initiatives to support the IL needs of the policy, research, and analysis community.[i] The House of Commons Library Services offer access to a range of information sources and relevant databases to offer authoritative materials to this community. House of Commons Library subject specialists[ii] are supported by research librarians,[iii] experts in the resources for specific policy areas. The House of Commons Library training team also offers a range of courses in commercial databases and parliamentary tools. Some research sections operate a rigorous peer-review mechanism so that each constituency query, each publication is factually accurate and impartial. Select Committee researchers are also offered IL training contextualised to be more inclusive in the sources they use to inform select committee proceedings.

The authors believe that by carefully selecting, examining, and using evidence in their own research outputs, the policy, research and analysis community help play a critical role in informing society and amplify marginal voices.

Information Distributors

UK Parliament publishes a wide range of information daily, ranging from written statements,[25] official Hansard records,[26] business papers[27] as well as research publications.[28] However not all of this information is strictly neutral and unbiased and as such they reflect

---

[i]This community groups under the same umbrella, all roles related to policy research and analysis across the House of Commons.
[ii]Subject specialists in the House of Commons Library denotes policy experts and statisticians working on enquiries and proactive research for Members of Parliament and their staff.
[iii]Research Librarians undertake research support and collection development to support the work of research sections in the House of Commons Library.

the core business of both houses: politics, and their business needs, information.

Here we are making a distinction in parliamentary information, between records and political statements: implicitly political and biased in their nature; a reflection of opinions shared on the floors of the House of Commons and House of Lords and the information that underpin the core business of UK Parliament: impartial and evidenced.

This task, for the lower house, is undertaken by the House of Commons Library. A prolific publisher, The House of Commons Library, has been producing impartial research informing the work of Members of Parliament (MPs) since 1946. This information is made available to the public through their website.

The House of Commons Library releases a range of research in formats suiting the needs of MPs from extensive research briefings to practical support for constituency caseworkers. All research is underpinned by a robust editorial policy striving for accurate and impartial publications information by evidence and expertise.

This research features heavily in parliamentary proceedings and is often cited on the House floor by MPs, 128 times in 2022.

Parliamentary engagement is usually limited and reaches a small, unrepresentative group.[29] The House of Commons Library strives to expend the impact of their work. The research is publicised through an active Twitter account, @commonslibrary, which totals 33.4k followers. The House of Commons Library research being public means that citizens have access to the same expert, impartial information and this informs their understanding of policy and current affairs. Through its research and proactive publication, the House of Commons Library empowers a more informed public in becoming involved parliamentary democracy.

PARLIAMENTS AS ENABLERS OF DEMOCRATIC PARTICIPATION

Political participation encompasses all the processes through which citizens 'influence the behaviour of those empowered to make decisions'.[30] In a democracy, political participation allows citizens the chance to be involved and active in the decision-making process that directly affects them.[31]

Traditionally, democratic participation is undertaken through a wide range of activities varying in nature and intention. Democratic participation can be passive[32] such as not signing up to the electoral register. It can be active such as taking part in national debates or assemblies, attending council meetings. Democratic participation can be reactive such as taking part in protests and strikes. Since 2014, democracy, rule of law, tolerance, mutual respect and individual liberties are taught as core 'British values' and encompass principles for democratic participation.[33]

There is a clear interest for parliaments in seeking engagement, views and opinions from citizens. First there is the need for parliaments to be aware of first-hand experience of the population: their understanding of current affairs, issues affecting them and invite scrutiny.

Parliaments therefore have a clear role in enabling encouraging and developing informed and reflective engagement and need to define clear avenues and opportunities to do so.

Parliamentary engagement may take different forms, according to typologies that indicate the degree of public involvement and influence. One model identifies five steps of public engagement with parliament: information, understanding, identification, participation and intervention. This suggests a succession of stages of public involvement that start with access to information about parliament and that may lead ultimately to the public actively contributing to parliamentary decisions.[34,35] But notwithstanding such models, in practice, relevant initiatives, where they take place, are often still in their early days and scholarly work about the relationships between parliaments and citizens (as opposed to, say their legislative and scrutiny functions) is still relatively sparse.[36] Parliaments have begun to develop the ways that they link with citizens,[37] not least to help address the dangers represented by public disengagement and lack of trust in parliamentary politics. Contributing to the work of parliamentary committees presents particular potential for involving the public in deliberations, although much remains to be done in this area.[38]

A recent analysis of parliamentary practices in Europe concludes that parliaments are selective in their public engagement activities, timidly or cautiously embracing the opportunities brought on by information and communication technologies to actively engage citizens.[39,40] The adoption of such technologies, and associated social media, cuts across and clashes to an extent with the traditional representative role of parliaments. Adopting new practices is therefore a challenge for them, requiring them to deploy resources, staff, financial and technological, as well as political will, to achieve meaningful public engagement.[41,42]

Nevertheless, there are cases of innovative engagement mechanisms, notably online discussion forums and digital debates on social media, as in Portugal and the UK; and crowdsourcing platforms that integrate citizens' views into the law-making process, as in Austria and Croatia[43,44] Pioneering efforts have been made by some national legislatures, as in Finland, where the Citizens' Initiative Act (2012) enables citizens to influence the legislative agenda, allowing the Finnish parliament to respond to public demand for more transparent, accessible and inclusive decision-making.[45] The outreach efforts of select committees of the House of Commons are outlined below. Sometimes, efforts at public engagement reflect a desire to reinforce the legitimacy and visibility of a parliamentary assembly, as exemplified by the European Parliament, where strengthening of links with citizens is an important political imperative.[46] Instances of parliamentary public engagement initiatives are by no means limited to Europe, as demonstrated by initiatives in Brazil[47] and Bangladesh.[48]

Parliamentary Engagement

We look again particularly at the case of the UK Parliament, which has arguably made significant progress in developing multifaceted and two-way communication with the public [Norton, 2012]. Indeed, according to an analytical frame devised to measure public engagement, the House of Commons has the highest score among a selection of 21 European lower parliamentary chambers.[49] Some forms of public engagement are well-established: contacting MPs or Peers (in the case of MPs, often interacting through a local constituency surgery) to discuss grievances and other issues affecting individuals – a practice that has grown especially over the past half-century[50]; and lobbying Parliament, either as an individual or a group, to support a particular policy or campaign.[51] Beyond these traditional approaches, more recent public engagement routes are of particular interest:

- E-Petitions, where members of the public call for a specific action from the UK Government or the House of Commons. This online practice was instituted in 2011 and petitions that reach 10,000 signatures get a response from the Government. Should petitions reach 100,000 signatures, they are considered for a debate in Parliament – in practice, they are almost always debated.[52]

- The House of Commons' Chamber Engagement Team provides a means for the public to keep abreast of parliamentary activities and to help facilitate communication between members of the public and MPs.[53] An archive on the Parliament website describes how the Team have provided avenues for people to contribute their experiences and views to parliamentary debates.[54]

- A crucial part of the UK Parliament's outreach is its learning programme, providing education services for schools, colleges, communities and home educators. These services take the form of face-to-face or online sessions with students and community or youth groups, educational visits and tours, teacher training; and a comprehensive series of online learning resources.[55] These activities underpin citizenship education and political literacy, and therefore bear some relationship to IL.

- Select committees of the House of Commons have played an important parliamentary scrutiny role since 1979. In 2012, reaching out to the public was formally recognised as one of their core tasks, notably through the medium of committee inquiries and their calls for evidence. Public engagement has developed significantly over the past 10 years, with activities including crowdsourcing input from the public; fact check forums; surveys and polling; deliberative workshops; citizens' assemblies; and promoting reports and recommendations as a means of reaching out to the public even after inquiries have concluded.[56] The UK Parliament website provides a clear and well-structured introduction about how members of the public can get themselves involved in the work of select committees.[57]

Going one step further in evidencing the need for information literate citizens to play a central part in government scrutiny, the UK Parliament pioneered the recruitment of lay members to the House of Commons Committee on Standards. Lay members have become an integral part of the Committee, sharing their experience and external perspectives through their IL skills. A recent recruitment campaign clearly stressed the essential requirement for applicants to have the 'ability to consider and review large amounts of information to come to sound evidence-based judgements'.[58]

The UK Parliament has progressed considerably towards engagement and participation, driving a more informed society to contribute to change. Many challenges still remain to engage hard to reach group through more diverse and inclusive initiatives such as the work of the Parliamentary Office for Science and Technology Knowledge Exchange Unit.[59]

CONCLUSION – PARLIAMENT'S CONTRIBUTION TO AN INFORMED SOCIETY

Parliaments have a unique role to play in educating citizens in IL for the benefits of an informed society and a healthy democracy. Looking at the example of the UK Parliament, it is clear that society has a wide range of ways to be involved and to develop IL skills through parliamentary engagement.

The UK Parliament, through the parliamentary policy, research and analysis community's own use and dissemination of information, has a central role in combatting misinformation and disinformation and to inform the political discourse in the wider informed society.

Parliaments also have every interest in encouraging parliamentary engagement to provide crucial scrutiny over their own proceedings, develop understanding of parliamentary activities and provide first-hand feedback to MPs.

REFERENCES

1. Secker, Jane. 'The revised CILIP definition of information literacy'. Journal of Information Literacy 12, no. 1 (2018): 156–158. http://openaccess.city.ac.uk/20572/.

2. UNESCO. Media and Information Literacy Policy and Strategy (2013). https://www.unesco.org/en/node/66602?hub=750.

3. Correia, Ana Maria Ramalho. 'Information literacy for an active and effective citizenship'. In White Paper prepared for UNESCO, the US National Commission on Libraries and Information Science, and the National Forum on Information Literacy, for use at the Information Literacy Meeting of Experts, Prague, The Czech Republic. 2002. https://www.researchgate.net/profile/Ana-Maria-Correia-2/publication/228765129_Information_literacy_for_-an_active_and_effective_citizenship/links/55d1bea408aee5504f68edf4/Information-literacy-for-an-active-and-effective-citizenship.pdf.

4. Line, Maurice B. 'Democracy and information: transmitters and receivers'. Library Management (2003). https://doi.org/10.1108/01435120310501059.

5. Lupien, Pascal, and Lorna E. Rourke. '(Mis) information, information literacy, and democracy: Paths for pedagogy to foster informed citizenship'. Journal of Information Literacy 15, no. 3 (2021). https://doi.org/10.11645/15.3.2947.

6. Smith, Lauren. 'Towards a model of critical information literacy instruction for the development of political agency'. Journal of Information Literacy 7, no. 2 (2013): 15–32. https://doi.org/10.11645/7.2.1809.

7. Griesbaum, Joachim, Daphné Çetta, Thomas Mandl, and Elke G. Montanari. 'What is information literacy and how to improve it?' (2021): 24–43. https://10.5283/epub.44935.

8. Khan, Sadia. 'Negotiating (dis) trust to advance democracy through media and information literacy'. Postdigital Science and Education 2, no. 1 (2020): 170–183. https://doi.org/10.1007/s42438-019-00072-9.

9. Alexander, Ross Cory. 'Political literacy as information literacy'. Communications in Information Literacy 3, no. 1 (2009): 3. http://archives.pdx.edu/ds/psu/22474.

10. Sánchez Vanderkast, Egbert J. 'Information literacy, a cornerstone of democratic society: A component of an information policy'. In European Conference on Information Literacy, pp. 79–85. Springer, Cham, 2013. https://doi.org/10.1007/978-3-319-03919-0_9.

11. Smith, Lauren. 'Towards a model of critical information literacy instruction for the development of political agency'. Journal of Information Literacy 7, no. 2 (2013): 15–32. https://doi.org/10.11645/7.2.1809.

12. Polizzi, Gianfranco. 'Information literacy in the digital age: why critical digital literacy matters for democracy', in Goldstein, Stéphane. (ed.) Informed Societies: why information literacy matters for citizenship, participation and democracy. Facet Publishing, London, pp. 1–23 (2020).

13. Lupien, Pascal, and Lorna E. Rourke. '(Mis) information, information literacy, and democracy: Paths for pedagogy to foster informed citizenship'. Journal of Information Literacy 15, no. 3 (2021). https://doi.org/10.11645/15.3.2947.

14. Line, Maurice B. 'Democracy and information: transmitters and receivers'. Library Management (2003). https://doi.org/10.1108/01435120310501059.

15. Byrne, Alex. 'Necromancy or life support? Libraries, democracy and the concerned intellectual'. Library Management (2003). https://doi.org/10.1108/01435120310464844.

16. Buschman, John. 'Good news, bad news, and fake news: Going beyond political literacy to democracy and libraries'. Journal of Documentation (2018). https://doi.org/10.1108/JD-05-2018-0074.

17. Jaeger, Paul T., and Natalie Greene Taylor. 'Arsenals of life-long information literacy: Educating users to navigate political and current events information in world of ever-evolving misinformation'. The Library Quarterly 91, no. 1 (2021): 19–31. https://doi.org/10.1086/711632.

18. Eckerdal, Johanna Rivano. 'Libraries, democracy, information literacy, and citizenship: an agonistic reading of central library and information studies' concepts'. Journal of Documentation (2017). https://doi.org/10.1108/JD-12-2016-0152.

19. Lor, Peter Johan. 'Democracy, information, and libraries in a time of post-truth discourse'. Library Management (2018). https://doi.org/10.1108/LM-06-2017-0061.

20. Kauhanen-Simanainen, Anne. 'Collaborative information literacy by government'. IFLA Journal 31, no. 2 (2005): 183–187. https://doi.org/10.1177/0340035205054883.

21. Henninger, Maureen. 'Government information: Literacies, behaviours and practices'. Government Information Quarterly 34, no. 1 (2017): 8–15. https://doi.org/10.1016/j.giq.2016.12.003.

22. Thorson, Emily. 'Information and Democracy: Public Policy in the News. By Stuart N. Soroka and Christopher Wlezien. New York: Cambridge University Press, 2022. 300 p. 34.99 paper'. Perspectives on Politics 20, no. 4 (2022): 1463–1465. https://doi.org/10.1017/S1537592722002936.

23. Oxford Languages. 'Word of the Year 2016' (2016). https://languages.oup.com/word-of-the-year/2016/ (accessed: 15/01/2023).

24. Secker, Jane. 'The revised CILIP definition of information literacy'. Journal of Information Literacy 12, no. 1 (2018): 156–158. http://openaccess.city.ac.uk/20572/.

25. UK Parliament. Written questions, answers and statements. https://questions-statements.parliament.uk/ (accessed: 16/01/2023).

26. UK Parliament. Hansard. https://hansard.parliament.uk/ (accessed: 16/01/2023).

27. UK Parliament. Commons business papers. https://commons-business.parliament.uk/ (accessed: 16/01/2023).

28. UK Parliament. Research publications. https://www.parliament.uk/business/publications/research/ (accessed: 16/01/2023).

29. Hansard Society. Connecting citizens to parliament: How Parliament can engage more effectively with Hard-to-Reach Groups (2011). https://www.hansardsociety.org.uk/publications/reports/connecting-citizens-to-parliament-how-parliament-can-engage-more (accessed: 24/01/2023).

30. Verba, Sidney. 'Democratic participation'. The Annals of the American Academy of Political and Social Science 373, no. 1 (1967): 53–78. https://doi.org/10.1177/000271626737300103.

31. Keutgen, Julia. 'Participatory democracy: The importance of having a say when times are hard'. Institute Montaigne (2021). https://www.institutmontaigne.org/en/analysis/participatory-democracy-importance-having-say-when-times-are-hard (accessed: 15/01/2023).

32. Chang, Chingching, and Chung-li Wu. 'Active vs. passive ambivalent voters: Implications for Interactive Political Communication and Participation'. Communication Research (2022). https://doi.org/10.1177/00936502211066001.

33. UK Department for Education. 'Guidance on promoting British values through SMSC'. (2014). https://www.gov.uk/government/publications/promoting-fundamental-british-values-through-smsc (accessed: 15/01/2023).

34. Leston-Bandeira, Cristina. 'Studying the relationship between Parliament and citizens'. The Journal of Legislative Studies 18, no. 3–4 (2012): 265–274. https://doi.org/10.1080/13572334.2012.706044.

35. Walker, Aileen, Naomi Jurczak, Catherine Bochel, and Cristina Leston-Bandeira. 'How public engagement became a core part of the House of Commons select committees'. Parliamentary Affairs 72, no. 4 (2019): 965–986. https://doi.org/10.1093/pa/gsz031.

36. Serra-Silva, Sofia. 'Beyond national boundaries in the study of digital public engagement: Interparliamentary institutions and cooperation in the Austrian and Portuguese national parliaments'. Policy & Internet (2022). https://doi.org/10.1002/poi3.326.

37. Leston-Bandeira, Cristina. 'Studying the relationship between Parliament and citizens'. The Journal of Legislative Studies 18, no. 3–4 (2012): 265–274. https://doi.org/10.1080/135723 34.2012.706044.

38. Hendriks, Carolyn M., and Adrian Kay. 'From 'opening up' to democratic renewal: Deepening public engagement in legislative committees'. Government and Opposition 54, no. 1 (2019): 25–51. https://doi.org/10.1017/gov.2017.20.

39. Serra-Silva, Sofia. 'Parliamentary online public engagement in the 21st century: A comparative perspective with a focus on Austria and Portugal'. PhD diss., Universidade de Lisboa (Portugal), 2019. https://www.proquest.com/openview/8103 0bb51d35228690c82765120c3991/1?pq-origsite=gscholar&cbl=2026366&diss=y.

40. Serra-Silva, Sofia. 'How parliaments engage with citizens? Online public engagement: a comparative analysis of Parliamentary websites'. The Journal of Legislative Studies (2021): 1–24. https://doi.org/10.1080/13572334.2021.1896451.

41. Griffith, Jeffrey, and Cristina Leston-Bandeira. 'How are parliaments using new media to engage with citizens?' The Journal of Legislative Studies 18, no. 3–4 (2012): 496–513. The Journal of Legislative Studies, 18(3–4), pp. 496–513. https://doi.org/10.1080/13572334.2012.706058.

42. Serra-Silva, Sofia. 'Beyond national boundaries in the study of digital public engagement: Interparliamentary institutions and cooperation in the Austrian and Portuguese national parliaments'. Policy & Internet (2022). https://doi.org/10.1002/poi3.326.

43. Serra-Silva, Sofia. 'How parliaments engage with citizens? Online public engagement: a comparative analysis of parliamentary websites'. The Journal of Legislative Studies (2021): 1–24. https://doi.org/10.1080/13572334.2021.1896451.

44. Serra-Silva, Sofia. 'Beyond national boundaries in the study of digital public engagement: Interparliamentary institutions and cooperation in the Austrian and Portuguese national parliaments'. Policy & Internet (2022). https://doi.org/10.1002/poi3.326.

45. Seo, Hyeon Su. 'Reaching out to the people? Parliament and citizen participation in Finland'. (2017). https://trepo.tuni.fi/handle/10024/100766.

46. Leston-Bandeira, Cristina. 'The pursuit of legitimacy as a key driver for public engagement: the European Parliament case'. Parliamentary Affairs 67, no. 2 (2014): 415–436. https://doi.org/10.1093/pa/gss050.

47. De Barros, Antonio Teixeira, Cristiane Brum Bernardes, and Malena Rehbein. 'Brazilian Parliament and digital engagement'. The Journal of Legislative Studies 22, no. 4 (2016): 540–558. https://doi.org/10.1080/13572334.2016.1235331.

48. Ahmed, Nizam. 'Parliament, public engagement and legislation in Bangladesh: a case study of Domestic Violence Act of 2010'. The Journal of Legislative Studies 24, no. 4 (2018): 431–449. https://doi.org/10.1080/13572334.2018.1540116.

49. Serra-Silva, Sofia. 'Beyond national boundaries in the study of digital public engagement: Interparliamentary institutions and cooperation in the Austrian and Portuguese national parliaments'. Policy & Internet (2022). https://doi.org/10.1002/poi3.326.

50. Norton, Philip. 'Parliament and citizens in the United Kingdom'. The Journal of Legislative Studies 18, no. 3–4 (2012): 403–418. https://doi.org/10.1080/13572334.2012.706053.

51. UK Parliament. Contact an MP or a member of the Lords. https://www.parliament.uk/get-involved/contact-an-mp-or-lord/ (accessed: 02/01/2023).

52. UK Government and Parliament. How petitions work. https://petition.parliament.uk/help (accessed: 02/03/2023).

53. UK Parliament. How you can join in. https://www.parliament.uk/get-involved/have-your-say-on-laws/chamber-engagement/how-you-can-join-in2/ (accessed: 02/01/2023).

54. UK Parliament. Engagement Archive. https://www.parliament.uk/get-involved/have-your-say-on-laws/engagement-archive/ (accessed: 02/01/2023).

55. UK Parliament. Learning. https://learning.parliament.uk/en/ (accessed: 02/01/2023).

56. Walker, Aileen, Naomi Jurczak, Catherine Bochel, and Cristina Leston-Bandeira. 'How public engagement became a core part of the House of Commons select committees'. Parliamentary Affairs 72, no. 4 (2019): 965–986. https://doi.org/10.1093/pa/gsz031.

57. UK Parliament. Have your say: select committee inquiries. https://www.parliament.uk/get-involved/committees/ (accessed: 02/01/2023).

58. UK Parliament. Lay Members of the Committee on Standards (2022). https://housesofparliament.tal.net/vx/mobile-0/appcentre-HouseOfCommons/brand-4/candidate/so/pm/3/pl/14/opp/3690-Lay-Members-of-the-Committee-on-Standards/en-GB (accessed: 16/01/2023).

59. UK Parliament. Working to support more diverse and inclusive engagement between UK Parliament and researchers. https://www.parliament.uk/get-involved/research-impact-at-the-uk-parliament/diverse-and-inclusive-engagement-between-uk-parliament-and-researchers/ (accessed: 24/01/2023).

10

QUESTIONS WORTH ASKING AND CONVERSATIONS THAT MATTER: GENERATING IDEAS IN COHESIVE COMMUNITIES

Tim Slack and Fiona Thomas

Very great change starts with very small conversations held among people who care.

–Margaret J. Wheatley[1]

QUESTIONS WORTH ASKING

Just Imagine

A public meeting in a neighbourhood community centre. Lines of chairs frequented by a scattering of local people and a higher proportion of public sector officers and agency representatives. On a raised platform at the front behind a table sits a group of local authority officers and elected members. They are there to consult on the community plan. A plan which has been drawn up externally to the community and is reacting to issues identified using statistics and external perceptions. The approach is based on problem-solving to tackle long-term issues. The meeting proceeds with a number of presentations followed by a question and answer session. Interaction is limited and the process tends towards a litany of complaints and solutions that are not feasible or affordable. Reactions to complaints foster defensiveness and external blame. The overall process leaves an air of dissatisfaction and frustration within the community attendees. They sense a missed opportunity where many of the voices within the community have not been heard or been able to contribute. A community plan is produced that 'ticks the boxes', meets the targets, and gathers dust until the next need for a community plan.

In a different part of the country a community summit is being held with people sitting around tables in small groups. There are neither presentations nor an externally written draft plan for approval. There is the buzz of conversation – noisy and full of interaction. Ideas and plans are being debated and shared around. People from different generations, backgrounds and roles are present. They're identifying the strengths of their community, talking about what they wish for, and what they can do differently by working together. New relationships are forming and solutions are emerging that are creative, aspirational and achievable. In the corner a group of artists are recording a 'visual minute' as a wall mural of the process, which will tour local venues to share the journey so far.

Focus on What's Strong, Not What's Wrong!

The difference between the two meetings arises from the use of Appreciative Inquiry (AI), which seeks the positive core of an organisation and builds from there, focusing on what's strong rather than what's wrong. Originating over 30 years ago, yet with its roots in ancient wisdom,[2] AI has been used with low-income cohesive communities across the world to generate new ideas and ways of working which improve daily life and wellbeing.[3] AI challenges the external perception of poor and disadvantaged communities as being in deficit and a problem to be solved. It recognises and encourages the innate resilience and ability of such communities to create their own solutions. Identifying the gifts, resources, and aspirations which people have, and working out what they desire for their communities or organisations sparks generativity – creating ideas and ways of thinking which are new. This chapter demonstrates how Appreciative Inquiry provides a framework for community ideas and creativity to flow.

Whose Ideas Are They Anyway?

One of the findings of the research[4] underlying the book *The Ideas-Informed Society: Why We Need It and How to Make It Happen* was that communities where there is low education and high cohesion do not see value in statements concerning tolerance and inclusion, ethical and sustainable practices of business, or the need to support physical and mental health. In this chapter, we postulate that such communities have their own way of expressing such beliefs and acting on them, valuing knowledge as wisdom rather than a consumer good. Appreciative Inquiry can act as the enabler to this view: Asking strength based, positive and generative questions, alongside a narrative approach releases creativity and enables the co-designing of solutions. The parallel and complementary concept of 'Positive Deviance'[5] plays an important part in releasing the innate energy and ideas already present, whilst visual minuting captures ideas and presents them in an accessible and inspiring way.

CREATIVE METHODOLOGIES

Appreciative Inquiry

The core principles which underpin Appreciative Inquiry were first developed in the 1990s by David Cooperrider and Suresh Srivastva (Cooperrider's advisor at Case Western Reserve University). Since then practitioners have described five additional emergent principles.[6] For the purposes of this chapter we have focused on the core principles and will mention them in examples of community activities:

- *Constructionist* – based on the theory of social constructionism, in which our individual realities are formed by our interpretation and perception. *Words create worlds.*

- *Simultaneity* – asking a question sets in motion a fundamental reaction, so the crafting of questions and the choice of words is important. *Inquiry creates change.*

- *Anticipatory* – our expectations and imagined scenarios lead us to make decisions that influence our present conditions and actions. *Image inspires action.*

- *Poetic* – we make sense of our lives through the stories we tell and hear, and we can choose to look into high points of learning and experience. *What we focus on grows.*

- *Positive* – momentum and change require large amounts of energy and this can come from positive effect and social bonding when we are at our best. *Positive questions lead to positive change.*

Although there's more to AI than the principles, they are a good place to start.

Positive Deviance

This concept is based on the observation that in every community or organisation, there are a few individuals or groups whose uncommon but successful behaviours and strategies have enabled them to find better solutions to problems than their neighbours who face the same challenges and barriers and have access to the same resources.

Communities which look homogenous from the outside or when described in tables of statistics are actually made up of unique individuals, each bringing their own insights to the task of daily survival. Together they make up communities which have assets or resources that they have not yet tapped. Positive Deviance enables a community or organisation to amplify uncommon behaviours or strategies discovered by community members among the least likely to succeed. These Positive Deviants are the spark of evidence to develop activities for sustainable behavioural and social change. The solution is already within – it just needs identifying and amplifying.

Visual Minutes

Visual minuters or graphic vocalisers are artists who, in real time, record through cartoons and drawings what is being said in a meeting or event. This approach has been used in a variety of settings from community planning to team building and culture change. The method has an impact that is generative and positive when used within disadvantaged communities. Participants often express their excitement about seeing their images, ideas and solutions appearing in a visual form before their eyes. These minutes are then used as part of community engagement events, funding proposals and assessment visits.

CONVERSATIONS THAT MATTER

Approaching Communities With a Fresh Perspective

Historical and traditional interventions can block and negatively interact with disadvantaged communities. Interventions must overcome the implicit and sometimes explicit assumptions about communities being steeped in deprivation which comes from a deficit belief and approach. Such inherited models often use 'management speak'[7] and come from a place of power and external decisions. What is ignored is existing resilience, adaptability and practical solutions already present or being explored informally. Appreciative Inquiry and Positive Deviance unearth the ways that already work and can move things forward.

A few years ago, one of the authors had the opportunity to attend a round table conversation with a CEO of a large funding organisation. The purpose was to explore how the organisation could relate better to the communities it served. One suggestion was to change the first question in the grant applications from the issues and problems to be addressed, and instead to inquire into what the community does well. This would bring to the surface its resilience and identify the successes to be built upon. Unfortunately, this approach was not taken up. The AI principle of simultaneity posits that the first question you ask is fateful, i.e. influential and potent, and will steer where the conversation will go. A first step in identifying and encouraging the creativity present in any community is to ask a question that is generative and positive.

Who holds the power or is perceived to hold the power can get in the way. An example of this came when working in inner city Liverpool using Appreciative Inquiry to co-design a community plan. The work had been commissioned by a local community organisation not the normal Local Authority or Housing Association. Using a combination of AI training for 25 residents and visual minutes, over 500 conversations in co-design days resulted in the creation of a the plan. The community organisation had been asked to meet with the City Council urban regeneration department, who wanted to include and adapt the plan into a wider masterplan. Putting the constructionist principle into action the community organisation commissioned consultants and asked them to attend the meeting, arguing that 'you are *our* consultants providing advice to *us*, not consultants appointed by the external organisation to their agenda. We trust you and have a relationship with you'. It was a valuable lesson in ensuring that community voices are heard. Co-designing and co-creating local solutions helps to shift the power position.

Big Local and the Dog Show

Big Local is a National Lottery programme providing 150 neighbourhoods with one million pounds each.[8] It is a bottom-up community-led project with the local community at the heart of the process. Each Big Local area has an external adviser and requires a community engagement process. Working with one of the Merseyside areas a local volunteer came up with the idea of a dog show as part of the engagement process. The show ran for three years and provided not only the opportunity for engagement on future community needs but also fostered community cohesion, provided a positive educational vehicle about dog care, increased participation in dog chipping, and contributed to resolving one of the very common community issues of dog mess. This was an issue high on residents' priority lists and beyond the scope of the normal planning process to deal with. Residents perceived it as the local authority responsibility to tackle through larger fines. The dog show was an example of using the 'poetic principle' (see the list of AI activities listed earlier) to focus on what was wanted. By celebrating dogs it provided an opportunity to change behaviours and educate pet owners. The result was less mess.

A Cross Generational Project

Making Jam is a simple project that fostered inter-generational relationships, built understanding about sourcing food, and encouraged environmental education. It was a youth project based in a Big Local area that took young people to pick blackberries on the local disused railway footpath. The next step was for community elders (aka 'your granny') to teach young people to make blackberry jam, followed by afternoon tea conversations. Its impact was much wider than a fun activity. The process encouraged local history conversations between community elders and young people. Local knowledge was shared and the young peoples' self-confidence and communication skills were enhanced. Participants began to have different perceptions about where food comes from and to appreciative nature more. It embodied the positive principle by starting small and snowballing. A bright idea produced multiple outcomes.

Mutuality and Voluntary Responses

One of the authors has lived on an ex-Council estate in South London for 16 years, which if statistics were the whole story could seem like a pretty dreary place. According to one survey based on the English index of deprivation statistics its highest score is 'average' for inside environment deprivation. On the other 8 scores it ranges from 'below average' to 'very bad'. And yet, that is not the impression gained from talking to neighbours and walking round the place. True, there are problems with fly-tipping, and everyone has routine grumbles about services. However, look beneath the surface and there are daily examples of imagination and neighbourliness which chime with Asset-based Community Development. This cousin of Appreciative Inquiry seeks out the positive core in neighbourhoods and flourishes through gifts, association and hospitality.[9]

Most of the social housing stock is owned by a tenant-led housing association which came into being in 2009, prompted by the desire of local residents to have something better than the service they were getting from the council. The founding Chair is a working-class child of the Second World War who was told by her teachers that she would never amount to much, and whose dyslexia was diagnosed years later. Having voted for transfer to the new association, the tenants were asked what housing improvements they wanted implementing first. Double glazing and new kitchens were installed by a dedicated team of fitters. Since then, the association has started building its own houses, including a complex of flats for single elderly people with social care needs which has released their three bedroom houses for families on the waiting list. Residents are the largest group on the Board.

One of the local churches has become a hub for community activities, through the persistent kindness of a previous minister. He used the authority of his role to welcome good ideas. As with many community efforts it is women who make it work. So the lunch club and the crafts group for older people are run in a voluntary capacity by women who are loved and respected. They also happen to have lived experience of physical and learning difficulties within their families. Belief in their capabilities and trust in their leadership abilities has created something which doesn't rely explicitly on paid external staff, although it does depend on the church keeping the building open.

Generating a Whole Community Plan Through Local Conversations

Rathlin Island, as the only inhabited island in Northern Ireland, is both a tourist attraction and one of the most important bird nesting grounds in Europe. Twenty years ago, the population had shrunk to barely more than 70. Through the work of the RDCA (Rathlin Development Community Association) supported by a wide range of stakeholders, the Island now has a thriving and expanding community of 160 with affordable housing, a range of community business and growing tourism economy. Up to five years ago the community planning was undertaken by external consultants in the traditional approach. The Islanders felt that the plan did not reflect community need and lacked community ownership. Following a long period of relationship building an AI approach was decided as the way forward, consisting of:

- Training a group of islanders in appreciative inquiry;

- Co-designing a set of questions with a planning group;

- One to one conversations, with more than 90 islanders;

- A project with the island primary school to look at the future of the island. This involved time travelling and the use of a model Tardis;

- Two community co-design events involving 40 plus islanders each time with visual minuters capturing the ideas and solutions.

The net result was a community-led plan as a recognised exemplar in community engagement. The emerging ideas led to a £1m project to restore the Manor House as a major island community building. The five different visual minutes have had a life beyond the initial project, providing an enduring image of the future of Rathlin Island as seen by the people who live there. Images inspired action, in an example of the anticipatory principle at work.

The COVID-19 pandemic of 2020–2022 significantly affected the island's economy. Recently a £5m vermin eradication project has been agreed as protection for the seabird colonies, through European Community funding obtained by the RSPB. Part of this has been a funded process to explore the economic impact of the eradication project, to identify economic solutions that can foster wellbeing and economic recovery. Once again AI will be used and a key part of this will be to co-design with islanders a social and economic review toolkit that can be implemented locally on an annual basis. This approach has provided a framework and process that hears as many voices as possible, builds local alliances and solutions from within that will have an impact. The process has also demonstrated that ideas and awareness on world needs are present within the Island community.

GENERATING IDEAS

Where Do Bright Ideas Come From?

We started this chapter by asking the reader to imagine two very different approaches to engaging low income communities in creating a vision for their future. In one, the ideas mostly come from outside, and may well be rather formulaic, using blueprints developed elsewhere. In the other, using AI, the ideas are generated from within the community and are unique to that context. They draw on wisdom from elsewhere without being constrained by other people's experience. We have argued that many of the essential resources needed to deal with the challenges facing poor or isolated communities already exist within the communities themselves.

The power of AI comes from drawing all the stakeholders into a conversation of equality, so that the staff of external agencies and local people sit alongside one another rather than being on opposite sides of the table. The conversational, narrative-based methodology of AI brings to the surface ideas which local people may have had without a channel for expressing them, as in the case of the ex-council estate in London, as well as generating new solutions such as the dog show through Big Local. Apparently cohesive communities often have positive deviants among them – people with ideas and solutions out of the accepted norms. The work on Rathlin Island is a good example of that. And in all the examples given here there have been moments of generativity when an impossible idea sparks off a new and feasible way forward.

The Appreciative Mindset

What is required are interventions that are built around long-term relationships, mentoring, loads of conversations, building confidence and thinking up practical examples suited to local circumstances and contexts. Intrinsic to these interventions has been the importance and value of training local people in the Appreciative Inquiry philosophy and techniques. AI tools and the appreciative mindset have provided the foundation for change and engagement from the community standpoint.

Tim Slack Appreciating People (www.appreciatingpeople.co.uk)
Fiona Thomas Appreciating Church (www.appreciating.church)

NOTES

1. Wheatley, M. J. (2002) Turning to One Another: Simple Conversations to Restore Hope to the Future. Berrett-Koehler.
2. The quote 'Excellence is a habit' is usually attributed to Aristotle. Authors Caelan Huntress and Frank Herron discovered that the natural origin of this quote is Will Durant, who was trying to explain Aristotle's contribution to philosophy in simple terms. Aristotle's original quote was: 'As it is not one swallow or a fine day that makes a spring, so it is not one day or a short time that makes a man blessed and happy'.
3. Global examples can be found through AI Commons. https://appreciativeinquiry.champlain.edu/.
4. Brown, C. and Groß-Opho, J. and Chadwick, K. and Parkinson, S. (2022) 'Achieving the ideas informed society: a Structural Equation Model for England', Emerald Open Research.
5. For a full description and examples of where this is being used. See https://positivedeviance.org/.
6. The Center for Appreciative Inquiry. https://www.centerforappreciativeinquiry.net/more-on-ai/principles-of-appreciative-inquiry/.
7. Words and expressions that are used by managers and in management theory, but may not be understood by ordinary people: *Relationship marketing' is management speak for*

selling products by offering discounts and benefits to existing customers. Cambridge Dictionary Online.
8. https://localtrust.org.uk/big-local/.
9. *The Abundant Community. Awakening the power of families and neighborhoods*. McKnight, J. and Block, P. Barrett-Koehler Publishers, Inc. (2010, 2012) Oakland.

11

AN ENTREPRENEUR'S JOURNEY: DELIVERING IDEAS TO CHANGE A VUCA WORLD*

Paul Lindley OBE

SOCIETY IN CRISIS

In the 1980s, recruits training for senior positions within the military at the US Army War College were introduced to a new way of describing the environment in which they would operate through the acronym VUCA.[1] VUCA stands for:

Volatile – where change is constant and instability is the norm.

Uncertain – where a lack of trends means that events are difficult to predict.

Complex – where problems are multi-layered and interconnected.

Ambiguous – where interpretations of events can vary.

If we consider a potted history of the twenty-first century to date, then VUCA seems a fitting description. Crises have arisen in all aspects of society: environmental, social justice, economic, political, public health, personal health, technology, war, terrorism.

---

*In writing this chapter, the author is grateful to Ruth Luzmore for her invaluable support.

Alongside this, the nature of change itself has changed. Across multiple aspects of the way we live, both individually and as communities, the speed of change has simultaneously increased and decreased.[2] We are frustrated by dawdling responses when events rapidly accelerate; for example the inadequate safeguarding protections to the ubiquity of social media in young people's lives or when they unexpectedly slow down such as to address flatlining industrial productivity.

In previous generations, moments of societal upheaval have invariably led to new ways of thinking, bold ideas and the possibilities of a tomorrow that is better than yesterday. Perhaps the publication of the Beveridge Report in 1942 and the subsequent founding of the welfare state in post war Britain is the most classic example. But the relentless onslaught of this century's challenges has barely given us time to catch our breath, let alone the time and space to collectively respond through our established institutions, so we can emerge as a thriving society. When predicament follows calamity follows catastrophe, the ability to plan for a better future is undermined, as is the belief in a secure, calmer future. We are failing to deal with the VUCA present and to sow seeds of hope and belief in a brighter future.

I worry in particular for those born in this century. They are a generation for whom a VUCA world is all they have ever known. Of course, learning to cope with difficulty in life is an important part of growing up and has been faced by generation after generation. But this generation of children's exposure to toxic stress and prolonged periods of adversity where caregivers, public services and governments have been unable to provide adequate support and security, are unprecedented. They also can have a negative impact on today's children's physiological development with lifelong consequences (The Center on the Developing Child, n.d.).[3] The causes of toxic stress will vary, for example through familial economic hardship, poverty or mental illnesses amongst other causes, but we must recognise that these are often symptoms themselves of a society in turmoil. Of course, not all children will experience the impact of an uncertain world in the same way or to the same degree, but theirs is a generation that has, so far, been dis-empowered from navigating the direction of their lives. They increasingly feel that they cannot shape their destiny or fulfil their potential.

Unfortunately, the VUCA world and its toxic stress causing environment is unlikely to recede anytime soon. Society, therefore, needs to accelerate its collective and pooled coping responses to create, and put into practice, new ideas to adapt to this environment. And quickly. Britain needs a thriving society and, as society is what happens when children grow up, it is in everyone's interest, whether parent or not, to invest in the wellbeing and healthy development of all our nation's children. To do this old ideas, tested and adopted in a different century, have proved inadequate in our VUCA world. We see this on a macro-level in the inability of collective leaders to tackle the climate and environmental emergency with sufficient alignment and speed, in the rise of populism undermining democracy right across the world and in the failings of capitalism to spread wealth and prosperity to meet the needs of the societies it serves as inequality grows. For children specifically in the UK, more are now living in both absolute and relative poverty than ever before, with more poor health: evidenced by rates of child obesity and demand for mental health services, and less access to spaces dedicated to supporting their needs (like gardens, youth clubs or Sure Start centres). We are in desperate need of new 'big' ideas for how to help our children, and nation, thrive and to encourage a culture that embraces change and added uncertainty that new ideas may create and but also solve. Collectively our institutions must be more entrepreneurial and our leaders need to embrace the two greatest characteristics that define the greatest entrepreneurs: curiosity and bravery.

IDEAS. WHERE DO THEY COME FROM?

When we have a new idea, why hasn't anyone thought of it before? How is it that some ideas develop into reality and others don't? Is it possible to solve national or global problems without new ideas becoming reality? I don't think so, and so they fascinate me.

Human beings are the only animal that can imagine something that doesn't exist and then have the ingenuity to communicate it, collaborate on it and revolutionise lives by inventing it – through innovation. Entrepreneurs do this all the time and evidence shows that ideas are most free-flowing, most embraced and most likely to be developed when the culture of a community encourages such communication, collaboration, inquisitiveness, ability to fail – learn – adapt and succeed.

I find it mind-blowing that a new idea, never before thought, can evolve into a new thing because someone has the imagination and ingenuity to make it so: and so create an invention or innovation that has the power in itself to improve the world. They take hold because of curiosity and bravery.

Was the person who first invented the wheel, the first to have the idea of a wheel? If not, why did the wheel inventor succeed where the wheel dreamer did not? What skills, support or collaboration did the inventor have that made all the difference? Let's hold that thought, in the context of curiosity and bravery and consider how we might think about the big ideas needed to improve children's lives that society through its culture could be persuaded to accept and adopt.

BIG IDEAS HELPING CHILDREN TO THRIVE

In recent decades, there have of course been many ideas and initiatives which have successfully increased the wellbeing of children (such as the fluoridisation of water, the Sure Start programme and the establishment of Wales' Future Generations Commissioner post) but although there haven't been enough of them to meet the challenges of a VUCA world, it is also worth being cautious of ideas which present themselves as easy fixes, and not pile straight in.

Take for example the 'baby box'. In the 1930s, faced with a need to lower infant mortality in the context of increasing birth rates, Finland began a public health experiment. All disadvantaged pregnant women were entitled to receive a 'baby box': a simple box filled with numerous baby-related materials which morphed into a safe place to sleep when emptied, for families living in poverty with no possibility of buying a cot. In order to receive this box, women had to engage with pre-natal care which also included anti-poverty programs. In the late 1940s, the programme was extended to all pregnant women. Finland significantly reduced its infant mortality rates and its baby box scheme was applauded in the media as a brilliant idea. Versions of the Finnish 'baby box' have since taken off in several countries. Indeed, after introducing the scheme in 2016, the Scottish government claimed that the baby box had reduced infant mortality. Numerous experts reacted to this claim however by warning that the baby box itself was only one part of an improvement in the healthcare system to which lower mortality could be attributed[4] and also against the potential misinterpretation that a baby was safer sleeping in a cardboard box than a crib.[5] Indirectly, they were clearly saying, through evidence they presented, be aware of simple solutions and ascribing cause and effect with a narrow focus, for everything in an ecosystem is connected or correlated.

There is also danger in the idea of lifting and transporting policies from other counties without fully understanding the wider system within which the policy was originally born. For example there has been much call (especially from 'the right') for the UK to adopt education policies from Singapore, where academic results are world class, children almost universally relish studying and the curriculum is wide and rigorous. However, before piling in and borrowing Singapore's education policies with the belief that they could transform British education and children's prospects, the wider system within which education policy has been set, has to be understood and also borrowed. For example, Singapore has a consensus about the purpose of education, which is not developed in the UK. It's purpose is much narrower ('preparing children for employment and citizenship') than that which the average British parent or indeed policy maker would recognise. In addition, in Singapore education is systemically aligned through all its constituent parts – from curriculum to textbooks to teacher training and more. The English system (education is devolved in the UK) is very fragmented in the voices and stakeholders influencing the whole education system. Further, Singapore recruits, trains and pays teachers exceptionally well. The UK does not. Finally, the Singaporean government exerts significant control over the decisions and freedoms of its citizens, and culturally this is accepted.[6] That is a long way from British culture and its citizens' relationship with their government. So, the Singaporean education policies, if adopted into the UK system are highly likely to fail. Context, culture and the big picture are critical for successful borrowing of ideas, as 'everything is connected'.

Finally, policymakers need to be very mindful, when executing new ideas designed to improve children's lives, that they are addressing the cause of the problem, not its symptom. Especially vital when the VUCA world means that it is often uncertain, complex and ambiguous as to which is which. Take for example education once more, education policy ideas to increase attainment and reduce inequality (and promote social mobility and opportunity) are doomed to fail (and have failed) without also addressing the drivers behind the inequality present in society such as poverty, housing or public health.

All these examples highlight two related problems I see when we seek ideas which aim to create positive change in society – which are vital for it to thrive in a VUCA world.

- The first is in the seduction of the appeal of a simple idea that is media friendly and logistically uncomplicated yet open to misinterpretation – sometimes with dangerous consequences.

- The second is in ignoring the wider VUCA context within which an idea is enacted. The nature of the world we inhabit is characterised by complexity where cause and effects are interconnected across a myriad of factors and entwined like a tangled ball of wool. For ideas to be sustainable, scalable and impactful, we need an ideas-informed society prepared to attempt to untangle that ball.

UNTANGLING THE BALL OF WOOL

As a teenager and a young man, my political hero was (and still is!) Senator Robert F Kennedy. He was a rare politician, as he enthusiastically embraced the possibilities of big ideas whilst recognising the uncertainly and complexity that they could set loose. He did so because he believed the risk was worth testing in order to create the better world he believed was possible. In his 1968 Presidential campaign, he constantly paraphrased George Bernard Shaw to articulate the hope new ideas gave him and how he wanted society to believe in possibilities and be informed and inspired by great ones. That quote is blu-tacked to my computer as I write: 'Some men *(sic)* see things as they are and ask why? I dream things that never were, and ask why not?'[7] It's a proposition that has been the challenge of my life and one to which I have constantly sought to address – by allowing myself to dream ideas, and then act upon them.

A PERSONAL JOURNEY IN MAKING IDEAS A REALITY

In 2004, I left my safe corporate career to act upon an idea that baby food could be delicious AND healthy, engage all a baby's senses and capture its parents' trust as being nutritiously complete and tasty. I spent 2 years wholly focused on converting the idea into a reality, and launched Ella's Kitchen, my brand of organic baby and children's food to the UK market. It was innovative, entrepreneurial and successful. Doubling its sales for each of its first 7 years to become the biggest baby food brand in the country and available right around the world. We constantly asked, 'why not?' with new ideas over recipes, ingredients, packaging, processing, marketing and even over the purpose of business itself. As a consequence, I became the UK's Entrepreneur of the Year before selling the company in 2013.

I then wanted to test how an entrepreneurial mindset could be embraced in other parts of life away from business. I involved myself in charity, social enterprise, education and public policy. I wondered how I could bring my learning, experience and ideas to inform change in other parts of society, especially towards problems of children's wellbeing, welfare, health or rights each of which are deepening in this VUCA world.

In finding some answers, and mindful of the pitfalls of unintended consequences and of the interdependence of so many issues – as already discussed, I wanted to share one specific project that embraces such ideas and possibilities and lives up to Kennedy and

Shaw's challenge in asking 'why not?'. It demonstrates a way of
seeking information, working with experts, engaging in new ideas
and thinking on multi-dimensional levels with promising signs of
social impact. The project focussed on reversing the alarming
growth of childhood obesity and unhealthy weight.

The most recent data from the National Child Measurement
Programme shows the highest annual rise of childhood obesity rates
since records began as well as 40% of 11-year-olds being
unhealthily overweight.[8] The tyranny of averages disguises the
horrifying fact that those living in deprived communities are twice
as likely to be overweight[9] – those most vulnerable in childhood are
most at risk.

At an individual level, childhood obesity can lead to: early onset
of conditions like type-2 diabetes, heart disease[10] and tooth decay;[11]
poor emotional health, sleep and lower educational attainment;[12]
and high likelihood of obesity in adulthood with associated risks of
disability and premature death.[13] The impact of unhealthy weight
going into adulthood goes beyond that of the individual with estimated cost to wider society being £27 billion annually.[14] This is a
problem we desperately need ideas to solve for society and the
individual's sake.

In 2018, I submitted my first job application in 20 years. It was
humbling when the Mayor of London, Sadiq Khan, appointed me
chair of London's brand-new Child Obesity Taskforce. His challenge, for a city that came bottom of the league table of healthy
child weight across major global cities, was to identify actionable
ideas to fundamentally change this. It was a project to try and start
unravelling that tangled ball of wool.

LONDON'S CHILD OBESITY TASKFORCE – A PLACE
FOR IDEAS

Here is what we could have done: Pull together a team of nutrition
experts to write a report of recommendations. But we didn't want
to do things the typical way. Instead I began putting together a team
of diverse individuals including: a professor of food policy, a head
teacher, a community engagement consultant, a regional director of

Public Health England, a Director of Children's Services, the Chief Executive of a major charity, an urban design and planning specialist, the founder of a London soup kitchen, a community organiser, an Early Years specialist, an expert in Digital Health, a brand manager and the CEO of a mental health charity. The individuals also represented life experience across the breadth of backgrounds and challenges Londoners faced, including that of living with obesity. The strength of this team was the range in both professional expertise and personal experiences all determined to offer new thinking about an old problem. My pitch to the mayor was 'with me you are going to get new ideas, some of which will fail. But those that do will be analysed and used to learn from, some of which will be adapted, iterated and reconceived to try again. Each time we do this we will get closer to solving the challenge. We have to try new ideas: if we keep doing what we always did we will always get what we always got. In this case increasing healthy weight'. He embraced this thinking.

We set about our task establishing a vision 'that every child in London should grow up in a community and an environment that supports their health and weight' and a purpose 'to unleash a transformation in London so that every child has every chance to grow up eating healthily, drinking plenty of water and being physically active'.[15]

Our ambitions and plans were built on three core principles:

1. *That children and their voices would be at the centre of everything we would consider.* This was because the one thing that needed to be done more than anything else was to listen to the voices of the children for whom we wanted to make a difference. My colleague, and vice chair, Professor Corinna Hawkes, put it brilliantly:

   I can't pretend to know what it's really like growing up in one of London's poorer neighbourhoods. I don't (unlike some of the other members of the Taskforce). But by getting down to the kids' level, I can begin to see the nature of the problem – and the potential solutions - much better. I can see that it's the way the negative influences combine in children's lives that make it so difficult to shift the problem. I can see that we need a connected set of actions around children as they go about their daily lives, actions that enable children of all ages to enjoy eating healthy diets, drinking water and moving more. I can see that we also need to address the nature of work, housing and poverty for their parents and other caregivers. I can see that we need children's help in designing the actions we know are important. It's no use asking food outlets to provide free water refills, for example, if children don't feel welcome in these places, or if new water fountains are placed in places seen as unsafe. If we are going to fix the system, we need to understand how people experience it on the inside.

When we start to think from the child's perspective, things become clearer. A child-centred approach is not about targeting individual kids: it's about understand-ing how the system around them can be changed in a way that meets them where they are. In changing the system, we can make a difference, helping kids grow up healthier, now, and for future generations.

(Hawkes, 2019)[16]

We went out and spoke to London's children eventually draw-ing their experiences together into four profiles of the daily realities of children living in low-income London families.[17] We began then to understand how London's children lived their lives and the interconnected influences that shaped their behaviours.

2. *To take a whole-systems approach to the challenge.* Multiple actions would be needed to tackle this problem, re-enforcing one another to reshape children's experience of nutrition and movement. The work on the profiles of a child's day identified the following environments which impact on their health: home, civic spaces (such as parks and leisure facilities), nursery and school, the streets they live and travel through, the media they

engage with, the retail spaces they walk by and use. These physical (and in the case of media often virtual) locations offered insights into the multitude of factors that create an 'obesogenic' system – one which makes it easier rather than harder to gain excess weight. At each of these locations we explored what the barriers for children being more physically active, eating healthily and drinking water were. Reasons included exposure to advertising on the streets, easy availability of fast food, high price of bottled water and lack of drinking fountains. The factors were also compounded by the reality of the everyday lives of their parents and caregivers, who due to housing, poverty and working pressures are less able to make decisions which help their child to be healthy.

3. *To be bigger and bolder in amplifying positive initiatives already happening.* I find this entrepreneurial approach of learning by doing, adapting and iterating, partnering and collaborating to be liberating. We knew we could link some, scale some and recommend minimum standards for others to build capacity across the city and be brave enough to trial and implement new actions – that might need to create their own evidence to measure impact and effectiveness.

As a result of this approach, we came up with an action plan to transform 10 aspects of the daily lives of children and parents in London. Each ambition had two calls to action which all together were split into three distinct impact areas:

- Providing skills and financial resources to families to give them the capacity to live better lives.

- Changing the environment in which children live their daily lives so they can eat healthily, drink more water and take plenty of physical exercise.

- Offering care and emotional support for children and their families so when they are struggling, they can easily find help that fits into their lives.

The interconnectedness of our calls to action was vital for success. It would be absolutely no good picking one or two and believing the job would be done. Every action we proposed had a knock-on effect to every other action. It was also no coincidence that our first actions were focused on eliminating child poverty in London (by a call to give the mayor the power to raise London's minimum wage to a living wage).

THE CHALLENGE OF AN IDEAS INFORMED AND INSPIRED SOCIETY

The journey charted in this chapter has been based on my belief that our VUCA world demands new ideas to enable a society to thrive, and that thriving societies are a consequence of thriving childhoods; and that big simple ideas often can be blind to unintended consequences and that most issues are connected to root causes. Building on this outlook I pursued the ideals of an ideas-informed society in the realm of children's health through my leading London's Child Obesity Taskforce. Through this whole experience I hold to two lessons.

- Firstly, that those who are for ideas which seek to intervene positively and successfully in the lives of our citizens, must take a holistic approach taking into consideration and attempting to influence the wider habitat that they are enacted. Everything is connected.

- Secondly and just as importantly, that those who are directly impacted by those ideas are central to the design and implementation of them. The most valuable experience is lived experience.

At the beginning of this chapter, I described the world we inhabit as characterised by a VUCA ecosystem – where toxic stress means that being 'ideas-informed' is challenging. Perhaps, through reflecting on the narrative and argument I have developed here, we need to reclaim the term VUCA from its negative connotations and shift it to one where uncertainty and complexity can bring ideas, opportunities and possibilities previously unimagined. Perhaps even, I could end the chapter by condensing its advice in creating an ideas-inspired society into four simple, three-word realities:

1. Be bravely curious.

2. Everything is connected.

3. Value lived experience.

4. Ask 'why not?'.

NOTES

1. Barber, H.F. (1992). Developing strategic leadership: The US Army War College experience. *Journal of Management Development*; 11(6):4–12. https://doi.org/10.1108/02621719 210018208

2. Dorling, D. (2021). *Slowdown*. New Haven: Yale University Press.

3. The Center on the Developing Child at Harvard University. (n.d.). Toxic stress. [online] Available at: https://developingchild.harvard.edu/science/key-concepts/toxic-stress/ [Accessed 26 April 2022].

4. Middlemiss, W., Brownstein, N.C., Leddy, M., Nelson, S., Manchiraju, S. & Grzywacz, J.G. (2019). Baby box distributions: public health benefit or concern? *Public Health Reports*. 2019 Jul/Aug; 134(4):328–331. https://doi.org/10.1177/0033354919847731

5. Watson, D., Ball, H.L., Reid, J. & Blair, P. (2020). Baby box: child welfare experts say use of sleep boxes could potentially put infants' lives at risk. The Conversation. [online] Available at: https://theconversation.com/baby-box-child-welfare-exp erts-say-use-of-sleep-boxes-could-potentially-put-infants-lives-at-risk-125512 [Accessed 31 January 2023].

6. Fletcher-Wood, H. (2018). Education in Singapore: which policies can England borrow? [Blog] Available at: https://improvingteaching.co.uk/2018/02/12/education-in-singapore-

8-which-policies-can-england-borrow/ [Accessed 31 January 2023].

7. Kennedy, R.F. (1968). Remarks at the University of Kansas, March 18, 1968. [Transcript] Available at: https://www.jfklibrary.org/learn/about-jfk/the-kennedy-family/robert-f-kennedy/robert-f-kennedy-speeches/remarks-at-the-university-of-kansas-march-18-1968 [Accessed 31 January 2023].

8. NHS Digital. (2021). National Child Measurement Programme, England 2020/21 School Year. [online] Available at: https://digital.nhs.uk/data-and-information/publications/statistical/national-child-measurement-programme/2020-21-school-year [Accessed 31 January 2023].

9. Public Health England. (2013). Obesity more likely in children from deprived areas. [online] Available at: https://www.gov.uk/government/news/obesity-more-likely-in-children-from-deprived-areas [Accessed 31 January 2023].

10. Biro, F. & Wien, M. (2010). Childhood obesity and adult morbidities. *The American Journal of Clinical Nutrition*; 91(5):1499S–1505S.

11. Public Health England. (2020). The relationship between dental caries and body mass index: child level analysis. [online] Available at: https://assets.publishing.service.gov.uk/government/uploads/system/uploads/attachment_data/file/844121/BMI_dental_caries.pdf [Accessed 31 January 2023].

12. The London Child Obesity Taskforce. (2018). Unhealthy weight in London's children. What we know. [online] Available at: https://www.london.gov.uk/sites/default/files/unhealthy_weight_in_londons_children.pdf [Accessed 31 January 2023].

13. Reilly, J. & Kelly, J. (2011). Long-term impact of overweight and obesity in childhood and adolescence on morbidity and premature mortality in adulthood: systematic review. *International Journal of Obesity*; 35:891–898.

14. Public Health England. (2017). Health matters: obesity and the food environment.

15. The London Child Obesity Taskforce. (2018). [online] Available at: https://www.london.gov.uk/programmes-strategies/health-and-wellbeing/londons-child-obesity-taskforce [Accessed 31 January 2023].

16. Hawkes, C. (2019). Getting kids to a healthy weight: is a child-centred approach right? City Hall Blog. [online] Available at: https://www.london.gov.uk/city-hall-blog/getting-kids-healthy-weight-child-centred-approach-right [Accessed 31 January 2023].

17. The London Child Obesity Taskforce. (2019). [online] Available at: https://www.london.gov.uk/sites/default/files/what_makes_it_harder_for_londons_children_be_healthier.pdf [Accessed 31 January 2023].

12

EDUCATION FOR DEMOCRACY: SCHOOLS AS COMMUNITIES OF INQUIRY

Vivienne Baumfield

> To *educate is to relocate ideas ... in a network of
> inferential relations, which will assist ... in developing
> new meaning (Derry)*[1]

What does an 'Ideas-Informed Society' need? The capacity of
social media to provide instant access to an ever growing volume of
information, opinions and observations presents both opportunities
and challenges. One of these challenges is the tension between a
concept of freedom as the exercising of individual agency without
any interference and an alternative view of freedom as the capacity
to participate in collective decision-making. For this alternative
view of freedom to be possible, an 'Ideas-Informed Society' needs
people with the willingness and confidence to engage in public
debate. If this participation is to be sustained, people need to
reconcile individual choices with the forging of common goals and
values by exercising the capacity to deliberate. John Dewey, the
twentieth century philosopher of education, identified the necessity
in a democracy for education to improve the methods and conditions of debate, discussion and persuasion. According to Dewey,
schools can support public deliberation by embracing learners'
cultural and personal differences and concentrating on building a

diverse community of inquiry rather than on creating standardised, routine training.[2]

In this chapter, I consider the potential of schools today to play a crucial role in promoting an 'Ideas-Informed Society' in an age of mass communication. Attention is given to the demands made on teachers' professional learning if they are to be active in co-creating knowledge for the public good with their students and the local community. Previous attempts to promote schools as communities of inquiry and the need for constructive alignment of curriculum, pedagogy and assessment, the three message systems of education,[3] are also considered to identify lessons for the future.

DEWEY, DEMOCRACY AND EDUCATION

Dewey is one of the most frequently cited authors in the field of democratic education[4] and the centenary of the publication of 'Democracy and Education'[5] stimulated reassessment of his contribution to current debate on the purpose of education.[6] In 1916, during the First World War, the pressing social issue was the question of American nationalism leading Dewey to emphasise education as the means of promoting a gradual, natural, progress towards a sense of mutual belonging and identity. For Dewey, there is an integral relationship between democracy and education; the degree to which society is democratic is indicated by the extent the specific and variable qualities of individuals in a community form part of social organisation. The state, therefore, has the responsibility for creating schools as communities for the effective realisation of the potentialities of every individual. The idea that it is within schools that children can become habituated and disposed towards democratic feeling and action runs throughout Dewey's work.[7] The means for achieving this aim are articulated in 'The School and Society' written in 1900[8] and two years later in 'The Child and the Curriculum'.[9] 'The School and Society' focuses on the importance of ensuring that the organisation of the school is congruent with changes in the social situation. By this, Dewey means that the relationship between school and society is dynamic and can be mutually beneficial provided that attention is paid to

ensuring that what is learnt is not dictated by the past or in antic-
ipation of what might be useful in the future but that the educational experiences have meaning for students in the present:

> *When the school introduces and trains each child in*
> *society into membership within such a little community*
> *... we shall have the deepest and best guarantee of a*
> *larger society which is worthy, lovely, and*
> *harmonious.*[10]

In 'The Child and the Curriculum', Dewey explores educational
formation as a process of gaining understanding by thinking
through the oppositions arising from the conflicting elements of
genuine problems. Learning is an active process requiring respon-
siveness to the claims made by other people in a shared social
context formed from the experience of different cultures and traditions. However, rather than making the effort this requires, for
most people it is easier to see the conditions in their separateness
and maintain one position at the expense of the other.[11]

By the 1920s, concerns were coalescing around the impact of
mass communication on the formation of popular opinion, the lack
of public interest in participating in democratic processes and their
ability to make the complex decisions required to govern in a
modern society. The publication of 'Public Opinion' by the influential political journalist Walter Lippmann[12] proposing that
decision-making was best left to those with the expertise and
interest in governing drew a response from Dewey in 1927 in 'The
Public and its Problems.'[13] Whilst Dewey acknowledged that it was
increasingly difficult to engage the public in matters of government,
he disagreed that the problem was simply one of lack of interest and
challenged the deficit view of the ability of people to make informed
decisions. In Dewey's analysis, democracy is based on participation
in the activities of popular government being educative, not on all
of the participants being 'experts'. Education is vital to releasing
personal potentialities and the ability to judge the bearing of the
knowledge supplied by others upon common concerns. The 'public'
forms around problems in which science and the results of experts
are put at the service of the people rather than being the preserve of
an elite group in society, however well-intentioned they may be.

What is needed is an experimental approach in which ideas are tools of inquiry, forming working hypotheses on what is to be done, not preconceptions based on dogmatic preconceptions. Promoting social inquiry through 'full and moving communication'[14] can become a transformative process creating the 'great community' that democracy requires by retaining the potency of local connectedness that had been displaced by rapid industrialisation whilst not becoming insular. The essential need is the recognition of embodied, social intelligence and improvement of the methods and conditions of debate, discussion and persuasion, 'That is the problem of the public'.[15]

Dewey said relatively little about teachers in his major educational writings, consequently the crucial role they play in his advocacy of the formation of a democratic society is not always fully recognised.[16] One exception is an address he gave to elementary school teachers during the time his 'laboratory school' at the University of Chicago was attracting attention.[17] In this address, Dewey emphasises the dependence of any school system on the quality and character of the teaching profession. He speaks out against the close supervision of teachers as this restricts the intellectual initiative, discussion and decision-making the work demands and concludes that the biggest obstacle to effecting any lasting change is their lack of freedom to exercise democracy in education.

TEACHERS AS PUBLIC INTELLECTUALS

The teaching profession has an important role to play in the realisation of the opportunities and the mitigation of the challenges of an 'Ideas Informed Society'. However, if the expertise of teachers is to perform a democratic function, they need sufficient autonomy to be insulated from the restrictions of external control but not so much that they risk becoming elitist, as has been the case in professions such as medicine and the law. In order to participate in the deliberations necessary for the formation of common goals and complete rather than compete with democracy,[18] teachers need to avoid the 'ossification of office' without acquiring the 'insolence of office'.[19]

In the 1960s, there was an expansion in the number of occupations seeking recognition as a profession leading people to question whether what we were experiencing was the 'professionalization of everyone'.[20] It was predicted that the development of knowledge societies would lead to even greater demand for professionals whilst at the same time creating barriers to the achievement of professional autonomy. The promotion of evidence-informed practice has been identified as the route to the professionalisation of an occupation through a blending of scientific with intuitive, experiential knowledge to develop an epistemology of practice.[21] The potential of a move to establish teaching as a profession through evidence-informed practice has been constrained by interpretations of what constitutes evidence, often construed as performance data, and a reluctance to engage in debate as to the purpose of education.[22] Consequently, recognition of the capacity of teachers to exercise judgement and participate in the co-creation of knowledge for the public good is restricted. We have seen that in the case of teachers, professionalisation can be contradictory and controversial in a situation in which, 'we do not really know how to make sense of professional control in anti-professional knowledge societies with changing public sectors'.[23]

Nevertheless, positioned at the intersection of research, policy and practice, professionals are mediators between experts and the public. Operating within multiple tensions, between theory and practice, between elitism and mass appeal and between academic specialisation and generalist inclusiveness, professionals can be 'public intellectuals' equipped to advocate for democracy in their service to the community.[24] Reductive views of teaching need to be challenged and the importance of provision for teachers' initial and continuing professional learning championed.[25] As Freire affirms, teaching is above all a professional task, the accomplishment of which requires

> ...*constant intellectual rigour and the stimulation of epistemological curiosity, the capacity to love, of*

creativity, of scientific competence and the rejection of scientific reductionism. The teaching task also requires the capacity to fight for freedom, without which the teaching task becomes meaningless.[26]

SCHOOLS AS COMMUNITIES OF INQUIRY

We can draw upon examples of successful approaches to promoting schools as communities of inquiry in which the interests of the individual and society can be integrated in the interests of democracy. At the classroom level, the work of Matthew Lipman, the developer of the Philosophy for Children (P4C) programme based on the work of Dewey and Vygotsky,[27] has had a positive impact in schools. Systematic reviews of published research[28] and evaluations in primary school[29] and secondary school[30] settings have demonstrated the benefits for students and their teachers. More recently, a Randomised Control Trial (RCT), considered by many to be the 'gold-standard' for empirical research, highlighted the capacity of classrooms constituted as communities of inquiry to integrate students of all abilities in learning together. Although the impact on improving attainment overall was modest, the researchers conclude:

However, for those who value reasoning for its own sake, this evaluation demonstrates that using curriculum time in this way does not damage attainment (and may well enhance it and reduce the poverty gradient in attainment) and so suggests that something like P4C is an appropriate educational approach.[31]

At the level of the whole school, researchers have shown taking an inquiry stance in approaches to teachers' professional learning through the development of school-university research partnerships to be beneficial.[32] Inquiry is the trigger and the leveller of any hierarchy of expertise as the mutual desire to find solutions promotes authentic collaborative effort. Focusing on creating conditions for conversations between teachers and researchers about how evidence from experience *and* from research supports the exercise of professional judgement can align what have been characterised as horizontal and vertical discourses[33] in a shared enterprise. The fundamental principle being for teachers and academics to find a shared interest in understanding a problematic situation and to study the enactment of potential solutions. As the external evaluation of a government sponsored initiative in England concluded:

> *It amounts to nothing short of the re-professionalisation of teaching as evidence informed. Based on this alone there would appear to be promise in the sponsorship of teacher/university networks.*[34]

Despite such promising, and recurring, indications of the feasibility of realising Dewey's vision for education in and for democracy, the failure to secure lasting change must be acknowledged. Underlying the intractability of making what many agree is a good idea in principle, a reality, is the problem of scale. How can the benefits accrued by initiatives at a local level be achieved across the education system? Unfortunately, rather than create conditions conducive to the proliferation of local initiatives, the tendency as societies modernise is to opt for 'massification' thus removing the very differences that are the impetus for creativity vital to a democratic society. Of course, a more localised, devolved educational system will require trust to be placed in the professionalism of teachers rather than in standardised measures of performance. It will also require approaches to the use of digital technology and social media that support communication not the formation of enclosed 'epistemic bunkers' by filtering information to echo what people already think.[35] The resolution to the most pressing public problems for Dewey then, and for us now, remains resolving the relation of the individual to the social if we are to realise the aims of an 'Ideas Informed Society'. As Freire reminds us, no one said it would be easy but failure to enable schools to be communities of inquiry in which the 'deliberative virtues'[36] contemporary society demands can be fostered is a price too high to pay.

REFERENCES

1. Derry, J. 'Dewey's Philosophy of Education:Representing and Intervening.' Chap. 8 In *John Dewey's Democracy and*

Education: A British Tribute, edited by S. Higgins and F. Coffield, 131–48. London: UCL IoE Press, 2016.

2. Levin, R. A. (1991). The Debate Over Schooling: Influences of Dewey and Thorndike. *Childhood Education*, 71–75.

3. Bernstein, B. (1999). Vertical and Horizontal Discourse: An Essay. *British Journal of Sociology of Education*, 20(2), 157–173.

4. Gutmann, A. (1999). *Democratic Education* (2nd ed.). Princeton University Press.

5. Dewey, J. (1916). *Democracy and Education: An Introduction to the Philosophy of Education*. Macmillan.

6. Higgins, S., & Coffield, F. (2016). *John Dewey's Democracy and Education: A British Tribute*. Trentham.

7. Cowan, S., & McCulloch, G. (2016). The Reception and Impact of Democracy and Education. In S. Higgins & F. Coffield (Eds.), *John Dewey's Democracy and Education: A British Tribute* (pp. 7–29). UCL IoE Press.

8. Dewey, J. (1907). *The School and Society. Being Three Lectures by John Dewey*. University of Chicago Press. (1900).

9. Dewey, J. (1902). *The Child and the Curriculum*. University of Chicago Press.

10. Dewey, J. (1907). *The School and Society. Being Three Lectures by John Dewey*. University of Chicago Press. (1900).

11. Dewey, J. (1902). *The Child and the Curriculum*. University of Chicago Press.

12. Lipman, M. (2017). The Institute for the Advancement of Philosophy for Children (IAPC). In S. Naji & R. Hashim (Eds.), *History, Theory and Practice of Philosophy for Children: International Perspectives* (pp. 1–9). Routledge.

13. Dewey, J. (2012). *The Public and Its Problems: An essay in Political Inquiry* (M. L. Rogers, Ed.). Pennsylvania State University Press. (1927).

14. Rakow, L. F. (2018). Family Feud: Who's Still Fighting about Dewey and Lippmann? *Javnost - The Public*, 25(1–2), 75–82.

15. Dewey, J. (2012). *The Public and Its Problems: An essay in Political Inquiry* (M. L. Rogers, Ed.). Pennsylvania State University Press. (1927).

16. Condliffe Lagerman, E. (1996). Experimenting with Education: John Dewey and Ella Flagg Young at the University of Chicago. *American Journal of Education, 104,* 171–185.

17. Dewey, J. (1903). Democracy in Education. *The Elementary School Teacher,* 4(4), 193–204.

18. Gutmann, A. (1999). *Democratic Education* (2nd ed.). Princeton University Press.

19. Walzer, M. (1983). *Spheres of Justice.* Basic Books.

20. Wilensky, H. L. (1964). The Professionalization of Everyone? *American Journal of Sociology,* 70(2), 137–158.

21. Noordegraaf, M. (2007). From 'Pure' to 'Hybrid' Professionalism: Present-day Professionalism in Ambiguous Public Domains. *Administration and society,* 39(6), 761–785.

22. Biesta, G. (2009). Good Education in an Age of Measurement: On the Need to Reconnect with the Question of Purpose in Education. *Educational Assessment, Evaluation and Accountability (formerly: Journal of Personnel Evaluation in Education), 21,* 33–46.

23. Noordegraaf, M. (2007). From 'Pure' to 'Hybrid' Professionalism: Present-day Professionalism in Ambiguous Public Domains. *Administration and society,* 39(6), 761–785.

24. Giroux, H. A. (2010). Bare Pedagogy and the Scourge of Neoliberalism: Rethinking Higher Education as a Democratic Public Sphere. *The Educational Forum.* https://doi.org/10.1080/00131725.2010.483897
    Schweizer, B. (2008). Introduction: Twentieth-Century Writers as Public Intellectuals. *Studies in the Humanities,* 35(2), 121–137.

25. Dickson, B. (2015). Scotland: Radical Alternatives in Teacher Education. In C. Brock (Ed.), *Education in the United Kingdom.* Bloomsbury.
    Dickson, B. (2020). ITE Reform at the University of Glasgow: Principles, Research-basis and Implications. *Wales Journal of Education,* 22(1), 257–280.

26. Freire, P. (2005). *Teachers as Cultural Workers.* Taylor and Francis.

27. Lipman, M. (2017). The Institute for the Advancement of Philosophy for Children (IAPC). In S. Naji & R. Hashim

(Eds.), *History, Theory and Practice of Philosophy for Children: International Perspectives* (pp. 1–9). Routledge.

28. Trickey, S., & Topping, K. (2004). Philosophy for Children a Systematic Review. *Research Papers in Education, 19*(3), 365–380.

29. Topping, K., & Trickey, S. (2007). Collaborative Philosophical Inquiry for Schoolchildren: Cognitive Gains at Two-year Follow-up. *British Journal of Educational Psychology, 77*(4), 787–796.

30. Williams, S. (1993). *Evaluating the Effects of Philosophical Enquiry in a Secondary School.* T. V. C. S. Project.

31. Gorard, S., Siddiqui, N., & See, B. H. (2017). Can Philosophy for Children Improve Primary School Attainment? *Journal of Philoosphy of Education, 5*(1), 5–22.

32. Cochran-Smith, M., & Lytle, S. L. (1993). *Inside/Outside: Teacher Research and Knowledge.* Teachers College Press. McLaughlin, C., Cordingley, P., McLellan, R., & Baumfield, V. (2015). *Making a Difference.* Cambridge University Press.

33. Bernstein, B. (1999). Vertical and Horizontal Discourse: An Essay. *British Journal of Sociology of Education, 20*(2), 157–173.

34. Kushner, S., Simons, H., James, D., Jones, K., & Yee, W. C. (2001). TTA School-based Research Consortium Initiative, the Evaluation, Final Report.

35. Furman, K. (2022). Epistemic Bunkers. *Social Epistemology,* 1–11. https://doi.org/10.1080/02691728.2022.2122756

36. Talisse, R. (2005). *Democracy After Liberalism: Pragmatism and Deliberative Politics.* Routledge.

PART 3

CREATIVITY, ARTS AND THE ENVIRONMENT

13

IN PRAISE OF INUTILITY: LEARNING FROM DICKENS

Judith Mossman

A persistent strand in public debate centres on what is useful and what is useless, and by extension, what should be paid for by the state and what should not. How can we assess the utility or inutility of ideas? What constitutes genuine utility? The problem for the ideas-driven society is that it is not always easy to tell what will, in the medium to long-term, be useful and what will not. Jeremy Bentham's famous definition of utility is distinctly capacious: 'that property in any object whereby it tends to produce pleasure, good or happiness, or to prevent the happening of mischief, pain, evil or unhappiness to the party whose interest is considered'.[1] That definition sounds very sympathetic to the idea that the category of usefulness might include the creative arts, yet the argument is frequently canvassed that spending on the arts is less important and more frivolous than spending on other areas of government. In some circumstances this is indeed a hard argument to combat; but it is important to bear in mind that what is useful does not invariably show itself to be so immediately. Nor does only one kind of utility exist. We might here remember the Chinese proverb: If you have two loaves of bread, sell one, and buy a lily. The bread is food for the body, the lily food for the soul. One enormous benefit of a society based on the best ideas (as one of the other essays in this volume argues, not all ideas are good ones) is that it is likely to keep an open mind about what constitutes genuine utility. Because if we make a mistake about what is useful, we can be lost. I move now to discuss an example of the effects of mistaken and true beliefs about usefulness: *Hard Times*.

THE *HARD TIMES* CAUTIONARY TALE

Hard Times (1854) rarely features on readers' lists of favourite novels, even among fans of Dickens. It is unremittingly grim, and the picaresque pleasures of *David Copperfield* and *Nicholas Nickleby* are muted. An array of largely unsympathetic characters suffers against the backdrop of Coketown, an industrial hell on earth. Yet its central themes nonetheless, I would argue, have value. It has a three-part structure, the parts named Sowing – Reaping – Garnering. It is tempting to read the novel as a tragedy with affinities with Sophocles' *Antigone*, though Dickens is light, generally, on classical references. Still, the novel's central figures, Thomas Gradgrind and his daughter Louisa, have something in common with Sophocles' Creon, brought low through the destruction of his family by his own inflexible ideology, and his niece Antigone, determined to bury her brother at all costs, despite his treachery to his city and family. Louisa's brother is still alive, and remains so; but she sacrifices herself in a marriage with an old and repulsive man to secure his advancement, and he remains her greatest emotional weakness.

Gradgrind's ideology is the worship of a narrowly defined reason enshrined in facts and his determination to reform education in his home town to eliminate fanciful elements and rely on the invincible purity and certainty of statistics, arithmetic and figures. This characterisation is of course spectacularly unfair to real scientists and mathematicians (and indeed to Jeremy Bentham, at the more pedantic parts of whose utilitarianism Dickens is certainly tilting), but Dickens does succeed in skewering Gradgrind's laserlike focus on education as a means to an end: 'Facts alone are wanted in life. Plant nothing else, and root out everything else. You can only form the minds of reasoning animals upon Facts: nothing else will ever be of any service to them'.[2] As the novel unwinds, Gradgrind, who is not a bad man, discovers to his own great cost that education needs to comprise more than facts, and aim at more than utility. Both his older children are destroyed by the lack of moral compass provided by their home life and their education. The qualities missing from Gradgrind's curriculum are embodied in Sissy Jupe, the daughter of an itinerant circus clown, whom Gradgrind takes in when her father deserts her. Although his motivation is to try whether the virtues of his system can rescue even so unpromising a specimen as Sissy (who struggles with arithmetic, cannot define a horse, and likes carpets with flowers on them – Gradgrindians are positively Platonic in their dislike of representational art), he is kind to her, and she repays him by saving the day. Her gratitude, and the importance she assumes in his family, is in stark contrast to the attitude of the unpleasant Bitzer, her fellow pupil in Gradgrind's school, who is thought very promising, but displays a solipsism so great that he consigns his own mother to the workhouse even though he is earning a wage. In a final confrontation, he threatens to deliver young Tom Gradgrind, who has embezzled money from his brother-in-law's bank, to the police. Emotional appeals and bribery both fail to influence him: Gradgrind tries one last argument:

> *Bitzer, I have but one chance left to soften you. You were many years at my school. If, in remembrance of the pains bestowed on you there, you can persuade yourself in any degree to disregard your present interest and release my son, I entreat and pray you to give him the benefit of that remembrance.*

> *'I really wonder, sir', rejoined the old pupil in an argumentative manner, 'to find you taking a position so untenable. My schooling was paid for; it was a bargain; and when I came away, the bargain ended'. It was a fundamental principle of the Gradgrind philosophy that everything was to be paid for. Nobody was ever on any account to give anybody anything, or render anybody help without purchase. Gratitude was to be abolished, and the virtues springing from it were not to be. Every inch of the existence of mankind, from birth to death, was to be a bargain across a counter. And if we didn't get to Heaven that way, it was not a politico-economical place, and we had no business there.*

So it is very specifically Gradgrind's educational philosophy, which privileges the transactional over the emotional and the imaginative, which lets him down at the end. Tom's ultimate saviour is the circus owner Mr Sleary, who is moved by Gradgrind's kindness to Sissy and uses his trained animals to distract Bitzer and get the wholly undeserving Tom away to the coast.

Critics might quite reasonably say that this plotting is almost pedantic in its symmetry, and that Dickens in his turn is being reductive. That point could fairly be argued; but nonetheless, there are echoes of the Gradgrind philosophy in UK education policy today, and it is not unreasonable, I think, to point them out. Successive UK education Secretaries of State have made almost annual pledges to crack down on so-called 'Mickey Mouse' courses. The definition of such a course is dictated, when one digs beneath the tabloid rhetoric, by the average graduate salary at six months and three-and-a-half years after graduation. The six-month survey was undertaken at population level, the follow up was a sample survey. Those courses which do not produce an average salary high enough to allow repayment of the loan taken to pay for the degree are, not unnaturally, a concern for those responsible for operating the scheme. And yet such an analysis clearly misses something. This is not the fault of the statisticians: HESA (Higher Education Statistics Agency), who compiles the surveys, took a great deal of trouble to evolve a methodology for measuring the contribution of all degrees to satisfaction in work later in life.[3] But the unsubtle version which one encounters in the press has had regrettable repercussions.

THE ARTS AND HUMANITIES IN PERIL

During 2022, a number of post-1992 universities, whose undergraduate bodies are mostly state-educated rather than from private schools, have closed or paused a range of Arts and Humanities degrees. James Graham OBE, a successful playwright who studied drama at the University of Hull, responded to the closures in a thought-provoking essay for the *New Statesman*.[4] He attributed them in large part (and I agree) to the falling off of student numbers caused directly by the reduction of arts subjects in schools and the strong steer away from creative subjects towards the 'facilitating subjects'. If people are not studying the creative arts at school, it would be surprising if they turned to them at university, especially when the tabloid version of the 'Mickey Mouse degree' narrative suggests that such degrees are not worth the considerable expense incurred. He also pointed to the issue that the HESA snapshot creates. In creative subjects, it often takes a while to become established as a professional:

> *Given the huge debt that students must rack up now to attend university, it's not unreasonable that the government is placing focus on quality and 'outcomes'. But its new metric – that graduates must find themselves in highly skilled employment a year after completing a course – is too narrow for artistic subjects. It took me years to sustain myself as a writer – so under the new measurements, my drama degree would have been deemed to have failed me.*

> *And yet, it didn't. Not every artist needs to go to university to become one, but I needed to. At a time when educational value wasn't solely measured on the speed it can deliver you into the workforce, my degree opened my eyes to a world far beyond what I had seen.*

THE POWER OF THE CREATIVE INDUSTRIES

Graham's points are well made – and he also hints at what may be lost when he points out that using 'Mickey Mouse' as a derogatory term is peculiar given the vast commercial success of that particular rodent. Graduate salaries in the creative industries are indeed not lavish; but the creative industries contribute enormously to the UK's economy and to its soft power. In 2019 the CBI recognised this in its report *Centre stage: Keeping the UK's creative industries in the spotlight*.[5] In 2017, the report noted, the creative industries were contributing £101.5 billion to the economy. The CBI's top recommendation was: 'The government should harness the valuable economic contribution of the creative industries by ensuring national policies are built with the sector in mind'. The report's authors noted the decline of arts subjects in schools and recommended that a creative subject be included alongside more academic ones in the 'EBacc'. They also recommended a revamp (yet to appear) of the terms of the apprenticeship levy to make it more fit for purpose for creative industries, with their smaller businesses and heavy emphasis on freelance work. At the time of writing these recommendations have yet to be adopted. An irony is emerging as a result of the withering of creative subjects in schools: for centuries, excellence in the arts provided a route out of poverty (I think of Haydn in the eighteenth century, Dickens in the nineteenth, and the actor Claude Rains in the twentieth). But in the twenty-first century, the reverse is becoming true – it is far easier to enjoy a stellar career in the arts if you are already comfortably off.

Of course, the creative industries, especially but not only the performing arts, suffered badly during the pandemic of 2020–2021 (though a few, such as computer gaming, actually grew during lockdown!). The UK government's cultural recovery fund made a real difference to many organisations, however, and in May 2022 the DCMS published figures which suggested that the sector was outperforming the economy as a whole in terms of Gross Value Added once more (though it was not quite back up to pre-pandemic levels).[6] In the light of the economic benefits the creative industries bestow, perhaps it is appropriate to consider whether they may in fact, despite appearances, be useful. In Dickens, this usefulness manifests itself both on the spiritual plane, and in practical terms when Mr Sleary uses his circus skills and personnel to rescue young Tom. Mr Sleary also defends his profession as fulfilling a basic human need (Dickens gives him a heavy lisp, which I have removed for ease of reading):

> *Don't be cross with us poor vagabonds. People must be amused. They can't be always a-learning, nor yet they can't be always a-working, they an't made for it. You must have us, Squire. Do the wise thing and the kind thing too, and make the best of us: not the worst!*

ONCE LOST, DIFFICULT TO RESTORE

Some policymakers in the UK are showing signs of following Mr Sleary's advice. Despite the pandemic, at the time of writing, the UK government in the form of the Department of Culture, Media and Sport, was still perceiving the creative industries as a potential tool for 'levelling up' the UK's economic inequalities.[7] Whether their supportive recommendations will convince the larger and more powerful Department of Education of the value of creative subjects in schools is another question. In January 2023, The House of Lords published a report entitled *At risk: our creative future*, which strongly suggested that not enough was being done to help the sector on several fronts.[8] Tellingly, one of the report's summary recommendations urged addressing blind spots in education and added: 'Lazy rhetoric about 'low value' arts courses risks deterring much needed talent from pursuing education and careers in the sector'. Quite. It was good to read later in the report: 'The Department for Education's sweeping rhetoric about "low value courses" is unhelpful. We agree that universities should provide good value for money. But the Department must also acknowledge that many of those going into the creative industries will work flexibly, in freelance roles, and take time to generate higher salaries. That does not mean their studies and subsequent jobs are less worthwhile'. It would be even better if one could be sure someone senior in the Department of Education would read it, and act upon it. There is no intention, apparently, to broaden the EBacc.

A further question concerns the humanities. The humanities are less 'amusing' in Sleary's terms, and therefore harder to monetise than the creative subjects, even though they are more favoured in the state secondary sector – at least for the time being. But English literature and history degrees have still come under the axe in the post-1992 sector almost to the same extent as the creative arts. At a time when a clear majority of the cabinet holds some kind of humanities degree, some reflection from these post-holders on the usefulness, both spiritual and practical, of their degrees would be welcome. Rehearsing here once again the many respects in which Humanities degrees provide valuable transferable skills would be unnecessary.[9] However, to give just one example, I am reminded of a famous quotation from a philosophy lecture by Professor J. A. Smith, as reported by Harold Macmillan (who read Classics) to Isaiah Berlin (who also read Classics before becoming a great academic philosopher), and recorded by the latter: 'All of you, gentlemen, will have different careers – some of you will be lawyers, some of you will be soldiers, some will be doctors or engineers, some will be government servants, some will be landowners or politicians. Let me tell you at once that nothing I say during these lectures will be of the slightest use to you in any of the fields in which you will attempt to exercise your skills. But one thing I can promise you: if you continue with this course of lectures to the end, you will always be able to know when men are talking rot'. While it is given to some to detect this without attending lectures, it is undoubtedly a very useful skill to be able to teach, and one highly important for success in every walk of life. Philosophy, and, even more so, Classics, are minority subjects now, and therefore vulnerable in the present climate, and while heroic efforts have just about kept Classics alive in state schools, and in parts of the post-1992 sector, no one knows how long that will last.

What is clear is that once subjects have disappeared from either secondary or tertiary educational establishments, it is extremely difficult to restore them. In restricting funding for the creative arts and the humanities, and deterring potential students, the state seems to be expressing a reluctance to pay for what is not deemed to be useful, in the face of clear evidence that it actually has been, is and will be. I fear, therefore, that if the Gradgrinds succeed this time in marginalising the Arts and Humanities for the vast majority of the population, there will be no Mr Sleary to come to the rescue. And we shall all be the poorer, literally as well as intellectually.

REFERENCES

1. Jeremy Bentham, *An Introduction to the Principles of Morals and Legislation* (1789).
2. *Hard Times* (1854), chapter 1.
3. This impressive piece of work, involving the work of a number of highly regarded philosophers, is available at

https://www.hesa.ac.uk/files/Graduate_Outcomes_History-y_and_Background_20200330.pdf. See esp. p. 9 on subjectivity. The survey was a big improvement on its predecessor, the DHLE. Accessed 21 December 2022.

4. 'In defence of Mickey Mouse degrees', *New Statesman*, 30 June 2022, https://www.newstatesman.com/quickfire/2022/06/defence-mickey-mouse-degrees-language-universities (accessed 28 November 2022).

5. The full report can be found at https://www.cbi.org.uk/media/3857/12527_creative-industries_hyperlinks.pdf (accessed 20 December 2022).

6. See https://www.thecreativeindustries.co.uk/facts-figures/positive-trend-in-gva-of-uk-creative-industries-from-pandemic (accessed 20 December 2022).

7. See the report published on 9 November 2022, 'Reimagining where we live: cultural placemaking and the levelling up agenda' at https://committees.parliament.uk/publications/31429/documents/176244/default/ (accessed 20 December 2022). The report noted issues with skills shortages in the creative industries, and also their considerable value for the placemaking agenda on which levelling up depends.

8. https://committees.parliament.uk/publications/33536/documents/182541/default/

9. See for example P. Holm, A. Jarrick and D. Scott, *Humanities World Report 2015* (Palgrave Macmillan 2015), esp. ch. 2.

14

THE POWER OF VISUAL IDEAS – CREATING A SENSE OF PLACE THROUGH ART

Rafael Klein

Over the course of my life as an artist, it has become clear to me that art can make an essential contribution to the ideas-informed society. This is perhaps most evident in works created for the public realm, but is also a large part of the enrichment of society through people living with art.

Working in sculpture, painting and film, I explore the ways personal narratives shape the world we inhabit, creating our sense of place and belonging. This central concern has also led me to make artists' books, which can form a core from which other artwork emanates.

It has taken me a long time to understand why telling stories about the world we inhabit has been so important to me. The journey towards this understanding has been a summary of my life as an artist.

An Overview of Some of the Books I've Created.

A BOY FROM BROOKLYN

I was born in New York, growing up in Brooklyn. For me, and probably for most second-generation Jews, the sense of where we come from, where we *might* belong, is complex and important.

My Jewish grandfathers immigrated to New York to escape pogroms and oppression in Poland and Austria at the turn of the century. After settling in the Lower East Side of New York, they sent for their wives. I know this because it is one of the very few things my father could tell me about his family background. When I asked him about his family origins, he claimed to know very little. When I asked my surviving grandmother about the family members who hadn't left, she would just say she didn't know. Whether this was an honest lack of knowledge or a refusal to visit such dark times didn't matter. To me it just created a black hole and a rootlessness. I had no family ancestry further back than the migrant Jews who had made it to New York.

Jews Hiding – Illustration From A Wanderer, Artists' Book Exploring My Background.

Growing up in Brooklyn, my father was part of the vibrant life of the street market. At the age of 10, he sold pickles from a barrel. I asked him if he worked on Saturday when he had no school:

> *No, on Sunday of course. What do you think, are you crazy? Saturday was Shabbat. I sold them until there*

*were none left. After the pickles, I got the idea to buy
lollipops and sell them off a pushcart. I would buy them
by the box, and sell them four for a nickel. That was
cheap! I would rent a pushcart, and sell the lollipops.*

**Lower East Side Market – Illustration From A Wanderer, Artists' Book
Exploring My Background.**

As a boy, I did have a strong sense of where I belonged. Coney
Island and the beaches have a strong identity. In the Brooklyn
suburbs, I was in America – and Coney Island was the classic
American amusement park, with the iconic hot dogs and roller
coasters. And once a year, usually just before summer ended and
the school year began, my family would spend the day there.

One hot August day, I lost my parents. The magical world of this
seaside funfair was a frightening and disorienting place seen
through the eyes of a lost eight-year-old boy. What was this strange
place of frightening rides, haunted houses and freak shows? I felt
uprooted, with no sense of where I was. The combination of fantasy
and reality made me forget I was still in Brooklyn. It was my first
experience of not knowing where I was, where I belonged – a
seminal experience for me – a feeling that would echo throughout

my life. ..... and that, I would eventually realise, was connected to
my background as a child of immigrants.

Many years later, I would return to this little boy lost sensation,
and try to gain some perspective on it through art. I created an
artists' book called *Coney Island*, which explored not just my
sensation of being lost and not knowing where I was, but also
focussed on a crowded, surreal world of dangerous rides, bearded
ladies and fantasy. In addition to the book, I created a series of
sculptures of the most memorable things in this unreal world. And
this storytelling through art was therapeutic. It helped me share the
experience, but also gave me a sense of coming from a real, if
strange, place.

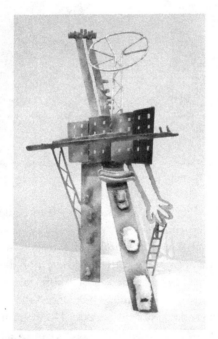

Hot Dog – Coney Island Sculpture.

MIGRATION

Brooklyn is no longer my family home. Americans migrate internally and my own family is no different. The distances are enormous; family separation and loss is a part of life. My parents and

my sister moved to Florida, and my brothers moved to California. Returning from the University of Chicago, I found myself back in New York City, beginning my career as an artist, but now with no family close by.

New York is a city of migrants, so I fit in well. I was now living in the East Village. Was I trying to return to the 'homeland' of my grandparents? Only a few blocks away stood the apartment of my grandmother – 194 Avenue C. But the Lower East Side was no longer the recreation of shtetl life of Eastern Europe. It was now a vibrant alternative cultural centre of small galleries, restaurants and rock venues. Without family or ancestry left in my home town, I used art to create a sense of place. I painted the street life, the buildings, the faces on the subway. I was defining my sense of place through paintings and sketches. However, I had lost my roots. I no longer felt that I belonged.

Subway – Observational Drawing While Riding the NY Subway.

When I visited my parents in their new home down in Florida, it felt like visiting an alien planet. Although it was largely populated by New York Jews, the towns and landscape were unrecognisable, crawling with swamps and alligators. Ordinary streets were indistinguishable from highways. From a compressed world in the inner city, this endless sprawl made little sense to me as a 'real' place.

On my return I unpacked the experience, trying to make sense of the place my family now lived through new artworks. My first large exhibition was at 112 Greene Street in Soho. I brought together a series of large relief sculptures about the false mythologies of America and called it 'Tin Temples'. It was an ironic look at American life, a sideways glance at iconic American places which really were just stories in the end - the movies, the highway, and of course, the dream holiday resort of Florida. I also created an artists' book, called *'Florida – Or You Can't Fight Progress'.*

Florida – A Large Relief Sculpture From 'Tin Temples', My Exhibition in 112 Greene St., Soho, New York.

The exhibition explored the lack of connection to a place of origin, the feeling of rootlessness, surrounded by 'invented' icons of what America really was. It struck a chord. 'Tin Temples' and 'Florida' were very well received, and the book found its way into important museum collections. The art I had created in response to a particularly American sense of living in a land of make-believe had created metaphors which resonated for many other people.

Having tried San Francisco, Los Angeles, Chicago and Florida I decided to move to Europe. After living in Italy for a year, I settled in London. But my inspiration as an artist often comes from my

American experiences – except now I am exploring 'Americana' from the point of view of an ex-patriot. Italy has also become, for me, a place which I examine and recreate through the stories I tell about it.

In fact, my neighbourhood in Brooklyn was half Jewish and half southern Italian. The sound of the immigrant older generations was part Yiddish and part southern Italian dialect. Before ever visiting Italy, I had loved the musical language of Italian operas. And now, when I spend some time there every year, it is the familiarity of the language which makes me feel at home.

In addition, Italy has been a place for my imagination to wander through my art. Dante, in his Divine Comedy, creates a richly detailed imagined world. This inspired me to recreate the journey through heaven and hell in a large series of sculptures and prints. It almost felt like a homecoming when I brought this to Dante's resting place in Ravenna, and to have the work embraced by the local people. A large sculpture made up of Dante's poetry is permanently sited there.

Angel Poetry – Permanent Public Sculpture for the Biblioteca Classense in Ravenna, Italy.

I have done many paintings and artists' books about the areas of Italy I have lived in, all with the magical quality of a fairy tale.

A PUBLIC SENSE OF PLACE

London has also inspired art which creates a sense of place. I have made many paintings of my particular area of South London, with its gorgeous parks and tree-lined streets. However, its most significant impact on my art is that it has been the place I began to create public sculpture. The wonderful experience of creating a permanent sculpture for a public space in my adopted home city makes me feel like I belong here in a unique way.

Public sculpture is a realm in which this story about place and belonging is incredibly important. All of my public sculptures have been collaborative in nature. For me, the most important aim of a public sculpture is to foster a sense of community ownership and to create a shared sense of place. I have developed a very particular process which I use to unleash people's personal ideas about the place they live, work or study. This process includes consultation, hands on workshops and often incorporation of ideas into the final artwork.

And within the process of working with diverse communities across the capital, I have discovered that I am not alone in needing to create a narrative about where I live in order to foster a sense of belonging. Many people benefit from the experience of creating a story through art about where they live. It fosters a sense of ownership, of belonging, and of identity which is important to us all.

A great example of this was a film project I made with former homeless clients of the charity Thames Reach. These were people who had finally been settled in flats, after long periods living rough. They took us to the areas where they used to sleep, and explained what life on the street was like. And in the process, they created a story of place leading to an idea of what home is. I eventually made a collaborative sculpture for the main offices of the charity, working with these clients, and creating a sculpture, *ASPIRE*, which tells the story of developing and growing in one's life.

Aspire – The Final Sculpture for the Head Office of Thames Reach.

When people live in a large block of flats, a collaborative project can create cohesion among diverse people, and foster ownership, identity, and a sense of belonging. This has been my experience in many projects I have created for different housing estates.

At the Mozart Estate, as part of a renovation, I worked first with elderly residents who brought photos and memorabilia which were permanently embedded into a 'Memory Wall' on the rebuilt estate. Then, children on the estate told stories about living there and made drawings about their lives. These were incorporated into permanent metal panels embedded in a new 'Story Wall'.

Similarly, at a school, a sense of belonging is a very positive experience for children, parents, teachers and staff. I worked with a school to create 'Alphabet Land', a book which explored cohesion understanding among children speaking three different languages – English, Bengali and Arabic.

It is a different sense of place which is created, but one which is no less important for a sense of tolerance, unity and pride.

I have been fortunate to work with many schools to create collaborative public art interventions which transform and enrich the experience of coming to learn, work and share in the school environment.

Kender Tree – Entrance Sculpture for Kender School, Lewisham, London.

A WANDERER

During this rich and varied career of helping people define a sense of where they live, I have continued to explore my own idea of where I fit in. If I feel a sense of belonging it is to my Jewish heritage more than to a country or an ancestral family. After all, rootlessness is a condition known to Jews throughout history.

My most recent artists' book and film is called *A Wanderer*.

I was born in America, and grew up in Brooklyn but now live in the UK and Italy, and have dual nationality. And recently it has been a task to find out why I am such a wanderer, why it has informed all of my work as an artist, and how my art has helped me to find a sense of belonging.

It is completely natural to want to explore your roots. After all, what defines us but where we are and where we come from? It's like all those advertisements – 'Check out your origins. Look into the past of your family. Learn about your ancestors'. So many genealogy sites to help you learn where you come from!

This search for a historic sense of where I am from inspired a long period of research into my family. I may never know what became of the family members who remained in Poland and

Austria. But the journey I have taken, both historic and imaginary, to try to picture what became of them, has been a meaningful experience for me, both as a man and an artist.

I tried to imagine what might have happened to family members who never migrated to New York. I pictured people who survived by hiding – in attics, in the Giełczyn Forest outside Łomża in Poland where my grandmother was from, in basements and abandoned barns. People making a safe world in unlikely places. And in the process, I have begun to come to terms with my own journey, and with my connection to my migrant Jewish family roots. It has been at times difficult, but has given me a new idea about where I belong, and how I am connected to an ancestry which is full of sadness, but also of joy, and which despite exile, migration, and oppression is incredibly rich in stories.

Empire State – A View From My Loft in Midtown Manhattan.

A Wanderer book and film https://rafaelklein.com/a-wanderer/

ART – EXPLORING IDEAS OF WHO WE ARE

The journey art has taken me on has led me to a place where I can fully appreciate how art is an essential part of the ideas-informed society. The enrichment that art provides is not limited to idle enjoyment but helps us form resilient ideas about our place in society and the world we inhabit. This has become especially apparent when creating work for the public realm. Public art, when developed in a collaboration with people who will live with the final work, provides a chance to explore ideas of who we are and what we share as a society. I believe this can be an essential tool in developing an ideas-informed society.

15

CURIOSITY AND STORIES: WORKING WITH ART AND ARCHAEOLOGY TO ENCOURAGE THE GROWTH OF CULTURAL CAPITAL IN LOCAL COMMUNITIES

John Castling and Jilly Johnston

I would have never visited the Spanish Gallery.

Jaz – transformative arts participant

This is our heritage, getting people involved in the community in projects like this is just wonderful.

Sue – community archaeology participant

Without having a past, you don't have a future: it's fundamental to your being, surely?

Stephen – community archaeology participant

In Bishop Auckland (North-East England), The Auckland Project is a charity using engagement with a wide cultural offer to bring about regeneration through, in part, actualising the benefits of increased 'cultural capital', a concept which closely overlaps with increased engagement in ideas-informed approaches.

As we will discuss throughout this chapter, there are many documented advantages of interaction with culture – and particularly the ideas inherent in various cultural sources which can positively affect both individuals and communities. This idea – that engagement in culture is powerful – is the starting point for our practices, and this chapter will outline the research that informs why we take this approach to culture-led regeneration, as well as exploring some examples of how we are going about that work. The Auckland Project have recently opened several high-quality cultural venues: the medieval Bishop of Durham's *Auckland Castle*, a *Mining Art Gallery*, a *Spanish [Art] Gallery* and (opening in 2023) a *Faith Museum* exploring the history of belief in Britain. There is, however, a challenge: Bishop Auckland is an area of high deprivation, and fixed negative mindsets about the present and past value of the town, alongside generationally held attitudes of detachment towards art, galleries and cultural spaces within the community present major barriers to cross. In this chapter we describe our approach to tackling these barriers within the disciplines of art and archaeology, suggesting that three powerful concepts are key to our successes: curiosity, community and narrative.

CURIOUS ABOUT CULTURE

In recent work on facilitating and achieving an ideas-informed society, Brown et al. conclude that education or 'life-long' learning is both the 'most appropriate' way to close the gap between the ideal and current situation in many countries in the West,[1] and one of five key barriers and enablers to the actualisation of ideas-informed societies.[2] They conclude that education must generate a 'desire to inquire, learn and question'. A key ingredient in generating this desire is provoking curiosity: 'Citizens are likely to engage with new ideas when they are curious'[3] and it is possible to 'foster states of curiosity', as evidenced by results of workplace studies.[4]

The concept of curiosity has been extensively debated within behavioural sciences, and certain insights are worth highlighting. Many scholars suggest curiosity is triggered by a 'knowledge gap' which can be both a catalyst for learning and as a worthwhile end in itself. Others don't see the need for this knowledge gap, instead defining curiosity more broadly as 'the desire for knowledge and information as well as exploratory, information-seeking behaviours'.[5] Some draw distinction between curiosity and interest, while others include interest within the concept of curiosity, but would distinguish different motives for learning.

However 'all theories agree that curiosity's immediate function is to learn, explore and immerse oneself in the interesting event. In the long term, curiosity serves a broader function of building knowledge and competence... Exploring new events fosters learning new things, meeting new people, and developing new skills. *Curiosity* can be defined as the recognition and pursuit of, and intense desire to explore novel, challenging, and uncertain events'.[6] This is similar to the definition adopted by Gino, that curiosity is 'the impulse to seek new information and experiences and explore novel possibilities'.[7]

Exploration is crucial in art and archaeology, and it is the possibility of fostering or stimulating curiosity which draws our interest. There is increasing evidence that curiosity is malleable and can be both prompted in short-term curiosity about specific subjects, and that individuals can become more curious in general. Curiosity can also be an important element of wellbeing, which is often intertwined with learning in the cultural sector. Also relevant is an observed link between curiosity and creativity, but as yet this link is not sufficiently understood beyond the fact that both involve novelty: 'Curiosity involves the pursuit of new knowledge and experiences. Creativity involves transforming existing knowledge, ideas, or objects into something novel and interesting'.[8] The pursuits of art and archaeology involve curiosity and creativity at their core and, significant for achieving ideas-informed society, touch on a multitude of other subjects: political, social, moral, spiritual and importantly – cultural.

'Cultural capital' has many varied understandings. Ofsted (the UK government's 'Office for Standards in Education, Children's Services and Skills') defines it as 'the essential knowledge that pupils need to be educated citizens, introducing them to the best that has been thought and said and helping to engender an appreciation of human creativity and achievement'.[9] This all-encompassing definition is too broad for our purposes, but neither do we consider cultural capital as merely a means to improving exam results attained simply by 'go[ing] to the theatre, museum, or historic places'.[10] The effect of cultural participation on academic achievement is still debated – numerous studies have determined that engagements in culture either can or largely do not positively affect educational outcomes.

THE POSITIVES OF CULTURAL ENGAGEMENT

Beyond exam results, cultural capital, which we understand as the intangible product of engaging in culture, can have positive benefits for people in multiple ways. The definition of 'engaging in culture' is equally slippery, but what the present authors mean by 'culture' includes visual/performance art, theatre, archaeology/history, literature, music, and crafts; and by engaging we mean visiting/viewing, reflecting on, learning about, or responding to cultural stimuli. In terms of our specialisms this engagement has been shown to have great advantages: 'The connections between participation in arts and culture and well-being have been demonstrated in a growing literature... [where] a prominent theme has been the potential of arts engagement to exacerbate or reduce health inequalities'.[11] A thorough review of the available literature on art and wellbeing recently concluded that 'evidence shows that visual arts activities, of various kinds, can reduce depression and anxiety and increase confidence and self-esteem'.[12] For those with mental health conditions, engagement with visual arts can 'encourage and stimulate re-engagement with the wider, everyday social world; and support in participants a potential renegotiation of identity through practice-based forms of making or doing'.[13]

There is an increasing recognition of the positives of engagement with the historic environment too, as well as moves to find better ways to demonstrate the link between heritage and wellbeing as these effects are often unappreciated amongst archaeology's public audiences. Several syntheses of the available data show that: 'Historic buildings and places, and associated activities and interventions, can have a wide range of beneficial impacts on the physical, mental and social wellbeing of individuals and communities'.[14]

These advantages are often celebrated primarily in terms of mental health benefits and more positive identity formations, with the former being particularly pronounced in archaeological projects. These are excellent aims, but fall short of connecting archaeology to wider benefits that might be gained by participants using archaeology to facilitate engagement in other cultural activities. The same is true in art, where there is 'a need to explore the role of social and cultural capital in shaping wellbeing outcomes in participatory arts'.[15]

However, in general areas with low education and high deprivation, two factors which relate to reduced engagement with ideas-informed living, participate in culture less. This is particularly important for The Auckland Project's setting.

Bishop Auckland is economically deprived. Fourteen of the town's 15 neighbourhoods are in the most deprived 34% nationally, including County Durham's most deprived neighbourhood.[16]

Nationally, those from the 10% most affluent areas are around three-and-a-quarter times more likely than those from the 10% least affluent areas to attend a public art display or go to see an exhibition of art, sculpture or photography – itself a prerequisite for a more active or meaningful engagement. For visiting a site of archaeological interest this is only slightly more balanced, with the most affluent tenth three times more likely to visit a site of archaeological interest than the least affluent tenth.[17]

There are many reasons suggested for this: the kind of work people and their families and communities do (both in terms of normalised behaviours and time to invest in relationships), lack of opportunities to engage, economic restrictions. Though research suggests the most likely barrier is social: 'if nobody else in our networks engages with high culture then we probably won't either'.[18] Conversely, those who are in networks where cultural activity is more common are more likely to have higher cultural capital despite work and economic circumstances which might usually predict low cultural engagement. It seems that the role of 'code-breakers', those who can gently decipher the unfamiliar world of cultural heritage, is an important one.

While literacy is often a crucial tool in decoding culture (as well as engaging in other elements of the ideas-informed society),[19] it is

important to remember that those unable to engage with written
words can, through inherent or developed visual literacy (i.e. being
able to 'read' visual sources) and concepts explored orally, still
engage with complex ideas. This is especially true when the power
of narrative is harnessed.

RELEVANCE THROUGH NARRATIVE

The idea of stories as powerful tools for communication has
become widespread. Its effectiveness has been celebrated in business
leadership, spatial planning design, life-long learning policy and
health care.

The work of psychologists suggests that storytelling is more than
just a powerful communication tool, but a means by which we
construct our realities and organise our experiences: 'we organise
our experience and our memory of human happenings mainly in the
form of narrative-stories... Narratives, then, are a version of
reality'.[20] It has even been argued that 'in a very fundamental sense
we exist and live our lives "in" and "through" stories... Stories do
not just provide us with a *sense* of who we are. To a large extent the
stories about our lives and ourselves *are* who we are'.[21]

Narrative approaches are so intertwined in museum interpretation that storytelling has been described as 'the real work of
museums'.[22] Approaches focussing on 'opportunities for individual
meaning making and narrative creation' are now popular in
museum practice.[23] The power of narrative approaches goes
beyond being useful for learning new information, and allows
audiences to be drawn into the stories, establishing connections
between the narrative content and their own stories and experiences. 'A story does what facts and statistics never can: it inspires
and motivates... The audience tunes in because they see themselves
woven into the story'.[24] In the context of museums, narrative
approaches have the power 'to make connections between museum
artifacts and images and visitors' lives and memories'.[25]

When engaging with cultural heritage, communicating in stories
'helps the visitor to interpret... the social and political context in
which the artwork [or object] was created. Visitors can also tell

their own stories, making connections between the artwork [and the past,] and their own concerns, knowledge and interests'.[26] When people tell stories of their own lives, they are 'not solely learning *from the narrative*; [there] is also the learning that goes on *in the act of narration*'.[27] By communicating the ideas embedded within particular artworks or archaeological discoveries through telling the story of Bishop Auckland's residents these ideas are not just interesting but become relevant and connected to the lives of our community.

Through the preceding two sections we have tried to briefly set out the case for *why* engaging with cultural ideas is something we need to encourage. There are individual benefits in health, well-being and learning from active participation in allowing ourselves to be shaped and informed by the ideas and narratives inherent in culture. But, more than this, the over-arching idea that communities can see positive change though engagement in culture is one that resonates with the subject of this book. We need societies informed by the powerful idea that cultural activity is more than a pastime, but a key to unlocking personal and community identities and regenerative futures.

BARRIERS TO ENGAGEMENT

Barriers to engagement with culture and the ideas therein can be summarised as those preventing *access* – both in terms of physical and intellectual accessibility, and those preventing *engagement* – such as background knowledge and experience to be able to make ideas relevant and processable. We find both these kinds of barriers in our work, but by helping to deciphering cultural heritage and empowering those who may be unfamiliar or feel it 'isn't for them', we can open access and encourage engagement.

Alongside the economic barriers – which as far as possible we overcome by making our participatory programmes free – there are three more specific barriers we encounter: perceived irrelevance, a required leap in knowledge, and a lack of culturally engaged social networks. The former correlates with the pattern of concern with immediate 'micro' interests for those with lower levels of education.[28] We frequently hear comments from non-participating locals akin to 'why do we need culture, just reopen the shops'.

So, having briefly discussed *why* the idea of engaging with culture is needed, we'll now briefly turn our focus to *how* we can overcome some of these barriers. Specifically, how we have found encouraging results when addressing relevance, knowledge gaps and disengaged social networks through the tools of inspiring curiosity, working within communities, and exploring through narratives.

OVERCOMING BARRIERS THROUGH ARCHAEOLOGY

Participation in archaeology can have positive impact upon well-being and engagement with ideas of identity and place.[29] However, opportunities for participation are better when they are more meaningful.[30]

Our approach to archaeological discovery acknowledges that while our staff and academic partners are knowledgeable, we don't know everything, and so foster an attitude that says, 'let's find out and explore that question together'. As we work with participants, we empower them to be the people who find out: each bucket-full of soil removed reveals the past more clearly, and we focus on giving the tools and confidences to enable us to regularly ask participants the question 'what do you think we're uncovering?' This makes contribution more valuable than prior knowledge, thereby encouraging confidence to learn and be curious, and highlights that participation is meaningful. Feedback from our 2021 community excavation participants shows 67% and 89% reported an increase in archaeological skills and historical knowledge, respectively. Others said that working with us had increased their confidence to try something new (48%), to speak to someone new or different to them, or to pursue independent learning (e.g. further reading, a course, a workshop, a local lecture etc.) (both 44%).

We also emphasise teamwork. Team-members become a community of archaeologists, which in turn builds their networks and improves access to the social capital required to benefit most from cultural capital. There can be problems: some of our participants are only able to attend infrequently so don't build strong connections. Still, 85% say they've felt part of a team through taking part in our excavations, and 100% that they are contributing to something important through participating.

We work hard to create a sense that the past we are exploring is 'our shared past'. Participants start with the story of our excavations, and the story of Bishop Auckland and its most powerful residents, the Prince Bishops of Durham, whose influence touched many elements of life in northern England and affected national and international events. We place our participants within that story, exploring with them how these stories are connected to their lives, experiences and identities – wherever they come from. They are therefore invited to consider themselves as a part of this narrative by involvement, not merely observation. For some this leads to a reflection on their own life stories, for others the story of Bishop Auckland's past becomes part of their identities. 50% of our 2021 excavation participants now volunteer elsewhere in the organisation, many sharing the stories they have uncovered with Auckland Castle's visitors, thereby become cultural 'decoders' themselves.

However, generally our 2021 participants come from more affluent post-codes in Bishop Auckland or elsewhere. Therefore our current project (the 'Bishop Big Dig'[31]) is working across Bishop Auckland (not just on The Auckland Project's sites) exploring how taking archaeological engagement out to people in the town, might 'increase [our community archaeology's] reach and diversity so that its benefits can be more widely felt'.[32] This project also includes children, who have potential to benefit significantly from engagement with archaeological learning.

OVERCOMING BARRIERS THROUGH ART

Our transformative arts projects seek to overcome barriers by developing a pull towards engagement that is stronger than an individual's reservation and fear of the unknown. We have found that it is often the case that the strongest pull is an innate curiosity, the *Statutory Framework for the Early Years Foundation Stage* suggests 'igniting children's curiosity' as a premise to build the seven areas of learning and development,[33] and we have found the use of 'playful' approaches to curiosity has had profound results. Playful approaches are proven to accelerate learning and create resilient, adaptive individuals. A task learned in play and 'in flow', which is a heightened state of curiosity, is mastered 20 times faster than by repetition.[34]

Playfully 'reimagining' artworks is a tool we often use. In the *Dalí: Surreal Worlds* project we worked with light artists to reimagine Dalí's famous *Christ of St. John of the Cross* – on loan to the Spanish Gallery in 2022. The artwork created was a large-scale spectacle situated in Bishop Auckland's market-place during an October evening food market, creating a talking point and stimulus for curiosity for town residents. The installation was created through meaningful participation from 120 Bishop Auckland children whose reimagining of Dalí's art became part of the artwork. This reimagining drew 4000 people to the market-place and resulted in the Spanish Gallery, which was open for free visits to Dalí's original artwork, attracting a record number of visitors.

Rooting art in individuals' narratives has also been successful. The *Can Any Mother Help Me?* project addressed a need for connection and fellowship felt by parents of young babies who were isolated and cut off from regular groups during the COVID-19 pandemic. We started offering remote support with creative packs and online sessions, which used a curiosity towards creativity as a tool for engagement. This grew into a small support group which widened with in-person meetings. Our approach focussed on the challenges these parents faced. The stories that were shared highlighted that the idea that being a 'good parent' was a heavy weight, with many parents feeling overwhelmed and 'not enough' – something that was emphasised by social media interactions. We responded by looking at a work from the Spanish Gallery – Murillo's *Virgin and Child* – and asking 'how useful is this image today?' By looking at the Virgin Mary through the eyes of an exhausted breastfeeding mother participants created an exhibition of photographic reimaginations of the painting. Connecting the image with individual narratives rendered it more 'real' and relatable to a diverse audience. In fact, during its run, the reinterpretations had more visitors than Murillo's original!

The project has subsequently grown though NHS local support groups, who are considering expanding it into a county-wide programme. We have consistently found that working in partnership with other organisations (e.g. NHS, Princes Trust, schools, youth and community centres, and local artists) breaks down barriers to engagement by presenting our sites and collections in a different narrative context – one that may not be as initially as unfamiliar as an art gallery.

Finally, we return to the acknowledgement of Jaz, one of our Transformative Arts participants with which we opened this chapter, that she – perhaps typical of many in the town – 'would have never visited the Spanish Gallery'. Jaz has since been part of three projects designed to engage 'hard to reach' members of the community. She started by attending a Baby Group run weekly in our community hub with her daughter, Al. Since joining the group she has been part of two projects which use creative activity to link with The Auckland Project's collections. Jaz has barriers to engagement (such as cost and transport) but through repeated engagements in creative projects and programs she now visits cultural heritage sites, exercises a sense of curiosity – exploring and being informed by the ideas inherent in art, and is an engaged part of the growing cultural offer in Bishop Auckland.

THE POWER OF CURIOSITY, COMMUNITY AND NARRATIVE

The Auckland Project is not merely about cultural venues: as a regeneration charity we seek to use culture to help bring about a Bishop Auckland which is, in the words of our founder Jonathan Ruffer, 'healthier, happier and wealthier'. In this chapter we have highlighted *why* culturally-fuelled-regeneration is a powerful and informed idea. For communities like Bishop Auckland it is an approach that we *need* for holistic positive change. *How* we're seeking to foster this ideas-informed society approach focuses on the power of curiosity, community, and narrative to encourage individuals to become learners engaged with the ideas through ensuring our local community feel welcome and valued in our cultural venues. We are on a long-term journey, monitoring the ways these approaches increase engagement in cultural capital and bring wider benefits to our local community. We believe, with what we've seen so far, that the results will be transformative.

REFERENCES

1. C. Brown, J. Groß Ophoff, K. Chadwick, and S. Parkinson, 'Achieving the "ideas-informed" society: results from a Structural Equation Model using survey data from England' (2022) *Emerald Open Research* at 16.
2. C. Brown, R. Luzmore, and J. Groß Ophoff, 'Facilitating the ideas-informed society: a systematic review' (2022) *Emerald Open Research* at 7–8.
3. C. Brown, R. Luzmore, and J. Groß Ophoff, 'Facilitating the ideas-informed society: a systematic review', 9.
4. F. Gino, 'The business case for curiosity' (2018).
5. E. Szumowska and A. W. Kruglanski, 'Curiosity as end and means' (2020) 35 *Current Opinion in Behavioural Sciences* 35–39.
6. P. J. Silvia and T. B. Kashdan, 'Curiosity and Interest: The Benets of Thriving on Novelty and Challenge' in C. R. Snyder, S. J. Lopez, L. M. Edwards, and S. C. Marques (eds.), *The Oxford Handbook of Positive Psychology*, (New York: Oxford University Press, 2017), pp. 482–92.
7. F. Gino, 'The business case for curiosity', p. 48.
8. M. E. Gross, C. M. Zedelius, and J. W. Schooler, 'Cultivating an understanding of curiosity as a seed for creativity' (2020) 35 *Current Opinion in Behavioural Sciences* at 77–82.
9. Office for Standards in Education, Children's Services and Skills, *Guidance: School Inspection Handbook* (2022) p. 226.
10. S. Stopforth and V. Gayle, 'Parental social class and GCSE attainment: Re-reading the role of "cultural capital"' (2022) 43 *British Journal of Sociology of Education* 680–99 at 686.
11. N. Daykin, L. Mansfield, C. Meads, K. Gray, A. Golding, A. Tomlinson, and C. Victor, 'The role of social capital in participatory arts for wellbeing: findings from a qualitative systematic review' (2021) 13 *Arts & Health* 134–57 at 2.

12. What Works Centre for Wellbeing, *Visual Art and Mental Health: Briefing* (2018) p. 2.

13. A. Tomlinson, J. Lane, G. Julier, L. Grigsby Duffy, A. Payne, L. Mansfield, T. Kay, A. John, C. Meads, N. Daykin, K. Ball, C. Tapson, P. Dolan, S. Testoni, and C. Victor, *Visual Art and Mental Health: A Systemic Review of the Subjective Wellbeing Outcomes of Engaging with Visual Arts for Adults ('Working-age', 15–64 years) with Diagnosed Mental Health Conditions* (2018) p. 3.

14. What Works Centre for Wellbeing, *Heritage and Wellbeing: Briefing* (2019) p. 2; For full detail see A. Pennington, R. Jones, A.-M. Bagnall, J. South, and R. Corcoran, *Heritage and Wellbeing: The Impact of Historic Places and Assets on Community Wellbeing - A Scoping Review* (2018).

15. N. Daykin, L. Mansfield, C. Meads, K. Gray, A. Golding, A. Tomlinson, and C. Victor, 'The role of social capital in participatory arts for wellbeing', 3.

16. Ministry of Housing, Community & Local Government, *Index of Multiple Deprivation: English Indices of Deprivation 2019* (2019).

17. *The Amazing Power of Networks: A (Research-Informed) Choose Your Own Destiny Book* (John Catt Educational, 2021) p. 88.

18. C. Brown, *The Amazing Power of Networks: A (Research-Informed) Choose Your Own Destiny Book*, p. 91.

19. C. Brown, R. Luzmore, and J. Groß Ophoff, 'Facilitating the ideas-informed society: a systematic review', 7.

20. J. Bruner, 'The narrative construction of reality' (1991) 18 *Critical Inquiry* 1–21 at 4–5.

21. I. F. Goodson, G. Biesta, M. Tedder, and N. Adair, *Narrative Learning* (Routledge, 2010) p. 1.

22. L. Bedford, 'Storytelling: the real work of museums' (2001) 44 *Curator: The Museum Journal* 27–34.

23. C. Ross, M. Carnall, A. Hudson-Smith, C. Warwick, M. Terras, and S. Gray, 'Enhancing Museum Narratives: Tales of Things and UCL's Grant Museum' in J. Farman (ed.), *The Mobile Story: Narrative Practices with Locative Technologies*, (New York: Routledge, 2014), pp. 276–89 p. 227.

24. D. Taylor, *The Healing Power of Stories: Creating Yourself Through the Stories of Your Life*, 1st ed. (Doubleday, 1996). p. 132.

25. Bedford, 'Storytelling', 30.

26. S. Valtolina, 'A storytelling-sriven framework for cultural heritage dissemination' (2016) 1 *Data Science and Engineering* 114–23 at 115; see also P. Schorch, 'Museum Encounters and Narrative Engagements' in S. Macdonald, H. Rees Leahy (eds.), *The International Handbooks of Museum Studies*, (Wiley, 2015), pp. 437–57.

27. I. F.Goodson, G. Biesta, M. Tedder, and N. Adair, *Narrative Learning*, p. 127.

28. C. Brown, R. Luzmore, and J. Groß Ophoff, 'Facilitating the ideas-informed society: a systematic review', 7–8.

29. Historic England, *Heritage and Society: Heritage Counts* (2019); What Works Centre for Wellbeing, *Heritage and Wellbeing: Briefing*; A. Pennington, R. Jones, A.-M. Bagnall, J. South, and R. Corcoran, *Heritage and Wellbeing: The Impact of Historic Places and Assets on Community Wellbeing - A Scoping Review*.

30. Chartered Institute for Archaeologists, *Delivering Public Benefit* (2021); B. Wilkins, 'A theory of change and evaluative framework for measuring the social impact of public participation in archaeology' (2019) 9 *European Journal of Post-Classical Archaeologies* 77–100.

31. C. Smith, C. Gerrard, and J. Castling, *The Bishop Big Dig Report* (2023), available at: https://collections.durham.ac.uk/files/r2rv042t15k#.ZHXoe-xKg1I.

32. C. Lewis, 'Heritage and Community Archaeology' in S. L. López Varela (ed.), *The Encyclopedia of Archaeological Sciences* (John Wiley & Sons, Inc., 2018), p. 5.

33. Department for Education, *Statutory Framework for the Early Years Foundation Stage: Setting the Standards for Learning, Development and Care for Children from Birth to Five* (2021) p. 8.

34. A. Griffith and M. Burns, *Outstanding Teaching: Engaging Learners* (Crown House Publishing, 2012) p. 10.

16

GETTING THE (POSITIVE) WORD OUT: THE IdeaSpies PLATFORM

Lynn Wood and Sabra Brock

THE POWER OF POSITIVE IDEAS

Positive ideas that could improve our lives are needed to fuel an ideas-informed society. All innovations are based on ideas.

However, positive ideas often fail to get our attention because negative news is a major problem in today's world. Our solution is a global platform that highlights clever and positive ideas at various stages of commercialisation. IdeaSpies is an open innovation platform that allows people to post, share, search, comment on and spark ideas that can make the world better.

This chapter outlines the origin, vision and approach of IdeaSpies. It describes the top two ideas in 2021 from amongst the thousands we are sharing, how IdeaSpies has been used, its benefits and our future plans.

DOOMSCROLLING VERSUS CHEERSCROLLING

As we monitor our social media feeds and other news outlets, there is no shortage of information seemingly designed to make us feel bad and sad.

An exhibition at the British Library in London early in 2022 showed exactly how much bad news dominates our lives. Called 'Breaking the News', it explained in detail what it is that makes an event 'news', utilising examples of 10 news categories. Only 1 of the 10 categories was clearly positive: that being *Celebration*. This sat along

193

amongst other more negative categories such as *Crime and sensationalism, Scandal, Conflict, Disaster, Power, Suppression, Satire, Chaos* and *Celebrity*.

Because reading negative news is so popular there's a term for it, *doomscrolling*. However, *doomscrolling* has its disadvantages, including:

- Giving you the impression that the future is gloomy;

- Making you feel anxious; and

- Preventing you from seeing ideas that offer you opportunities in life.

Writer Maura Thomas cited nineteenth-century philosopher and founding father of modern psychology, William James, as saying, 'My experience is what I agree to attend to'. She went on to explain that your attention determines your experiences, and the experiences you have dictate your life.[1]

So, instead of doomscrolling, let's consider its opposite, *cheerscrolling*. The Urban Dictionary defines cheerscrolling as visiting sites that provide positive news and make you feel good.[2]

Where are these positive ideas concentrated? Thousands of positive ideas can easily be found on IdeaSpies.com. It is a digital library and, as such, a valuable resource for those who want to solve new or old problems in new ways.

Screen Shot 1. IdeaSpies Home Page.

THE CREATION AND DEVELOPMENT OF IdeaSpies

IdeaSpies was co-founded in 2015 by Australian Lynn Wood and American Dr Sabra Brock during a trip to Canada. A travel guide sparked the idea by saying, 'Promote what you love rather than bash what you hate'. Wood developed IdeaSpies as a web platform with the help of many volunteers. Dr Brock is now on the Advisory Board.

The idea for IdeaSpies was that it should be a place for showcasing the positive ideas happening right now around the world, explained simply, to serve as an antidote to negative news. The name was chosen as it features both ideas and the importance of looking out for them, with the concept first tested as a Facebook page.

IdeaSpies has been developed as an open innovation platform for clever ideas, new discoveries and original thinkers. Its ideas are drawn from volunteer Editors of 19 topics ranging from AgTech to Wellbeing. Ideas are posted in 100 words or less, with eye catching images or videos, so they are easily understood and shared. Initially it was developed on Wordpress; then, when it reached over 2,000 ideas posted, a bespoke platform was developed so it could scale further.

Over its lifetime, IdeaSpies has received rigorous and detailed testing to ensure it is easy to use and secure. Many students, particularly from Macquarie University in Sydney, have contributed to the design as part of their IT courses. Two student groups looked at how the user experience could be improved and later, two groups checked the security, including by trying to break into the platform. They did break in and we fixed it. It was particularly important for IdeaSpies to be easy to use and secure for the UpRising student programme, discussed later in this chapter.

THE EVOLVING STRUCTURE OF IdeaSpies

Initially, IdeaSpies was open for anyone to post an idea, and they were all posted together. The platform was designed to ensure that it was simple and easy for anyone around the world to post a positive idea, explained simply with an image. Over time, topics for ideas could be identified and ideas were grouped into these topics on the platform.

Early on Wood was advised to create voluntary Editors who could contribute ideas in their specific fields of expertise, but it took several years for the opportunity to be realised. It started when Wood thought the timing was right and asked a colleague, Jill Storey, who had founded a crowd funding organisation called ReadyFundGo, whether she could recommend anyone as an Editor. Storey knew a person who might be interested in being the Editor for agricultural technology. He agreed; then others were invited who had posted positive ideas well on IdeaSpies. They posted ideas in addition to all others able to post. Then more people asked to join as Editors. They saw the usefulness of the platform in amplifying their voices in their chosen fields and enjoyed the positive association it offers.

IdeaSpies then developed and published an Editorial Policy, which is

> *IdeaSpies shares ideas that do good. They are explained in posts of 100 words or less, designed to attract busy people who are curious and looking for ways to improve our lives.*
>
> *They can be ideas happening now, ideas being developed, a different way to think about something or a new concept. They should offer a solution to a problem.*
>
> *Whenever you see something and think 'that's clever' it should be on IdeaSpies.*
>
> *Our vision is to be the pre-eminent source of innovative ideas for all Australians and around the World.*

As IdeaSpies became more popular however, more people started posting ideas that did not fit our policy. We then therefore restricted posting to our Editors, Advisory Board and selected others such as students in our UpRising programme.

The Advisory Board was chosen from people already supporting IdeaSpies who are leaders in their fields. It comprises seven members and has been serving since 2019. Members have high level experience in Government, Industry, Education, Publishing, Law and Innovation.

IdeaSpies is now a curated platform and quality of ideas posted is important. Due to the quality of ideas it is being syndicated around the world to organisations interested in keeping up to date with positive news in the topics we cover.

IdeaSpies has been designed to attract positive people with positive ideas whose values focus on being:

- Supportive. Supporting those who have ideas that can improve our lives,

- Curious. Asking how the world and our lives could be better,

- Optimistic. Looking for the good in everything and everyone,

- Observant. Seeing opportunities in life and explaining them simply and

- Proactive. Taking a constructive viewpoint, framing issues to explore possible solutions or alternatives.

We use the acrostic SCOOP to help us remember our values given they are so important to us.

BENEFITS OF IdeaSpies

Key supporters were asked in 2022 about the benefits they received from having joined IdeaSpies. There were two overarching themes in their answers - *Community* and *Ideas*:

Community-related comments on the value of IdeaSpies included:

- Joining a powerful group of like-minded people who are passionate about helping others to succeed;

- A powerful group of Editors;

- One-stop shop of curated ideas from leaders in their fields;

- An emphasis on global citizens making global differences;

- A thriving ecosystem of some incredible people across different industries; and

- A community of innovators and collaborators that encompasses people from all walks of life and from all over the globe.

Idea-related comments on the value of IdeaSpies included:

- Sharing positive ideas that boost optimism;

- Advocacy for a better world;

- A place with an emotional sense of wellbeing and gratitude;

- A digital library of positive ideas;

- A very useful free resource to search if you want to keep up with innovation;

- A voice for positive ideas that could make the world happier and more sustainable;

- A counter to gloom and doom; and

- Value in tracking trends across industries and communities to help explore and dream for a better world.

'The real benefit of IdeaSpies is the democratisation of ideas', observed David Thodey AO, Chair of technology companies Xero and Tyro and Chair of the IdeaSpies Advisory Board, 'Great ideas, research, and innovation can come from anyone – so often the best ideas do not have a voice. IdeaSpies provides a platform for people to share ideas that create a better world'.

TOP IDEAS

The two most popular ideas on IdeaSpies in 2021 based on most clicks were about COVID-19 and a student project called UpRising. The UpRising initiative is discussed in the next section as a case study.

The COVID-19-related idea resulted from Wood wondering one weekend in June 2021 why Australia did not have a public plan for dealing with COVID-19, so she drafted one. She called it a Positive Pandemic Plan (PPP) and posted it on IdeaSpies. It listed 10 points in 100 words. She shared it on social media, attracting a lot of attention. Many commented on and encouraged the plan. They were very concerned that all travel, even for Australians, had been halted in an effort to keep the country COVID free (and be well-positioned for the upcoming elections).

Coincidentally, soon after the IdeaSpies post, the Australian Government published a plan. Finally, Australians were able to return home for Christmas in 2021 if they were vaccinated, as recommended in Point 10 of the IdeaSpies plan.

A Positive Pandemic Plan (PPP)

 27 June 2021 by **IdeaSpies**   👍 45

Screen Shot 2. Most Popular Idea in 2021.

CASE STUDY: THE UPRISING SCHOOLS INITIATIVE

The UpRising initiative came about because of the effort of an enterprising high school teacher in Sydney, Richard Hainsworth. The New South Wales (NSW) school curriculum for Design and

Technology specifies that students must engage in a year-long major design project (MDP) in which they identify a genuine societal need and create an innovative solution. The ideas are often brilliant, but interest in them dies at the end of the school year, and as a result, projects are simply discarded in the cupboard or rubbish bin.

Hainsworth's Design and Technology class was already using IdeaSpies as a source of inspiration for their ideas. It was pointed out to him that they could also post their ideas on IdeaSpies, meaning they might also receive helpful comments from people outside friends and family. Rather than just offer this advantage to his own students, he shared the idea with colleagues at the voluntary association of Design and Technology teachers (The Institute of Technology Education (iTE)) so more students could benefit from it.

The safety and positivity advantages of IdeaSpies were very important criteria in the iTE's decision to support a trial of Hainsworth's idea in NSW. Unlike larger social media sites, such as Facebook and LinkedIn, comments on IdeaSpies are collected in one place with the post and can be easily referenced while allowing the students to remain anonymous. Additionally, all posts on IdeaSpies are positive and any comments are constructive. Students could change their posts, based on the comments they received from many people supporting the UpRising initiative, plus use the posts as public evidence of their talents in seeking further education and job opportunities.

Volunteer teachers who are iTE members set up a registration system so teachers could enroll their students, following school and parent approval. A maximum of 50 students was set for the pilot in 2021. It culminated in a year-end event where the effort and talents of all the students were celebrated. Seed funding and mentorship were then subsequently awarded to three students to take their projects beyond their schooling years.

Testimonials from students were extremely positive:

> *UpRising was a great tool to use as it allowed more individuals to see my project idea and helped me develop the idea through their feedback...this really helped me guide my path. (Kindness Bank)*

For the first time in my life I felt that my ideas had a following. (RoboticRover for Safe Delivery of Humanitarian Aid in Warzones)

Teachers were also positive with one commenting that the UpRising initiative helped prepare students for 'the world outside the school. Our students have learnt new skills in communicating with the business, entrepreneurial and research sectors they were previously not completely aware of'.

UpRising - connecting young designers with industry

Screenshot 3. Second-Most Popular Idea in 2021.

THE FUTURE OF IdeaSpies

The IdeaSpies vision is to be the pre-eminent source of innovative ideas for Australians and globally. Increasingly the IdeaSpies database of ideas and users is becoming an asset that can be leveraged to ascertain which ideas have traction: for instance, in terms of historical trends (e.g. hydrogen) or specific innovations (e.g. wearable solar cells). The COVID-19 idea category, for example, documents the stages of dealing with COVID-19 from when solutions as ideas were first identified.

Three main opportunities are currently being explored for IdeaSpies:

1. An IdeaSpies Kiosk in innovation centres, libraries and museums

Because IdeaSpies is a digital library it could be showcased in traditional libraries and museums to demonstrate how there are many positive ideas around the world that are solutions to current day problems. A positive view of the future is particularly important for the younger generation, so they are encouraged to create it.

An IdeaSpies Kiosk has already been set up at nandin, the ANSTO (Australian Nuclear Science and Technology Association) Innovation Centre in NSW. The kiosk shows how useful IdeaSpies is in searching ideas related to topics or keywords, explained simply. It can stimulate further ideas and help with research as well as idea development. In this way it can serve as a catalyst to more thinking about problems, issues and ideas as solutions.

2. Expansion of the UpRising initiative

While the UpRising initiative is currently restricted to 50 students in NSW, it could be expanded to more students around Australia so students can post their school Design and Technology project ideas on IdeaSpies and get useful feedback on them, just as they do in NSW. While many schools offer virtual learning environments within their own schools, the UpRising initiative offers a safe and positive virtual environment to test ideas outside a school and globally. It enriches learning by giving students the opportunity to take control of their own learning, safely circulating ideas they post to get comments from wider circles of influence.

3. Other uses

- Support other school and university projects involving innovation in Australia and worldwide by giving students the opportunity to get helpful comments on them, without the restraints in the UpRising programme of having the students approved to post by schools and teachers;

- Encourage positive discussion on sensitive subjects such as nuclear and hydrogen, just as it did with COVID-19 in 2021;

- Showcase examples of cooperation on innovation between countries, reinforcing the importance of collaborating on positive ideas globally as well as within countries;

- Connect research ideas at universities with business and industry that can help commercialise them;

- Connect major organisations seeking solutions to problems with people in other organisations who can solve them, e.g., problems related to climate.

These new uses could feature any brand with the full functionality of the existing platform. Organisations could rebrand IdeaSpies with their own identity, topics and descriptions.

It is planned that the current IdeaSpies platform will remain free as a public good. While it has received considerable support from volunteers over the past few years, corporate and government support will ensure we can achieve the vision for IdeaSpies to be the pre-eminent source of innovative ideas for all Australians and globally.

SUMMARY

In Summary: The IdeaSpies Contribution to an Ideas-Informed Society

The world needs more emphasis on positive ideas to counteract our bias towards noticing negative news. Positive ideas can fuel progress towards an ideas-informed society.

IdeaSpies is a platform with thousands of positive ideas, submitted by a broad range of people. It is easily searched and an ideal basis for innovators looking for ideas to support and build on.

We are encouraging people to change their habits from doomscrolling to cheerscrolling.

Our vision is for IdeaSpies to become the pre-eminent source of innovative ideas for all Australians and globally.

NOTES

1. James, W. (1890). As quoted in Thomas, M. (March 15), 2018 *Harvard Business Review*. Accessed October 2, 2022, from https://hbr.org/2018/03/to-control-your-life-control-what-you-pay-attention-to.
2. Unwanted Life (2021). *Urban Dictionary*. Accessed September 6, 2022, from https://www.urbandictionary.com/define.php?term=Cheerscrolling.

17

HOW TO SUCCEED IN A VOLATILE WORLD? UTILISING THE 7 PILLARS OF POSITIVE RESILIENCE TO MAKE THE IDEAS-INFORMED SOCIETY A REALITY

Belinda Board

BOUNCING BACK OR BOUNCING FORWARD

There has been no shortage of things to worry about in recent times: what with war in Europe, political polarisation, the energy crisis, global food shortages and soaring inflation and cost of living. Layered onto earlier shocks of a deadly global pandemic and supply chain chaos, it seems like there are so many different problems coming at us from so many different angles. It's a challenge just knowing which to focus upon. We are living in perhaps the most challenging environment ever faced; one of extreme volatility, uncertainty, complexity and ambiguity (VUCA).

Such volatile times test our fortitude. In response, some are 'digging deeper', working ever harder to simply stay afloat, while others are changing their approach to positively pursue the opportunities.

Indeed we see two distinct approaches emerging. The first approach adopts a 'Reactive, dig deeper', mindset and concentrates on investing ever increasing amounts of effort into farming a single track of survival. In other words, doing the same thing that's always been done, just digging deeper to do even more of it. This 'bounce back' approach is characterised by a focus on the here and now, utilising tried and tested methods and ideas, doing short term interventions and shoring up defences to reduce, or ideally prevent any permanent damage. This short-term reactive rationale offers little more that temporary respite as people wait and watch conditions unfold. Mental health statistics across the globe make sober reading, even for the ardent supporters of this approach.

But we see a second approach emerging as well. This approach adopts a 'Proactive, positive change' mindset, and concentrates on investing effort to galvanise thriving outcomes. This 'bounce forward' approach embraces the volatility to catalyse positive change and new opportunities. This future-focused approach offers bold, forward momentum that places the owner squarely in the driving seat. To succeed, it requires people to engage with new ideas, new realities, new expectations, new beliefs, new norms and new behaviours.

Many of us have been inspired by stories of ordinary people dealing with indescribable challenges and tragedies with determination and optimistic resolve. Stories of bending and adapting and creating positive change – from often seemingly impossible circumstances – are testament to the notion that many people, despite adversity and challenge, generate positive, constructive outcomes and can actually flourish.[1]

Our 10+ years of research on workplace resilience across hundreds of private and public sector organisations has been studying these two approaches and the results are clear: reactive, 'bounce back' approaches tend to deliver average performance and can lead to missed opportunities, frustrations, and disengagement; while proactive, 'bounce forward' approaches can deliver top quartile performance, high well-being, and high engagement. Individuals and communities with higher levels of positive resilience are more likely to be able to engage with new ideas, utilise an experiential mindset, have an optimistic attitude, make smarter decisions and choices, look for opportunities to learn and adopt more progressive beliefs and norms. Positive resilience provides the psychological mechanism required make the goal of an ideas-informed society a reality.

THRIVING RATHER THAN JUST SURVIVING

So what distinguishes these two mindsets and how can individuals, organisations and societies benefit from better understanding these ingredients? At Peoplewise, through both our academic research and practitioner experience working with organisations to be more effective, we have identified seven factors that differentiate people who thrive rather than merely survive. Together, these seven factors combine to form Positive Resilience a vital 'muscle' for operating in a VUCA world and one that creates a platform for positive change and progress at every level of society.

Positive Resilience offers individuals the opportunity to reach their full potential for both happiness and success. It offers organisations the opportunity to realise long-term competitive advantage, by helping them to be more flexible, more adaptive and more open to new ideas, growth and positive change. It offers society, via government think tanks and policy makers, the opportunity to fulfil their obligations to citizens to protect and provide by adopting an approach that is wholistic, engaging and relevant. Amid the environmental, social and political crises facing societies and communities today, Positive Resilience offers the psychological mechanism for citizens that will close that gap between the ideal of the ideas-informed society and the current reality.

The premise of the 7 Pillars of Positive Resilience is simple – resilience, 'bouncing back' and utilising the same old ideas and methods, is not enough if we are to build individuals, organisations and societies that can grow and thrive in a sustainable and enduring manner. Who wants to go back to many of the pre pandemic practices that already seem obsolete and outdated – who, for example, wants to go to the GP's ever again for a prescription that could easily be handled over the phone? Who wants to have a mandatory 5-day office-based work week again?

POSITIVE RESILIENCE

The 7 Pillars of Positive Resilience represent seven factors that together create an operating system, be it personal, organisational, or societal, that is characterised by delivering positive change. People who embody Positive Resilience aren't superhuman. Nor do they conform to a mythical 'faultless' persona. Adversity, challenge, and stress plague us all to varying degrees at various points in our lives. So, how can we account for individual differences in how people cope with and manage adversity, challenge, and stress? The answer lies in the 7 Pillars of Positive Resilience which together enable us to go beyond merely coping and recovery, by providing a platform for growth and development. Positive Resilience is not an inherent quality that we either have or do not have. Rather, it involves thinking patterns, feelings, behaviours, actions, and strategies that can be learned and developed. How we live our lives, through our daily habits is the key to growing positive resilience and each pillar is easily constructed by living and mastering straightforward daily practices.

Positively Resilient people are hopeful and optimistic. They adapt and cope with demanding environments with a clear sense of purpose and coherence. They show a sense of adventure, courage, and self-understanding, use humour, have a capacity for hard work; and possess the ability to cope with and find outlets for emotions.[2]

This chapter looks at the 7 Pillars of Positive Resilience as critical mechanisms that allow people and society to flourish, and to bounce forward and grow from challenging circumstances. Building a strong operating system of positive resilience is not only good for individuals it is essential for organisations and society as a whole. Being deliberate and persistent in creating the 7 pillars will produce innovation and growth and contribute to creating a more ideas led society.

PRP PILLAR 1 – PURPOSEFULNESS

Purposefulness inspires commitment and dedication towards a goal or objective. The ability to see the value in what we do and to know what we are striving for helps to build the endurance required to maintain focus and determination to push through any challenge that we may face to achieve a fuller and better future.

Our research has shown that Purposefulness is critical for being inspired, committed, and dedicated towards a goal or objective. The ability to see the value in what we do and to know what we are striving for is essential for building the endurance required to maintain focus and determination to push through any challenge that we may face.[3] In an ideas-informed society, which represents the notion of an upward trajectory of societal progress, those with higher levels of Purposefulness will be more likely to realign their values, motivators and behaviours in response to new progressive beliefs and norms.

Recent events have demonstrated just how central Purpose is to people. The paradigm of the 'great resignation', a term coined by Anthony Klotz, an associate professor of management at Texas A&M University, describes the phenomenon of a great number of employees voluntarily quitting their jobs since March 2021. After an extended period of not working, of working from home with no commute, or working under extreme pressures, many people reassessed their work-life balance and work-life priorities. Purpose is at the heart of this revolution. Research indicates that it is not money, but purpose, meaning and ability to be one's true self at work, that are most important for those considering a job change.[4]

A recent study by WeSpire[5] found that Gen-Z is 'The first generation to prioritise purpose over salary. They read Mission Statements and Values documents to select where they work and want their employer's values to match their values. They expect consistency and authenticity and will call you out, often publicly, if they don't see it. They will leave companies they believe are hiding or putting too much spin on bad news, ignoring their negative environmental or social impacts, or that have toxic workplace cultures'. The message is clear, more important than remuneration packages, employees want to work for an organisation whose values and culture align with their own and offer growth, connection and meaningful work.

For organisations, now more than ever before, creating a culture where there is a strong sense of purpose, engagement and purposeful commitment to one's work and the organisation is crucial. That is what the Purpose pillar of Positive Resilience offers employees – something people want to be part of, and something that will evolve and realign in response to new progressive beliefs and norms in communities and societies.

At a societal and organisation level, governments and leaders are increasingly recognising that the pursuit of profit and economic growth is no longer enough. The idea of corporate and societal purpose is not new but has re-entered public discourse in recent years. There is renewed language, regulation and focus on long-term value creation, investment and stewardship of our environment, people and society. In a world recovering from the legacy of the 2008 banking crisis and the COVID-19 pandemic, and facing digital disruption, economic volatility, social inequality and environmental crisis, governments and organisations must harness the power of purpose. When individuals are able to reframe their challenges and tasks as opportunities to help others and make a difference, our lives and our work feel more significant.[6]

PRP PILLAR 2 – PERSPECTIVE

Perspective enables us to build a positive, courageous outlook and stay optimistic in the face of adversity Perspective encourages us to look at the bigger picture, consider where we are in relation to the problem, and how we can go about solving it, rather than resigning ourselves to 'the Fates'.[7]

Having Perspective is a core foundation for what differentiates those hungry for new knowledge, positive change and better opportunities, no matter what challenge or circumstance is faced. Our research has shown that Perspective is critical for enabling us to look at the big picture, consider where we are in relation to a problem, and to focus with an optimistic outlook on how we can go about solving challenges, rather than resigning ourselves 'to the fates'.[8] Optimistic people tend to work harder and be more productive, probably because they can more clearly see the options for how to achieve the goal, they are working towards.[9] Optimism doesn't accept failure. It's also good for your physical health. A study conducted by the University of Illinois found that optimistic participants were 76% more likely to have an 'ideal' health score.[10]

Having an optimistic outlook is not the same as pretending that everything is perfect all the time. Unrealistic optimism can lead to bad decisions,[11] or lack of effort[12] and can set a person up for disaster just as surely as pessimistic catastrophising.[13] It is important to cultivate flexible and realistic optimism, that is, 'optimism with its eyes open'.[14] This has been shown to help people set hopeful yet realistic goals and cope effectively with setbacks and problems.[15]

The world's refugee crisis has shown that 89.3 million people worldwide were forcibly displaced at the end of 2021 as a result of persecution, conflict, violence, human rights violations or events seriously disturbing public order.[16] Yet, despite this unimaginable suffering and loss, research has shown that refugees demonstrate a remarkable degree of resistance to mental health difficulties.[17] For this population, despite having every right to be hijacked through their extreme emotional turmoil and resource loss, research actually shows a remarkable degree of resistance to mental health difficulties and stress. This incredible finding is attributed to the ability to maintain a forward looking, optimistic outlook that utilises the Perspective mechanism to shape positive and forward-focused – 'bounce-forward' – attitudes and actions in relation to substantial loss and instability faced.

For organisations, Perspective is the driver for new knowledge, positive change and transformation. Utilising Perspective allows organisations to take a wide, forward focussed, and optimistic view of the future enabling them to step beyond the default way of thinking to innovate and create new opportunities and strategic value propositions, even from apparent setbacks and challenge.

Time and time again, we have seen examples of where creativity, disruptive innovation and societal progress results from setback and crisis. The space race revolutionised portable computer software and hardware, as well as developments in medical imaging techniques, durable healthcare equipment, artificial limbs, water filtration systems, solar panels and countless more. World War II largely gave rise to momentous advances in numerous technologies and medicines.

As we look forward, the ability to harness Perspective will allow societies and economies to grow and evolve. As collective societies today, we are seeking new perspectives, new paradigms and revitalised optimism for a better future. Today's powerful social change movements reflect the collective desire to take refreshed perspective with hope for the future and focussed action for transformational change. Whether it's the *Black Lives Matter, #Me Too*, human rights, indigenous land rights, Net Zero Agenda or LGBTQ+ equality movements, the shift in the collective voice and optimism for the future is loud and clear. Moreover, with hope comes targeted deployment of resources to drive real positive change in areas that really matter.

PRP PILLAR 3 – CONTROL

Control allows us to manage our emotions, rather than our emotions controlling us. The ability to stay calm under pressure, manage our impulses and emotional reactions allows us to engage in rational thinking and deliver optimised performance. It is about being able to rapidly regain your equilibrium when faced with setbacks or pressure so you're able to respond rather than react.

Our research found that people with strong Control have developed effective strategies to deal with becoming overwhelmed by their emotions – often referred to as Emotional Hijack. They can regulate their reactions to help them to think more clearly, be more creative, and make decisions that take the wider perspective into account.[18] They are therefore able to choose more rational and effective responses to situations, make better decisions, and work more effectively with others. Without emotional Control, individuals are unlikely to consume or use knowledge in an instrumental, logical or rational way.

Individuals with a lower level of Control have been shown to have stronger reactions to higher levels of distress and longer recovery time from stressful events.[19] They have fewer or lower quality relationships[20] and are less likely to reach out for help.[21] They may also adopt negative or less effective coping strategies, such as repeatedly going over a situation in their head or avoiding social support rather than reaching out for help.[22] In today's volatile, uncertain, complex and ambiguous (VUCA) world, we can't predict the future, but we can prepare for it, and choosing to respond, rather than react, is key to the ability to unlock recovery and personal growth from setbacks.

For companies, emotional control is important during times of organisational change or when dealing with difficult employee situations. Workers often look to leaders for examples of how to behave, especially during times of turmoil or ambiguity. Therefore, leaders need to prepare to present a calm, rational front. When leaders have high emotional control, they are seen as more likeable,[23] ethical[24] and working in the interests of the organisation. Good leaders know that emotions play an important role in building a strong operating system. They can be used to frame new events or situations in a positive way. Leaders can express confidence in an individual by showing positive affect towards them. Research shows that leaders who heavily suppress their emotions are less satisfied in their work, are more likely to want to leave their organisation,[25] and can have a negative impact on their direct reports.[26] To be in control of one's emotions is not about suppressing all emotions, but rather consciously choosing which emotions are appropriate in any given situation, and authentically harnessing emotions to garner buy-in and motivation from others.

The recent COVID-19 pandemic has highlighted the importance of emotional control at the collective societal level to enable new ideas and progress to flourish. During this extraordinary time, we have witnessed the emotional toll, panic and trauma that accompanies any crisis. And yet, we've also seen the governmental and collective public response that emphasised the need to foster public trust, offer hope, and cultivate cohesion and compassion to enable society to adapt and rebuild in a calm and rational manner.

The next 25 years will bring radical change that will impact us significantly: inflation, poverty, political instability, social justice, biodiversity, sustainability, human rights, emerging technology – the list goes on. We must be able to understand and shift our emotional reactions and public narratives linked to our underlying hopes, fears, emotions, and pre-existing identities. We must be able to build a voice for the next generation, create a constructive forum for diverse perspectives, and be compassionate towards ourselves and others. At a societal level, the Control pillar of positive resilience is essential for ensuring that we engage in calm and rational productive responses, rather than counter-productive emotionally charged reactions, to weather the challenges of the twenty-first century and deliver progress.

PRP PILLAR 4 – CONNECTEDNESS

Connectedness creates psychological safety, belonging, cohesion, cooperation, and coordination, all achieved through a focus on building and maintaining high quality connections and relationships with others. The ability to find belonging and identity through different roles and support networks allows people to give and receive more meaningful support and endure and succeed through any challenge.

Our research has shown that Connectedness is critical for being able to recognise and leverage the value of strong networks with varying social ties in bringing rich sources of support and guidance, along with the opportunity to be altruistic and make a difference to others. Individuals high in Connectedness feel a strong sense of belonging and actively build and maintain relationships across multiple contexts. In organisations, strong vertical and lateral interconnections across the business, minimise siloed working. It is only in these conditions that mutually beneficial relationships, knowledge sharing, cross-functional thinking, skills development, new ideas and innovation can flourish. All essential building blocks for cultivating new and relevant future capabilities.[27] In an ideas-informed society, knowledge and progress require strong connections across citizens to proliferate and drive change.

The value of connection is seen in all realms of the world. Human beings are social and codependent animals, and studies have shown that deprivation of social interaction can have grave consequences on a person's psychology. Social interaction is not exclusive to humans, as many animal species are known to live in social groups – herds, prides, packs, pods, hives etc. – and the communal benefits for both predators and prey far outweigh living solitary lives. As human beings, our ability to learn and thrive is dependent on the community and eco-system in which we exist.

Individuals who are low in Connectedness may experience feelings of isolation in times of difficulty which only intensifies the experience of stress. They may adopt a more insular style of working which can be self-limiting and can negatively impact their ability to learn effective coping strategies from others. Connectedness is not just about having a support network to draw upon. Helping others through altruism and social behaviour is associated with greater wellbeing, health and longevity, resilience to stress and success.[28] One of the best ways to help ourselves feel more positive is to help someone else.[29]

Connectedness is about both the quality and variety of our relationships. A large amount of research into happiness, wellbeing and resilience over the past 20 years agrees that meaningful close relationships are critical for human flourishing.[30] Those who are strongly socially integrated, having a wide variety of satisfying and meaningful relationships with others, not only have better mental health and a higher sense of wellbeing, but also better physical health.[31]

However, our relationships and experiences at work are not always positive, and workplace cultures do not always support business or employees to flourish. A recent study by Society of Human Resource Management (SHRM)[32] found that toxic workplace cultures are experienced by almost two thirds of working Americans, resulting in a cost of turnover due to poor workplace culture exceeding $223 billion in the US alone. A toxic culture is most commonly characterised by a breakdown in relationships – namely through an absence of open and transparent communication. Organisations simply cannot achieve their goals without employees who are engaged, productive, connected and fulfilled at work. The best people managers engage in active listening techniques, striving to understand their employees and clarifying information as necessary so those employees can better understand the messages being conveyed. Strong workplace cultures often begin with 'values blueprinting' – a candid conversation about beliefs and principles. Once those values are blueprinted, two-way communication remains an important step in identifying what works at work and what doesn't. The best workplace cultures are built on the collaborative partnership of C-suite executives, HR professionals and people managers who bring their own unique perspective and capabilities in the discussion, co-creation and evolution of workplace policies and practices.

More broadly, building and maintaining relationships in multiple areas of life takes effort, but pays dividends when we are struggling.[33] In today's digitally dominated society, colossal portions of our lives our lived online. Technology in all its forms has indisputably changed the world. In the positive, it has provided a lifeline for isolated individuals and provided unpreceded opportunity for boundaryless and rapid transfer of new ideas and information. Social media and technology have connected people personally and professionally, given friends and loved ones another avenue of long-distance contact, and bought people from all corners of the world together in discussion of interests, ideas, debate and advancement of causes. However, in the negative, it has provided an anonymous platform for verbal abuse, peer pressure, and in some domains the digital connection is a poor substitute for physical connect. As organisations navigate increasingly digital and hybrid working experiences, they must focus on nurturing authentic communication and meaningful, positive interactions that produce innovation and growth.

PRP PILLAR 5 – GROWTH

Growth allows people to view uncertainty and adversity as an exciting challenge and opportunity to learn. The ability to reflect upon the situation, then test out reflection by putting learning into practice creates a superior ability to grow from mistakes and use past experiences to develop increasingly adaptive strategies.

Our research has shown that the fifth pillar of positive resilience – Growth – is critical for thriving and surviving. This pillar refers to an individual's inclination to learn from experiences and adopt a growth mindset. Famously coined by Carol Dweck, a growth mindset is the belief that your basic qualities are things that you can cultivate through your efforts, your strategies, and help from others.[34] Individuals with a growth mindset see difficulty and failure as opportunities to learn and develop, not as evidence of fixed inability, and respond by trying harder, experimenting with new idea and methods, and not by giving up.

To be positively resilient to a constantly changing environment we must invest in our curiosity and desire to explore and to learn about ourselves and the world. This idea is incapsulated by the duality of homeostasis, i.e., the self-regulatory process within all cells and organisms that seeks to stability to survive, while on the other hand must adjust and evolve to changing conditions. If homeostasis is successful, life continues. Yet as the environment changes, the mechanisms must adapt to avoid disaster, death and even extinction of the organism.

We found that individuals high in growth embrace learning experimentation and questioning based on a deliberate intent to understand other perspectives and ideas, in addition to implementing formal post-event reviews and self-reflective practices aimed specifically at learning from experience.[35] Leaders that drive a high performance, positive culture create an environment with a thirst for continuous learning and growth because their teams feel safe to take on more challenging tasks, and they take the time to give constructive developmental feedback on an ongoing basis.[36] Attractive cultures promote being curious and an adopting of experimental mindsets. Experiential learning boosts retention scores by 90% and creates a culture that inspires employees to engage with education, development, and innovation.[37] Fulfilling one's talents and potentialities is inherently motivating to us as human beings and continues to be a major cultural factor that employees consider when deciding to stay or go. There is no doubt that investing in building a positive culture with growth mindset at the heart will positively impact organisation's ability to retain and attract high value talent.

The challenge for society and organisations is how they will create the environment that allows individuals to be genuinely curious, open to change and to proactively engage in learning experiences. Our research has found that the crucial difference between success and failure lies in the perception of one's own ability to learn and grow, which drives the desire to do so.[38] The global pandemic has highlighted the societal and individual need and desire for the Growth pillar of positive resilience.

Unprecedented restrictions, setbacks, difficulties, stress, and suffering tested everyone in the world. And yet, while initially some might have embraced the chance to pause and reset, as the pandemic progressed it was clear that people, especially young people, craved positive change and progress, for themselves and the society they live in. Without a doubt, the global pandemic demonstrated the basic human desire to learn and grow; the desire for 'thrive' and 'not just survive'.

As organisations now face into the unprecedented disruption of the fifth industrial revolution, which is dawning upon the world in unforeseeable ways as we increasingly utilise Industry 4.0 technologies including Artificial Intelligence (AI), Big Data (BD), the Internet of Things, digital platforms, augmented and virtual reality, and 3D printing. The upcoming Society 5.0, known as the super-smart society, may be the final bridge between machine and man and is anticipated to change the face of white and blue-collar jobs in unprecedented ways.[39] In preparation, some organisations are responding by investing in the recruitment and development of transferable skills, with growth behaviours at the heart of the strategy, over the more traditional job knowledge and skills paradigm. No matter what happens in the future, it is apparent that this fundamental paradigm shift in technology will require individuals, in any job, in any part of society, to actively engage in learning and Growth behaviours.

PRP PILLAR 6 – COPING

The Coping pillar describes how well we are coping with the pressures of our environment. It includes our ability to find the ideal balance between pressure and performance: our optimal performance zone.

Our research has shown that Coping – our ability to perform at our best – is critical for being able to use stress and pressure as energy to rise up to challenges with added motivation and focus.[40] People high in Coping feel stimulated, engaged, and positively fulfilled by their life and work, and push themselves out of their comfort zone, feeling confident in their ability to cope and perform.

With higher levels of Coping, people will be more likely and more able to engage in the search for progressive ideas and beliefs.

Being busy implies a certain degree of stress, challenge, and pressure. People who are busy are happier and have more meaningful lives than those who aren't.[41] One study found that any kind of stress is a high predictor of a meaningful life,[42] with the most common effects of stress including strength, growth, and resilience.[43] However, to maintain performance in our optimal performance zone, we must all negotiate and balance pressure and performance. There is a clear relationship between the impact of good stress, which elicits healthy and positive reactions, otherwise known as 'eustress'[44] and distress, which elicits unhealthy or negative reactions.

People high in Coping harness their response to pressure to gain a number of benefits: energy to rise to a challenge or deliver sustained performance in flow,[45] motivation to connect with others, and desire to learn and grow.[46] So long as we are not overwhelmed by our 'fight or flight' instincts, we can choose to see the stress we are experiencing as a positive challenge, rather than a threat.

However, if we push ourselves too far, for too long, and the pressure that we experience exceeds our ability to cope, then we can become overburdened, and performance will begin to decrease.[47] This is the overload performance zone. Operating in this zone puts people at risk not only of burnout, ill health, high workforce turnover, absenteeism, lowered morale and reduced efficiency and performance, but also potentially death.[48] Our research shows that people low in Coping may feel overwhelmed and move into this overload performance zone as external pressures increase if they do not build their coping skills and overall Positive Resilience.[49]

As people seek more meaningful work and purpose-driven organisations, our research shows that high performing organisations support people's ability to cope by maintaining a good balance of pressure and performance, where people are challenged and stretched but also supported with adequate resources and safeguards against burnout.[50] Leaders who effectively drive positive cultures are champions of creating the optimal conditions for all their team members to perform productively, cope effectively cope and remain engaged. They understand that this looks different from one individual to the next, regularly check-in and take action to ensure workload is manageable and remains motivating.

In today's increasingly hybrid and remote working world, organisations are facing new challenges in to how they manage and support their employee's work so that is stimulating and stretching yet manageable. Organisations and employees must engage in constructive dialogue and continuous feedback loops. Outside the work environment, we should look for ways to simplify our daily pressures, and focus on activities and hobbies that stimulate, engage, and build confidence.

PRP PILLAR 7 – WELLBEING

Wellbeing refers to the daily habits and strategies that we engage in to maintain physical and mental health and live our lives to the full. It is the ability to build, maintain and restore our reserves of energy that allows us to dig deeper, renew and rejuvenate from setback and challenge.

Our research shows that one of the most effective approaches to building Positive Resilience is to engage in healthy habits around sleep, eating and exercise.[51] People high in Wellbeing are typically able to respond effectively to stressful situations, using proactive mental and physical wellbeing strategies to build energy and psychological strength. Like hibernating animals and plants in nature, human beings need to maintain and build the optimal physical and mental conditions to maintain and restore our fragile but precious sense of life. To realise an ideas-informed society, Wellbeing will be critical. Without strong physical and mental health, while citizens may be more likely to benefit, they are also less likely to be able to engage with new ideas, make smarter decisions and choices, and adopt more progressive beliefs and norms.

In today's fast paced world, we often underestimate the impact of our bodily state on our mental functioning. We may try to handle our busy lives by sleeping less. Unfortunately, this is highly counter-productive, as it results in less effective decision making, lower creativity, negative moods, lower work engagement, higher unethical behaviour, and lower performance, not to mention more obesity, greater risk for coronary heart disease and higher risks of injury, motor vehicle crashes and early death.[52]

The cost for society and organisations is clear. In 2020–2021, approximately 822,000 UK workers were affected by work-related stress, depression or anxiety, accounting for 50% of all work-related ill health.[53] The costs of poor mental health in the UK workplace are estimated at £45 billion, with £7 billion in absence costs, £27bn in presenteeism and £9bn in turnover costs.[54]

The key idea – that Wellbeing as a pillar of positive resilience offers opportunity for us to reach our full potential for both happiness and success – is gaining momentum. Now, more than ever before, people are investing in their own wellbeing. Recent Global Wellness Institute[55] research published in 2021 reveals the wellness market grew to a record $4.9 trillion in 2019, up from $4.3 trillion in 2017, and predicted to reach $7 trillion by 2025, fuelled by the pandemic and a shift in societal values and behaviours.

In organisations, employees increasingly expect wellbeing to be integrated not the DNA of organisational life. Our research has found that successful organisations have personal accounts of team members that attest to genuinely believing that their manager cares about and successfully supports their wellbeing as well as role models a healthy work-life balance.[56] This creates a positive environment that nurtures a culture of self-care, where everyone is encouraged to engage in healthy habits and coping strategies and look after their physical and psychological wellbeing. Gone are the days of generic employee assistance and benefits programmes. Organisations at the vanguard are investing in bespoke wellbeing programmes that truly make a difference and measure wellbeing as a KPI reported alongside financial, performance and customer metrics.

Prioritising employee wellbeing creates a positive workplace culture and reinforces employee satisfaction and loyalty. It's also good for business. Without a positive organisational culture businesses will inevitably struggle to effectively build, attract, and retain the future capabilities they need to fare well in the decade to come. By integrating true wellbeing programmes, organisations will enjoy competitive edge not only in the war for talent, but also to creating a positive culture that fosters employees' ability to cope optimally, with a sense of holistic wellbeing and ability to deliver marginal gains and step-change in innovation and performance.

At a societal level, the UK government has announced £500 million investment in mental health recovery plan as part of the wider government agenda to build back better from the pandemic and ensure everyone is able to access the support, they need.[57]

Reactive measures are no longer enough. As a society and collective of responsible individuals and organisations, we must acknowledge and take action to encourage engagement in daily healthy habits that form the foundation of maintaining mental and physical health so that we can embrace volatility to catalyse positive change, new ideas and new opportunities.

GAINS FOR INDIVIDUALS, GOVERNMENTS AND SOCIETY

Our research has recognised that Positive Resilience is not just about individuals and their ability to maintain a proactive positive change mindset that allows to actually bounce forward and grow from challenging circumstances. Moreover, building a strong operating system of Positive Resilience is essential for organisations and society as a whole. To make the ideas-informed society a reality within this volatile world, we need citizens and communities to utilise the 7 Pillars of Positive Resilience.

Understanding an individual's culture, context, and the families, organisations, and communities within which they live and work, forms the backdrop to developing the right environments with the right resources and mechanisms where people embrace new ideas to thrive, not just survive. Being deliberate and persistent in creating the 7 Pillars of Positive Resilience will produce innovation and growth and contribute to creating a more ideas led society.

Peoplewise coined the term 'Collective Positive Resilience' to describe a resilience strategy that influences the whole ecosystem towards delivering top quartile performance, high wellbeing, and high engagement. Collective positive resilience is defined as '...the cooperative determination and bonds that bind groups together, and facilitates recovery, adaptation and growth from adversity, threat and challenge'. The 7 Pillars of Positive Resilience represent 7 factors that together create an operating system, be it personal, organisational, or societal, that is characterised by delivering positive change. This psychological mechanism is at the heart of realising the benefits of an ideas-informed society. It involves everyone working together towards a common purpose with shared values and goals, developing strong relationships of mutual trust and psychological safety, a sense of collective efficacy, effective processes for the group to handle conflict and a broad optimistic outlook.

The combination of the impact of the global pandemic on working patterns, alongside the resulting economic downturn and serious threats to many industry sectors has underlined the need for organisations to focus on building out positive organisational cultures to positively adapt to change. In aspiring towards an ideas-informed workplace environment, creating positive cultures will provide businesses with the capacity to be forward looking, open to new ideas, reinventive with their business strategies and models, and highly adaptive to deliver the change that will inevitably be needed over the next decade. The 7 Pillars of Positive Resilience will enable organisations to successfully build positive cultures, with ideas-informed philosophy at the heart, to allow organisations to thrive and progress within our volatile, uncertain, complex and ambiguous (VUCA) world.

Organisations with the foresight to invest in building an ideas-informed community will gain huge opportunity to realise sustained performance and long-term competitive advantage whatever adversities, challenges, and setbacks arise. By utilising the 7 Pillars of Positive Resilience, workplaces can create cultures and strategies that will deliver long-term financial viability, high performance, growth and employee engagement and satisfaction.

At societal level, the role of government is to protect, serve and progress. In today's volatile world, governments are under increased pressure to act quickly and at scale. By reimagining how they work and investing in the infrastructure that align to the key principles of the 7 Pillars of Positive Resilience, they can create positively resilient societies and public services that actively and critical engage with new ideas, make smarter decisions and choices, and adopt more progressive beliefs and norms. By utilising the psychological mechanisms of the 7 Pillars of Positive Resilience, individuals, organisations and societies will ensure that they can make the ideals of the ideas-informed society a reality and be fit for purpose for the next decade and beyond.

REFERENCES

1. Board, B., & Brown, J. (2010). Barriers and enablers to returning to work from long term sickness absence: Part 1-A Quantitative Perspective. *American Journal of Industrial Medicine*, *1*, 1–19.
   Feeney, B. C., & Collins, N. L. (2015). A new look at social support: A theoretical perspective on thriving through relationships. In *Personality and Social Psychology Review* (Vol. 19, Issue 2).
   Jayawickreme, E., & Blackie, L. E. R. (2014). Post-traumatic growth as positive personality change: Evidence, controversies, and future directions. *European Journal of Personality*, *28*(4), 312–331.
   Jayawickreme, E., Infurna, F. J., Alajak, K., Blackie, L. E. R., Chopik, W. J., Chung, J. M., Dorfman, A., Fleeson, W., Forgeard, M. J. C., Frazier, P., Furr, R. M., Grossmann, I., Heller, A. S., Laceulle, O. M., Lucas, R. E., Luhmann, M., Luong, G., Meijer, L., Mclean, K. C., ... Zonneveld, R. (2021). *Post-traumatic growth as positive personality change: Challenges, opportunities, and recommendations. August 2020*, 145–165.
   Kashdan, T. B., & Kane, J. Q. (2011). Post-traumatic distress and the presence of post-traumatic growth and meaning in life: Experiential avoidance as a moderator. *Personality and Individual Differences*, *50*(1), 84–89.
   Tedeschi, R. G., & Calhoun, L. G. (2004). Posttraumatic growth: Conceptual foundations and empirical evidence. In *Psychological Inquiry* (Vol. 15, Issue 1, pp. 1–18). Routledge.

Tedeschi, R. G., Shakespeare-Finch, J., Taku, K., & Calhoun, L. G. (2018). *Posttraumatic growth: Theory, research, and applications.* Routledge.

2. Chmitorz, A., Kunzler, A. M., Helmreich, I., Tüscher, O., Kalisch, R., Kubiak, T., Wessa, M., & Lieb, K. (2018). Intervention studies to foster resilience – A systematic review and proposal for a resilience framework in future intervention studies. *Clinical Psychology Review, 59,* 78–100.

Masten, A. S., & Barnes, A. (2018). Resilience in Children: Developmental Perspectives. *Children, 5*(7), 98.

Southwick, S. M., Bonanno, G. A., Masten, A. S., Panter-Brick, C., & Yehuda, R. (2014). Resilience definitions, theory, and challenges: Interdisciplinary perspectives. *European Journal of Psychotraumatology, 5.*

Southwick, S. M., & Charney, D. S. (2018). *Resilience: The science of mastering life's greatest challenges* (2nd Editio). Cambridge University Press.

Wu, G., Feder, A., Cohen, H., Kim, J. J., Calderon, S., Charney, D. S., & Mathé, A. A. (2013). Understanding resilience. Frontiers in Behavioral Neuroscience, 7(January 2013).

3. Board, B., Adcock, N., & Hancock, R. (2021). 7 Pillars of Positive Resilience: Realising happiness and success. White paper.

4. Cohen, A. (2021). 'How to quit your job in the great post-pandemic resignation boom', Bloomberg Businessweek, available at: www.bloomberg.com/news/articles/2021-05-10/quit-your-job-how-toresign-after-covid-pandemic.

5. Wespire (2021). The 2021 State of Employee Engagement. White paper.

6. Smith, E. E. (2017). The power of meaning: Crafting a life that matters. Random House.

7. Board, B., & Brown, J. (2010). Barriers and enablers to returning to work from long term sickness absence: Part 1-A Quantitative Perspective. *American Journal of Industrial Medicine, 1,* 1–19.

8. Board, B., & Brown, J. (2010). Barriers and enablers to returning to work from long term sickness absence: Part 1-A

Quantitative Perspective. *American Journal of Industrial Medicine*, 1, 1–19.

9. Sharot, T. (2012). The Optimism Bias: Why we're wired to look on the bright side. Hachette UK.

10. Hernandez, R., Kershaw, K. N., Siddique, J., Boehm, J. K., Kubzansky, L. D., Diez-Roux, A., ... & Lloyd-Jones, D. M. (2015). Optimism and cardiovascular health: multi-ethnic study of atherosclerosis (MESA). *Health Behavior and Policy Review*, 2(1), 62–73.

11. Carver, C. S., Scheier, M. F., & Segerstrom, S. C. (2010). Optimism. In *Clinical Psychology Review* (Vol. 30, Issue 7, pp. 879–889).
Seligman, M. E. P. (2006). *Learned Optimism*. Vintage Books.

12. Kappes, A., and Oettingen, G. The emergence of goal pursuit: Mental contrasting connects future and reality. *Journal of Experimental Social Psychology*, 54(2014), 25–39.

13. Board, B., & Brown, J. (2010). Barriers and enablers to returning to work from long term sickness absence: Part 1-A Quantitative Perspective. *American Journal of Industrial Medicine*, 1, 1–19.

14. Seligman, M. E. P. (2006). *Learned Optimism*. Vintage Books.

15. Luthans, F., Avolio, B. J., Avey, J. B., & Norman, S. M. (2007). Positive psychological capital: Measurement and relationship with performance and satisfaction. *Personnel Psychology*, 60(3), 541–572.

16. UN Refugee Agency (UNHCR); UNHCR Global Trends 2021. UNHCR – Figures at a Glance.

17. Ellis, B. H., Winer, J. P., Murray, K., & Barrett, C. (2019). Understanding the mental health of refugees: Trauma, stress, and the cultural context. In *The Massachusetts General Hospital textbook on diversity and cultural sensitivity in mental health*, 253–273.

18. Board, B., Adcock, N., & Hancock, R. (2021). 7 Pillars of Positive Resilience: Realising happiness and success. White paper.

19. Armstrong, A. R., Galligan, R. F., & Critchley, C. R. (2011). Emotional intelligence and psychological resilience to negative

life events. *Personality and Individual Differences*, *51*(3), 331–336.

20. Brackett, M. A., Rivers, S. E., & Salovey, P. (2011). Emotional intelligence: Implications for personal, social, academic, and workplace success. *Social and Personality Psychology Compass*, *5*(1), 88–103.

21. Armstrong, A. R., Galligan, R. F., & Critchley, C. R. (2011). Emotional intelligence and psychological resilience to negative life events. *Personality and Individual Differences*, *51*(3), 331–336.

22. Salovey, P., Bedell, B. T., Detweiler, J. B., & Mayer, J. D. (1999). Coping intelligently: Emotional intelligence and the coping process. In C. R. Snyder (Ed.), *Coping: The psychology of what works* (pp. 141–164).

23. Nelson, P. D. (1964). Similarities and differences among leaders and followers. *The Journal of Social Psychology*, *63*(1), 161–167.

24. Kalshoven, K., Den Hartog, D. N., & De Hoogh, A. H. B. (2011). Ethical leader behavior and Big Five factors of personality. *Journal of Business Ethics, 100*, 349–366.

25. Côté, S., & Morgan, L. M. (2002). A longitudinal analysis of the association between emotion regulation, job satisfaction, and intentions to quit. *Journal of Organizational Behavior, 23*, 947–962.

26. Kafetsios, K., Nezlek, J. B., & Vassilakou, T. (2012). Relationships between leaders' and subordinates' emotion regulation and satisfaction and affect at work. *The Journal of Social Psychology, 152*, 436–457.

27. Board, B., & Brown, J. (2021). Barriers and enablers to returning to work from long term sickness absence: Part 1-A Quantitative Perspective. *American Journal of Industrial Medicine, 1*, 1–19.

28. Curry, O. S., Rowland, L. A., Van Lissa, C. J., Zlotowitz, S., McAlaney, J., & Whitehouse, H. (2018). Happy to help? A systematic review and meta-analysis of the effects of performing acts of kindness on the well-being of the actor. *Journal of Experimental Social Psychology, 76*, 320–329.

29. Ko, K., Margolis, S., Revord, J., & Lyubomirsky, S. (2019). Comparing the effects of performing and recalling acts of kindness. *The Journal of Positive Psychology*, 1–9.

30. Feeney, B. C., & Collins, N. L. (2015). A new look at social support: A theoretical perspective on thriving through relationships. In *Personality and Social Psychology Review* (Vol. 19, Issue 2).

31. Holt-Lunstad, J., & Smith, T. B. (2012). Social relationships and mortality. *Social and Personality Psychology Compass*, 6(1), 41–53.

32. Society for Human Resource Management (SHRM). The high cost of a toxic workplace culture. How culture impacts the workforce – and the bottom line.

33. Southwick, S. M., & Charney, D. S. (2018). *Resilience: The science of mastering life's greatest challenges* (2nd Editio). Cambridge University Press.

34. Dweck, C. S. (2017). *Mindset* (Updated). Robinson.

35. Board, B., & Brown, J. (2010). Barriers and enablers to returning to work from long term sickness absence: Part 1-A Quantitative Perspective. *American Journal of Industrial Medicine*, 1, 1–19.

36. Board, B., Adcock, N., & Hancock, R. (2021). 7 Pillars of Positive Resilience: Realising happiness and success. White paper.

37. Board, B., Adcock, N., & Hancock, R. (2021). 7 Pillars of Positive Resilience: Realising happiness and success. White paper.

38. Board, B., Adcock, N., & Hancock, R. (2021). 7 Pillars of Positive Resilience: Realising happiness and success. White paper.

39. Sarfraz, Z., Sarfraz, A., Iftikar, H. M., & Akhund, R. (2021). Is COVID-19 pushing us to the fifth industrial revolution (society 5.0)? *Pakistan Journal of Medical Sciences*, 37(2), 591.

40. Board, B., & Brown, J. (2010). Barriers and enablers to returning to work from long term sickness absence: Part 1-A Quantitative Perspective. *American Journal of Industrial Medicine*, 1, 1–19.

41. McGonigal, K. (2015). *The upside of stress: Why stress is good for you, and how to get good at it.* Vermilion.

42. Baumeister, R. F., Vohs, K. D., Aaker, J. L., & Garbinsky, E. N. (2013). Some key differences between a happy life and a meaningful life. *Journal of Positive Psychology,* 8(6), 505–516.

43. McGonigal, K. (2015). *The upside of stress: Why stress is good for you, and how to get good at it.* Vermilion.

44. Kupriyanov, R. V, Sholokhov, M. A., Kupriyanov, R., & Zhdanov, R. (2014). The Eustress Concept: Problems and Outlooks. *World Journal of Medical Sciences,* 11(2), 179–185.

45. Nakamura, J., & Csikszentmihalyi, M. (2020). The experience of flow: Theory and research. In C. R. Snyder, S. J. Lopez, L. M. Edwards, & S. C. Marques (Eds.), *The Oxford Handbook of Positive Psychology, 3rd Edition* (pp. 279–296). Oxford University Press.

46. McGonigal, K. (2015). *The upside of stress: Why stress is good for you, and how to get good at it.* Vermilion.

47. Nelson, D. L., & Simmons, B. L. (2004). Health psychology and work stress: A more positive approach. In J. C. Quick & L. E. Tetrick (Eds.), *Handbook of occupational health psychology* (pp. 97–119). American Psychological Association.

48. Hannigan, B., Edwards, D., & Burnard, P. (2004). Stress and stress management in clinical psychology: Findings from a systematic review. *Journal of Mental Health,* 13(3), 235–245. O'Connor, D. B., Thayer, J. F., & Vedhara, K. (2021). Stress and Health: A Review of Psychobiological Processes. *Annual Review of Psychology,* 72(1), 663–688.

49. Board, B., Adcock, N., & Hancock, R. (2021). 7 Pillars of Positive Resilience: Realising happiness and success. White paper.

50. Board, B., Adcock, N., & Hancock, R. (2021). 7 Pillars of Positive Resilience: Realising happiness and success. White paper.

51. Board, B., Adcock, N., & Hancock, R. (2021). 7 Pillars of Positive Resilience: Realising happiness and success. White paper.

52. Barnes, C. M., & Drake, C. L. (2015). Prioritizing Sleep Health: Public Health Policy Recommendations. *Perspectives on Psychological Science, 10*(6), 733–737.

53. ONS. Personal well-being in the UK QMI Newport: Office for National Statistics. 2016.

54. Deloitte (2020). Mental health and employers. Refreshing the case for investment.

55. Global Wellness Institute (2021). The Global Wellness Economy: Looking Beyond Covid.

56. Board, B., Adcock, N., & Hancock, R. (2021). 7 Pillars of Positive Resilience: Realising happiness and success. White paper.

57. UK Department of Health and Social Care. Mental health recovery plan backed by £500 million. Press release [Published 27 March 2021].

18

AS WE SIT IN THE IN-BETWEEN

Benjamin Freud and Charlotte Hankin

THE AGE OF NUMBERS

This is the age of numbers, big and small. Some big numbers are unimaginably big: by 2025, it is estimated that we will generate 463 exabytes of data every day. (An exabyte is 2 to the 60th power bytes.) We are approaching the rate at which the volume of human knowledge will double every 12 hours. Just to put that in perspective, at the turn of the twentieth century, human knowledge was doubling every 100 years. The really big numbers are made up of tiny numbers; binary digits of 1's and 0's. Some numbers are getting smaller, like the years we have left before we can reverse climate breakdown.

Other numbers need to become smaller: from 4°C to 1.5°C or even 0°C. Then there are two small numbers that are gigantic numbers: 4 and 6 – the Fourth Industrial Revolution and the Sixth Mass Extinction. This is the age of numbers, when species die out at 100 to 1,000 the speed of the normal extinction rate, when 69% of wildlife populations disappears in 52 years. This is the age of infinite possibilities in tension with the only one viable (literally) path for the human species: appreciating that we are all in this together so that we may reverse climate breakdown.

WE ARE ALL IN THIS TOGETHER

No matter our backgrounds, no matter how we identify, where we find ourselves in this moment, we are all in this together. Despite some still denying climate breakdown, while others are too far removed from the scientific discourse because they have more pressing needs to survive in the right now, we are all in this together. Climate breakdown is the one thing that today connects all humans to all other living things. It is our collective story, written every time we experience extreme climate events as well as banal ones – and it feels like what was once extreme is now banal. It's our collective story, yet too often the voices of the Global North monopolise the mic and we can't hear those of the Global South. Their extremes are too often whispers in the media.

This sense that we are all in this together won't only come from information at our disposal. We have all the information we need. We have too much information. For this first time in history, we have a problem of information over-abundance rather than scarcity. An ideas-informed society is made up of individuals who sift through ideas, not by looking for some objective standard – there is none – or waving everything off as relativism – that is a trick of prestidigitation – but by responding to conditions through the ideas. Ideas are not Platonic ideals, they are unfinished pieces of clay that we manipulate together no tricks allowed. We are all in this together even when past ideas have cultivated separateness. To give a new twist to Albert Einstein's quote, the ideas that have led us to the brink of climate breakdown will not reverse it. In the twenty-first century, an ideas-informed society is a society with new ideas and new ways of living them, together.

FUGITIVES AND SANCTUARY

This is a time of change, non-linear change. It always has been, really, but this is one of those rare liminal moments in history when what we thought we knew no longer holds. What was heads is tails and tails is heads, and both at once. Rather than fight to keep the familiar, we must flee, flee so we can find a place to sit, far away.

This flight from the familiar, this escape from the dominant narrative is also the story of the fugitive. These times require from us the courage to escape the pull, to be fugitives and provide sanctuary to other fugitives.[i] These times require us to find sanity by dispelling the illusion that what is has always been, by breaking the effigy of staticness. This is the time to write many narratives, fleeing from any dominance.

In sanctuary there is the opportunity to sit and imagine. The imagining we have in the now, born of the experiences of the past, channels the energy to bring about the futures. Past, present and future entangled into one as the discourse we employ places boundaries on what might emerge. This draws on the idea of complementarity in quantum physics: the worlds are full of probabilities, but which will be realized dependent on how we measure them (*measure* in its etymological sense of ascertaining dimensions, limiting). We are more than responsible for our choices, as the existentialists had us believe, operating as separate beings condemned to be free.[ii] We are response-able for the cuts we make in the universe to create the assemblages of which we are part, within which we intra-act with the worlds, within which we are not the solid in the centre but the liquid that swirls in the non-permanent container through which, in that moment, we choose to regard reality. In other words, our ethics are the ways in which we decide what matters and what doesn't, what to respond to and what not to ignore. Our ethics are what we leave out, not what we leave in.

When we become conscious of what we leave out, why we leave out, we nurture the soil for an ideas-informed society to thrive. When we cultivate our response-ability, we appreciate that we are all in this together and ideas are no longer things we come up with in our heads, but embodied fields within which we all find ourselves. Post-truth has no place in our communion. We don't all have to agree, but we come to care, because we are all in this together. Information emerges as the in-formation of a collective.

Because these are times for urgency and for slowing down, together.

---

[i] Terms and notions I take from Bayo Akomolafe.
[ii] Jean-Paul Sartre, 'Existentialism Is a Humanism'.

Back to the 4 and the 6: the collapse of spacetime and matter no longer belongs to the realm of theoretical physics. It has become our everyday reality emerging from technology and species extinction, connected, among other things, by climate breakdown. This moment that exists here with all of us is between the 4th and 6th, between an Industrial Revolution that blurs the line between life and technology, and mass extinctions that draw lines between life and death. We find sanctuary in between blurred and fresh lines. It is here that we can witness the stories of our connections and relationships, of the fluidity of who we are, of who *we* are as relational becomings – no longer distinguished or distinguishable as individuals or as categories, but rather as possibilities (probabilities?), as events that are, were and have yet to become. Let us sit in this space, in this moment, and find ways to rework the suffering into affirmative becomings, into regenerative ecologies.

As we sit here, we discover we now have the power of teleportation, we can even be in several places at once. Our experience of quantum superposition is the new reality. How else would you describe logging onto a Zoom call where your face and voice appear on four continents at the same time? You are in an office in Buenos Aires, a living room in Leeds, a café in Yokohama and a park in Minneapolis. All at once. When we are in many places at once, we must make sure that we don't get lost or that we don't get caught in the paradox of travelling vast distances but remaining trapped in the smallest of echo chambers. An ideas-informed society is one of refuge from the noise, not from the plurality of voices and the listening of open hearts.

THE NEW VISTAS OF DIGITAL TECHNOLOGY

There is no distinction between the digital world and the real world. We have a symbiotic relationship with digital technology: we have come to depend on it for recommendations, directions, collaboration, creations, information, communication, flirtations, disseminations, procuration, alimentation, relaxation and incarnation. The next time you sit on a bus, a train, in a waiting room or at a coffee shop, note how many shoulders are hunched, necks long, eyes captives of the screen. Those embodied subjects you see are immersed in the digital reality that is simply reality. There is nothing not real about the marks we leave through our interactions – nay our intra-actions – with our devices: information exchange and knowledge production in different forms. More to the point, how is my conversation with you on Zoom, perhaps separated by an ocean and half a continent, not real even if your face and voice come to me in reconstructed 1's and 0's? How is my ability to share my reaction to your words with a funny little yellow face drawing not expressive? How is the music Siri selects for you thanks to its algorithm not somehow a part of you?

We have the power of teleportation and we will need it, because the age of transportation is ending. Leave that to the second half of the previous millennium. Trade, travel and traffic will have to be reconceptualised, reengineered and relived. The planet cannot sustain the carbon byproducts of a neoliberal globalised order, or rather, the kind of planet we want cannot, for the planet will outlive all homo sapiens no matter how we respond to *our* crisis of climate, not the planet's. We are not trying to save the planet, we are trying to save ourselves and perhaps even millions of non-human species; this is a noble enough endeavour. We may have the power to teleport, but so do events many thousands of kilometres away. They land on our doorsteps as floods, fires and pandemics.

CONFRONTING CHOICES

As spacetime melts away, we draw new maps as we notice the new landscapes in the gap between the 4th and the 6th. We notice that we are entangled in these landscapes and that we shift along with them, that the maps we use are as useful as they are useless. The map is not the territory, in the words of Alfred Korzybski, and we realize that when we give primacy to relationships and not to entities, the markings on the map – those representations – will always be secondary.[iii] How can you capture the flow of a river? How can you observe it when you are the river?

[iii]Alfred Korzybski, *Science and Sanity*.

As we start to come down from this vantage point, we ask ourselves what we might find in the valley below, what this might mean for us, not as individuals nor as humans, but as members of the biocollective – every living thing that has an interest in the healthfulness of the planet. We find that we now live in the strangeness of the new reality, one that has infinite perspectives as we abandon the self, that representation that we held dear, and turn to the interconnectedness of all things. When we live in the in-between, in between the 4th and the 6th, in between moments and epochs, in between what is 'you' and what is 'I', we become because we no longer hold onto the static being. We appreciate that society is not the sum of individual parts but the networks that connect, the information that travels between us, which is dynamic and responsive.

When we arrive in the valley we confront the choices we make – nay the responses we have – when faced with the enfolding of the digital and the physical into one reality, the understanding that there is no longer (has there ever been?) a difference between our inter/intra-actions with the digital and our interactions with the analogue. Both create assemblages, all of which are moveable and moving, both leave marks on us and the world, both are worldly. If the Fourth Industrial Revolution melds the digital and the analogue, what will be our response? Will we resist this as so many genera-tions of resistors to technology have tried to hold back the flow? Or will we use our energy to direct the flow?

When we arrive in the valley we confront our responses con-cerning how to redirect our patterns of production, consumption and relations to bring about ways of organising that do not violate the planetary boundaries and maybe even move us towards life-affirming mindsets that are regenerative, where love for, of and with life fuse into one guiding star. What would it take to move towards this civilization? How will we reconsider humans and non-humans both as our kin? How will we gain a different appreciation of *we*? What will our society look like if we extend it to non-humans and the more-than-human? How will our ideas lead to new in-formation?

When we can travel at fibre optic speeds, we extend our horizons into the infinite. There is nowhere in spacetime we cannot reach, so long as there is a connection to data and someone has generated the code to gain access (in this case, I mean the software and hardware). Yet when temperatures rise at faster than geological speeds, we must narrow our horizons to the local. We recreate (bio-)regional economies of production and consumption and rekindle our relationships with life around us. In the gap between 4th and 6th, we sit in two spacetimes at once: the fantastically infinite and the primordially finite.

USING TECHNOLOGY TO HELP US NURTURE AND FLOURISH

Let's satisfy the wanderlust for people, places and ideas by taking advantage of digital technologies. Let's go to all these places at once and listen to voices from all over the world, sharing ourselves in festivals of exchange. Let's put on our headsets and walk through the halls of the Louvre as our physical bodies are left at home. Let's be the first people to have to grapple with the problem of overabundance of information rather than its scarcity.

Let's live the good life by appreciating all that is around us rather than seeking to fill it with all this stuff from far away. Let's grow food locally and become friends with our neighbours (all those life forms above and below land). Let's make things here and not way over there, and just make less of it. Let's have more conversations about what matters in this part of the world, always with an eye to the distant, but seldom do we physically displace ourselves.

We leave fewer footprints when we don't journey far with our physical bodies and journey farther with our digital ones.[iv] We can eat an apple grown in the orchard 5,000 m down the road while conversing with someone's digital form 5,000 km away. We can get to know the birds that fill our ears with song by stepping outside as well as stepping into the Metaverse. What we cannot do is keep up this pace of physical trade, travel and traffic nor the price paid by consumption, convenience and conspicuousness.

[iv]Of course, we will have to build to figure out how sustainable data farming as the digital sector generates more greenhouse gases than the aviation sector.

We aren't looking for a techno-solution. There are none. We are looking for techno-means. We are looking to use technology in ways that help the biocollective thrive, without the hierarchy of progress, the values of shinier is better. Technology is a means – whether it's a pruner or a processor – to enrich, to care for, to nurture. Technology not just as a means to provide for our unfettered desires, rather one that allows us all to live well, as a biocollective. We respond to the world through love for the many worlds we inhabit, all connected in the web of life.

We aren't looking to live in caves huddled around a fire either. We find ways to feed the *we* and not the *I*, appreciating we are of nature, entangled within that web and that pulling on one strand of silk, it will be vibrate throughout. We live well, comfortably, with joy and satiation, not gluttony. We value relationships over things. We value the *we* and the *I* equally because they are the same. We value regeneration over extraction.

RIPPLES AND WAVES

What will it take for a world to emerge that is connected to the infinite and to the finite, this cosmolocalism in which we make use of our powers of teleportation to connect with those far away and self-organise to reconnect with those within touch? It will take courage, moral courage. It will take each one of us to make a ripple, so that the many ripples we each make amplify into a wave, and then a tsunami. It will take courage to tell another story, to create another narrative. It will take courage to stand up, stand out and stand alone. But we will not be alone. Our story is the stories of many, the stories of those who want to thrive, who want to find abundance not in things but in relationships, *with* interconnections.

We have the courage to be fugitives of a narrative of extraction and separation. We run, we hide, we find each other in between the 4th and the 6th, where spacetime collapses and we start anew, but not anew. We take what we can carry and no more, but we do not carry alone. We carry these stories with us and stay with the trouble.

PART 4

EDUCATION AND EMPOWERING YOUNG PEOPLE

19

IDEAS-INFORMED? – IDEAS ARE NOT ENOUGH!

Valerie Hannon and Anthony Mackay AM

CRISIS IN EDUCATION AND THE NEED FOR TRANSFORMATION

There is today a disconnect between our mass education systems and the new world of disruption and hyperchange that confronts us. It is becoming more apparent, and more deeply concerning. Whilst we live now in an age of unbelievably rapid technological advance, we increasingly fear losing control over it. We create the power of Artificial Intelligence but deeply fear the unintended consequences. We know that profound job disruption is coming, but cannot quite discern the contours. Unanticipated conflict and violence disfigure our world, disrupt supply chains and further deepen inequality. We recognise the power of pandemics to upend our lives, and wonder what the next one will be and whether we will survive it. Yet a further indicator of the new phase into which humanity has entered is contestation around what constitutes truth or factual knowledge. Above all, we have failed to act collectively to control the climate emergency, and know that the next radical, destructive shift in the condition of the planet may be just a butterfly's wingbeat away.

Yet how have education systems adapted to acknowledge this new reality? The answer is: hardly at all. The paradigm for education has remained largely unchanged. The challenge for too many education systems is that they have not recognised the implications of this new phase of human existence for their own purpose – and therefore for what and how children learn.

Many international bodies are leading the call for a radical rethink of the purposes, values, practices and intended outcomes of public education systems.[1] In September 2022, for the first time, the UN convened a summit[2] on The Transformation of Education – transformation, not improvement or reform. The vision statement[3] of the Secretary General is apposite here:

> *The crisis in education requires us to fundamentally rethink its purpose and curricula...*
>
> *In a world of rising tensions, fraying trust and existential environmental crises, education must help us not only to live better with each other, but also with nature ... Young people are also keenly aware that humanity faces existential threats in the form of the triple planetary crisis: climate change, pollution and biodiversity. Throughout the Summit process, they made clear that they want to know more about these issues and to become part of the solution.*
>
> *... Education transformation requires the collective commitment and action of visionary political leaders at all levels, parents, students, teachers and the public at large.*
>
> Antonio Guterres

One dimension of this initiative is to bring education into a new relationship with the economy and work in an AI-driven, hyper-connected age. However, there are other equally or more important dimensions:

- creating a generation that can pursue and maintain planetary survival;

- education to achieve more equitable societies; and

- learning that enables young people to discover who they are, what their purposes are, and to exercise agency.

The transformation required goes beyond ideas. For sure, ideas are needed now more than ever, enabling us to reframe the past, envisage our futures and apply imagination to the challenges and opportunities those potential futures hold; but ideas are not enough. Some of the most despotic, revolting periods of history have been characterised by societies being gripped by a set of powerful ideas skilfully promoted by authoritarian leaders.

SO WHAT MORE IS NEEDED?

Now more than ever, young people need the capacity to evaluate competing ideas, and to apply a set of values to them that tend – in the 'long arc of the moral universe' (to use Martin Luther King's phrase) – towards justice: environmental, societal and racial, and personal. Also, crucially, they need educational experiences that equip them to acquire the courage to shape what lies ahead. Moreover, it is important that they acquire competencies beyond the cognitive. In addition, our societies surely need to be infused with levels of emotional intelligence sadly lacking in both public and private life. The lamentable state of politics in many jurisdictions attests to the former. Multiple sources of data give evidence of the latter: societies are facing ever rising rates of depression, anxiety and other emotional states that are beyond the reach of ideas.

A vision of a transformed education is thankfully taking shape in many contexts.[4] For it to gain traction and accelerate, however, it depends upon leadership of a completely new order – that is the key lever to create the future that humanity needs.

Leadership is the key ingredient. The importance of leadership is starkly revealed when people face objective threats and dangers; when old ways of working are no longer viable. Thus the major management consultancies and leadership thinkers in business have turned their attention to the implications of these tumultuous shifts.[5]

The literature on educational leadership is vast; but writers, scholars and activists increasingly recognise the crucial importance of a vision for a transformed education system, reflecting a judicious mix of bold new ideas and powerful old ones.

The powerful ideas of the last decade incorporate multiple insights, fundamentally highlighting the human dimensions of leadership. Perhaps these may be captured as

- the emphasis on education leaders as leaders of learning, and as *learners,*

- the notion that leadership must be inclusive, distributed and co-creative,

- a focus on personal qualities such as honesty, authenticity and humility,

- leadership needing to demonstrate moral integrity and

- underpinning social-emotional competencies, such as empathy.

These are qualities easily described, yet acquired and exercised only with great effort.

However, in addition, the predicament humanity now faces demands leadership of a different order, and is the subject of this chapter.

Such leadership will require both internal and external change.

The external change entails a political shift in which legitimacy flows from authentic stakeholder engagement. A new politics entails new concepts of participative democracy, of community action and the power of networking.[6]

The internal changes demanded of leaders call for the authorising of self. System change is related to self-change. Authentic, powerful leadership emerges from leading oneself, ahead of seeking to lead others. Alongside this, humility and courage are required to lead in a direction that counters vested interests, apathy, outdated world views and fear.[7]

NEW MODELS FOR LEADERSHIP IN EDUCATION

If leadership is key, what are the forms of specifically *education* leadership that are needed for the future? We discern five directions that will distinguish the new breed of leaders the situation requires.[8] This will be leadership that

1. mobilises new voices to craft a fresh narrative – to create a collective story focused on learning for the purpose of human and planetary thriving,

2. reframes and reprioritises equity as a fundamental dimension of liveable, just futures,

3. engages entire ecosystems in pursuit of powerful ideas-led, values-driven learning,

4. commits to and manages responsible experimentation and innovation and

5. is 'futures literate' and enables others to become so.

Leadership for a New Narrative

Genuine transformation of education depends on the creation of a new public narrative – one that locates learning in a wider societal context. Without it, the pervasiveness of the old narrative remains hidden – how it permeates thinking and assumptions. The old paradigm of learning is locked in through a tacit narrative of 'success'. One current dictionary[9] defines success as wealth, fame and power. This does reflect a widespread view. A new narrative about the purpose of learning – one which is expansive, informed and profoundly moral – is now the central business of leaders. We think the concept of thriving offers a fertile way forward. There is not space here fully to outline the key features of the new narrative for education that is adequate for the times: indeed, part of what we urge is a free and fresh debate about this. However, surely the outlines are not in dispute: thriving at planetary, societal, inter-personal and intrapersonal levels. If we address what each of these now means to us, a new public narrative about education clearly emerges, but it will depend on an interrogation of our values. What is it that we really hold dear? The debate around values is perhaps one of the most urgent that we need. We should also note that in exploring it, we need to go beyond ideas, into something more visceral and profound.[10]

However, in addition, the new public narrative for education so urgently needed is not one that is simply articulated by leaders alone, however visionary. It needs to be co-created and crafted through the engagement of many voices. This endeavour is being explored on a number of fronts – for example, as a result of the UN Summit on Education Transformation, Big Education Conversations.[11]

Leading for Equity

In most education systems, even where overall education standards (on the old metrics of standardised academic tests) are rising,[12] inequalities remain or are rising. Such metrics, of course, provide a narrowly restricted lens through which to assess the issue. We need to broaden the focus so as to encompass the variety of inequalities that beset us: income/wealth; social class; race; caste; gender; sexuality; neurodiversity – indeed, the multiplicity of ways in which humans are differentiated hierarchically, to advantage some and disadvantage and oppress others.

The issue of equity is profoundly important for humanity's future. It is not a 'nice-to-have'; but rather, it is fundamental to thriving at all the levels set out above. Equity is essentially about what it is that is valued and how. Whilst 'equity' has in the past been simplistically conceived of as, variously, equality of opportunity or outcomes, it did not get to the heart of the question. It is now apparent that the overarching goal of thriving cannot be achieved without rethinking equity. The planet itself has been put at risk by an ideology of greed, consumption and acquisition. In terms of reaching towards a peaceful planet, the dehumanising of groups in a culture of dominance is what has led, and continues to lead, to the precariousness of peace. Also, when it comes to thriving societies, scholarship[13] shows that wealth does not determine equity. Societies with a larger gap between rich and poor are bad for everyone – including the well-off.

Inequality – or the dominance paradigm – manifests itself in a number of ways, not just the economic (though that is usually a marker).

As the *Black Lives Matter* and *#MeToo* campaigns have shown, violence against people of colour and women continues to blight prospects for a thrivable future for all.

So, we need leadership for equity if we are to shape thriving future societies. Leaders in the future need to be advocates for inclusion and diversity, for racial equality; fiercely anti-racist and anti-sexist; agents of change, activists intervening to attack institutional barriers to equity and to achieve the power shifts that are necessary to produce justice for all. This takes courage; not just good ideas.

Leading Within Learning Ecosystems

The traditional silos of schooling are no longer adequate to the challenge of providing the range, diversity and personalisation of learning opportunities that young people now need if we are all to thrive. Many more organisations and sectors need to be involved. One way to think about this is to reconceive of 'education systems' (usually top-down hierarchical arrangements of management, in a segmented sector) as learning ecosystems.[14] Learning ecosystems bring together *diverse* providers – not only schools and colleges – but also non-formal learning institutions, private sector organisations, the creative and cultural sectors, businesses and tech companies – to create new learning opportunities. To realise education transformation, education has to become 'everybody's business'. In the new conditions we face, schools cannot do everything: they need to integrate themselves in nets of learning opportunities. This is what leadership in ecosystems means. Also, it requires a different mind- and skill-set: one that values collaboration and knows how to promote it.

Leading Innovation

Now, education leaders – especially system leaders – need to be committed to experimentation, innovation and knowledge exchange, not only in an individual's own learning environment but on behalf of the wider system. This entails understanding methods of innovation and how they sit alongside the use of research. It also means involving users – especially learners – in the effort. COVID-19 showed how critical it is for great leaders to be able to iterate, adopt and adapt. The leadership of innovation is not a competency for which professionals in education are classically prepared. It now needs to become a part of the leadership repertoire. The good news is that a range of well-evidenced and developed methodologies now exists and is readily available to be deployed in the endeavour. These methodologies may not be standard in leadership development programs; but their use is growing, new approaches are emerging and expertise is becoming more widespread.

Leadership That Is Futures-Literate

Current conditions are reframing what defines good leadership. The old idea of determining a clear vision and pursuing it (with some gestures towards the impact of changed circumstances) seems too brittle a stance for leaders in the future.[15]

As Smith puts it,

> *Leadership must enable a culture that supports the freedom to think and plan in non-linear ways, and views uncertainty as a material to build with, not as a risk to be mitigated.*

Everything that we have argued for in this chapter derives from the contention that it is the absolute duty of educators to look forward in an informed and balanced way to a future very different from the past: one which, although they might not themselves experience it fully, their students undoubtedly will.

Therefore, leaders need to become 'futures-literate', in order to help their communities become so. Public discourse is replete with images of futures imagined, projected or pronounced to be a fait accompli. Often these are also presented as binary false choices – of dystopia or utopia. At a time when economic visions, belief systems and cultures are all up for grabs, there is a need to work out the contours of a future framed according to our values. That is why the tools and processes of futures thinking are so valuable – to leaders in particular. Toolkits, frameworks and processes are now readily available – if leaders reach out for them.[16]

This approach must not be seen as a narrow exercise in prediction. Rather, if it is understood as an effort towards understanding the nature of change, of expanding the imagination, and of strengthening people's capacity to shape change, then a different picture emerges. This is about learning to be anticipatory of trends and forces that can both promote and produce deeper learning, and of those that threaten a flourishing future. It is about overcoming fear and inspiring hope – issues at the very heart of any leadership.

Engaging with ideas of possibility – and especially bringing imagination into play – are fundamental.

ENABLING THE NEW LEADERSHIP

What does all this look like in practice? One programme that has been working with leaders of education systems in this way has been the Global Education Leadership Partnership.[17]

Since 2019, this has been an effort to bring together system leaders to build their own capacity to become transformational. Genuinely global, the programme has gathered leaders together on every continent to address an agenda that is fundamentally set out by the five signposts for education set out above: the exploration of new purpose; the pursuit of genuine equity; deploying innovation; building ecosystems; and accessing and engaging in futures thinking. Leaders from across the world have been engaging in these ideas, but – to the proposition being explored by the chapters in this book as a whole – we have learned that this endeavour is about more than ideas. It entails a fundamental revision of values. It depends upon moral courage: the courage to advocate for and pursue policies that are challenging and require empathetic introduction and painstaking preparation. It takes skills of advocacy and persuasion – and it needs resilience.

CONCLUSION – GALVANISING ACTION

In this contribution, we have argued that the potential power of an ideas-informed society – good ideas, virtuous ideas for the common good and the public interest – depends upon leadership that enables the shifts that make it happen. However, 'making it happen' requires thought leadership, convening power and advocacy that moves people. There is a good case for suggesting that the transformation of education is akin to the imperative of action on the climate emergency. Ideas, data and forecasts need to be converted into goals that galvanise action, engage with an ever-growing movement and – hopefully, in time – result in a transformative shift. One might be tempted to fear that, just as with the climate crisis, high-blown rhetoric expressed by leaders at international gatherings does not get translated into real action, but withers and disappears on contact with domestic political realities. That is why courage and imagination are so critical in this piece. The lack of political imagination brought to bear in both these domains is a major obstacle.[18]

We applaud and support the drive towards an ideas-informed society: but we believe that it is not enough.

NOTES

1. See, for example, UNESCO (2022) A New Social Contract, UNESCO, Paris. https://en.unesco.org/futuresofeducation/ and the OECD's work on Education and Skills 2030 https://www.oecd.org/education/2030-project/.
2. https://www.un.org/en/transforming-education-summit.
3. https://www.un.org/sites/un2.un.org/files/2022/09/ sg_vision_statement_on_transforming_education.pdf.

4. Hannon, V and Peterson, A K (2021) THRIVE: The Purpose of Schools in a Changing World, Cambridge University Press, Cambridge, UK; and Mehta, J and Fine, S (2019) In Search of Deeper Learning: The Quest to Remake the American High School, Harvard, Cambridge, MA.

5. See, for example, Five New Operating Principles for the Age of Disruption by Sweetman, K and Cragun, S, at dukece.com/insights/five-new-operating-principles-age-disruption; Three Vital Skills for the Age of Disruption by Krishnan, K, for the 2019 World Economic Forum. Accessed at weforum.org/agenda/2019/09/3-vital-skills-for-the-age-of-disruption.

6. Timms, H and Heimans, J (2018) New Power, Macmillan, London.

7. Scharmer, O (2013) Leading from the Emerging Future: From Ego-System to Eco-System Economies, Penguin Random House, New York.

8. Hannon, V and Mackay, A (2021) The future of educational leadership: Five signposts, CSE Leading Education Series, Paper 04, August 2021, Centre for Strategic Education, Melbourne.

9. Merriam Webster.

10. Carney, M (2021) Value(s): Building a Better World for All, Harper Collins, New York.

11. https://www.bigeducationconversation.org/.

12. Taking Australia as an example, see Bonnor, C, Kidson, P, Piccoli, A, Sahlberg, P and Wilson, R (2021) Structural Failure: Why Australia Keeps Falling Short of its Educational Goals, UNSW Gonski Institute, Sydney.

13. Pickett, K and Wilkinson, R (2010) The Spirit Level: Why Equality is Better for Everyone, Penguin, London.

14. Hannon, V, Thomas, L, Ward, S and Beresford, T (2018) Local Learning Ecosystems: Emerging Models, WISE, Toronto; and Luksha, P, Spencer-Keyse, J and Cubista, J (2020) Learning Ecosystems: An Emerging Praxis for the Future of Education. Accessed at learningecosystems2020.globaledufutures.org.

15. Smith, S (2020) How to Future: Leading and Sense-Making in an Age of Hyperchange, Kogan Page, London.

16. For example, UNESCO (2020) Futures Literacy: A Skill for the 21st Century, UNESCO, Paris. Accessed at en.unesco.org/futuresliteracy.
17. https://www.gelponline.org/.
18. Mulgan, G (2022) Another World is Possible: How to Reignite Social and Political Imagination, Hurst and Co, London.

FURTHER READING

Bentley, T and Singhania, A (2020) Leading through crisis: Resilience, recovery and renewal, ACEL Monograph No 60, Australian Council for Educational Leaders, Sydney.

Fullan, M (2018) Nuance: Why Some Leaders Succeed and Others Fail, Corwin Press, Thousand Oaks, CA.

Fullan, M and Gallagher, M (2017) Transforming Systems, Deep Learning and the Equity Hypothesis, a paper prepared for the Learning Policy Institute, Stanford University. Accessed at https://fuse.education.vic.gov.au

Krznaric, R (2020) The Good Ancestor: How to Think Long-Term in a Short-Term World, The Experiment, London.

Rose, T (2022) Collective Illusions: Conformity, Complicity and the Science of Why We Make Bad Decisions, Hachette, New York.

Shallowe, A, Szymczyk, A, Firebrace, E, Burbidge, I and Morrison, J (2020) A Stitch in Time: Realising the Value of Futures and Foresight, RSA, Peru, October. Accessed at https://thestaffcollege.uk/wp-content/uploads/2021/02/rsa-stitch-in-time.pdf

Stiegler, B (2021) The Age of Disruption: Technology and Madness in Computational Capitalism. Accessed at https://newint.org/features/2017/11/01/robotization-dangers

20

UNLEASHING IDEAS THROUGH YOUTH LED SOCIAL INNOVATION

Katherine Crisp

PASSION AND FRUSTRATION

This chapter will explore the role that child- and youth-led social innovation programmes can play in developing an ideas-informed society. Firstly, some definitions. A *social innovation* is, quite simply, a new idea that can benefit society. *Youth-led* social innovation has agency at its core with young people defining the challenges, the solutions and leading the process to put them into action. A structured *youth social innovation programme* will typically involve young people working in teams to identify social challenges, design solutions and have the opportunity to unlock support (such as funding, mentorship, networks) to put solutions into action. It will typically involve a mix of facilitated, self-guided and peer learning.

In particular, the chapter will consider the opportunities and the barriers, which form the combined cocktail of passion and frustration that led to my recent founding of Social Innovation for All, a social enterprise seeking to unleash the creative potential of children and young people to address social challenges.

The passion arises from the experience of leading the global scale up of UNICEF's youth social innovation and social entrepreneurship programmes, namely UPSHIFT and ImaGen Ventures. The passion is infectious: from the young founder of a club for children with autism in Ho Chi Minh City who was driven by the lack of social and learning opportunities for her brother; to the young woman in a remote and dusty town near the Tajik-Afghan border who had co-developed a community recycling project, but perhaps more importantly, had gained the confidence to speak eloquently in front of a packed room full of strangers; to the two young men from Darfur in Sudan who wanted to bring employment and opportunity to their community and were themselves experiencing their first journey outside of their country, trying to understand and be understood, not just in terms of language, but also in how to conduct yourself in a work environment, in a different culture, with new people. All essential skills they needed to learn to make their dreams a reality.

It is clear that young people are often driven by social purpose and have many ideas along with the energy to invest in making their ideas happen. But, according to Nesta,[1] 98.5% of the UK's school population do not get the opportunity to participate in programmes that support invention and innovation. Those that do are typically in the South of England (including London) and already from more privileged backgrounds. Hence the frustration.

This is where more widespread enablement of youth-led social innovation opportunities could play a crucial role, bringing a structured approach to problem identification, solving, ideation and implementation. By giving young people the skills, opportunities and platforms to work together to learn how to invent and to innovate, whilst focusing on social challenges, we would take a crucial step towards building an ideas-informed society. The focus of this chapter is England, as the Nesta research recognises greater existing opportunities in Scotland and because Wales is currently implementing curriculum reform.

WHY ADOLESCENCE IS KEY TO AN IDEAS-INFORMED SOCIETY?

Adolescence is the transition between childhood and adulthood, the timing and length of which has varied historically and across cultures. In the UK adolescence is typically defined as 10–19 years old and whilst this definition (with good reason) has more recently stretched to 24 years old[2]; we will focus here on under 18s, as this largely corresponds with secondary education.

Arguably, adolescence provides the ideal window to start to give young people the skills and opportunities to drive an ideas-informed society. Adolescence marks a crucial phase of human growth and development, second only in importance to infancy.[3] The maturation process in the adolescent brain both creates new pathways and strengthens existing ones, shaping who we become as adults.

There is relatively a well-established understanding of early childhood brain development. However, it is only within the last 50 years that research started to reveal continued brain development into adolescence.[4] This means there has been far less attention paid to the second most significant phase of brain development although it is synonymous with increased self and social awareness, a focus on peers (instead of parents), increased ability to plan and multi-task, improved problem solving and greater risk taking.[5] This creates a developmental window and an opportunity to focus on harnessing and developing skills of creativity, problem solving, critical thinking and collaboration, which arguably are not prioritised within the formal education system in England (along with many other countries).

The rationale for social innovation programmes focused on adolescents isn't about creating game-changing social innovations, such as the Big Issue or Park Run. It is about being intentional in developing the 'muscles' of creativity, innovation and citizenship during adolescence. By putting ideas into action (and, at times, failing), young people learn essential skillsets, develop new mindset, become more resilient and gain confidence. By focusing on social issues they put citizenship (already a core area of the curriculum) into action. By enabling these opportunities within schools, we would be able to reach a whole generation; increasing by nearly 100 times the pool of future innovators, levelling the playing field and creating millions of seedling ideas for positive social change.

A POLICY DISCONNECT OR A POLICY OPPORTUNITY?

To achieve a vision of reaching every adolescent schools are key; 8.9 million children and young people are in education in England in 2020–2021, 3.5 million of them adolescents in secondary schools.[6] However, in England, as in most other countries, innovation and education policy are developed in separate government departments with limited overlap. To build an ideas-informed society, starting with children and young people, the approach needs to change.

Education policy, curriculum and examinations in England, as in many other countries, focus on subject specific knowledge. The need to build transferable skills is generally recognised as important by all stakeholders from schools to employers to young people. The Skills Builder Partnership is a UK based global movement of employers, educators and impact organisations working together to ensure that one day, everyone builds the essential skills to succeed. Their Framework identifies eight 'Essential Skills' of Listening, Speaking, Problem Solving, Creativity, Staying Positive, Aiming High, Leadership and Teamwork. However, these skills are not the main focus of the national curriculum, are not considered by examinations or school league tables and only tangentially evaluated within the Education Inspection Framework in relation to personal development.[7] The formal education curriculum in England concentrates on the mastery of essential knowledge across an increasingly narrow compulsory range of subjects[8] with the accountability systems incentivising a focus on attainment scores. Secondary teachers are subject specialists who tend to operate within their specialism, rather than having the time or incentives to plan cross-curricular learning. Whilst there is an expectation that schools deliver a broad and balanced curriculum, 'broad and balanced' is not defined and there are many points of tension for schools in delivering this. These include budget and staffing constraints, the focus on increasing participation in the defined set of EBacc subjects,[9] along with an increasing number of schools teaching GCSEs over 3 years, instead of 2, thereby narrowing the curriculum offering 1 year earlier.[10]

There is clear potential to link cross-curricular innovation opportunities to a range of different subject specific curriculum goals, including English, DT, Computer Science, Humanities and PSHE, as well as the more typical STEM subjects. However, due to the tensions discussed above the integration is often subject specific and/or limited to small groups of students to enable incorporation into the school calendar.

However, this is in sharp contrast to the regularly cited needs of employers, with forecasts suggesting occupations requiring inter-personal skills, critical thinking and problem solving will continue to grow[11] and with employers increasingly assessing these types of skills as an integral part of their recruitment processes.[12] And these same skills that are so valued by employers are a key part of realising the vision of an ideas informed society.

The lack of focus and accountability within schools mean that invention and innovation activities are typically enrichment or extra-curricular, rather than a core part of the curriculum. They depend on motivated teachers and usually only attract a small and self-selecting group of students. This is truly an opportunity lost!

Meanwhile, the UK's innovation policy and strategy[13] focuses primarily on business, Universities and increasingly place-based innovation, which is about leveraging a region's institutions and industry to drive innovation in relation to local or regional challenges and opportunities. The people dimension of this policy relates largely to immigration and senior leadership development. Whilst there is commitment within the UK's R&D strategy to undertake a review of youth engagement,[14] this is a tiny step towards considering the long-term benefits of building children and young people's skills as innovators in order to foster a larger and more diverse pool of innovators, as advocated by Nesta.[15]

Nesta highlights the opportunity to foster a more diverse and wider pool of innovators by creating policy incentives, evidence and an ecosystem that supports schools to develop invention and innovation skills. If this can be combined with a focus on social challenges (aka youth-led social innovation) adolescents can be given the skills, opportunities and mindset to explore and tackle social challenges, building their 'innovation muscle' to become confident creators of an ideas informed society.

LEARNING ACROSS BORDERS

Whilst there are multiple examples at local or sub-regional level in England of schools based social innovation programmes, there are no nationally scaled programmes with reach comparable to long established schools-based enterprise programmes, such as the Prince's Trust or Young Enterprise. However, the good news is that these examples do exist in other countries and we will explore the model and learnings of two such examples through case studies on UPSHIFT and the Young Social Innovators Programme.

Case Study – UPSHIFT in Action in India

UPSHIFT is UNICEF's flagship youth social innovation programme, which was initially piloted by UNICEF in Kosovo and subsequently scaled globally with the support of UNICEF's Office of Innovation.

It is a youth skills development programme that rapidly unlocks youth potential to create tangible change in their lives through identifying issues in their local communities and designing entrepreneurial solutions to address those issues. UPSHIFT combines human centred design workshops, mentorship and, in some cases, seed funding, to equip young people to adopt a problem-solving mindset and a persevering attitude. They build a set of practical skills and attributes like grit and determination that enable them to succeed. This not only makes them effective at addressing issues in their communities, but also gives them confidence they can apply throughout their lives. UPSHIFT works with youth as a partnership, teaching young people skills and practices, but using their voices and ideas to shape the programme in return.

By the end of 2022, UPSHIFT had already changed the lives of 3.1 million young people across 45 countries, achieving rapid results. UPSHIFT's approach adjusts to each context and country, ensuring each child and young person can use their unique understanding of their community to make a difference. Although the programme started outside of education systems, it is now being integrated into education systems in nine different countries, with the example from India being highlighted as a case study that would be relevant for the English education system.

The UPSHIFT programme in India is being delivered in four states (with a combined population of over 200 million people). The programme itself is only in its third year of operation but already over 270,000 adolescents, typically aged 10–14 years old have completed the UPSHIFT course. It is delivered in schools through a trained teacher facilitator, working at any one time with a group of up to 25 adolescents, with work underway to increase the reach to full year groups in each school through integration into the curriculum. Teachers receive training and are supported through a digital platform that has content for both students and teachers, including videos, adaptive quizzes and worksheets. As part of their learning journey students apply design thinking to design their own social innovation ideas, with teams submitting their ideas through the digital platform, and the teams with the most promising ideas attending in person bootcamps at the district and then state level. This blended approach leverages technology to enable wide-spread skills building, whilst also being able to identify and nurture a small number of teams in-person, to develop the most relevant, acceptable, replicable and scalable youth-led social innovations.

India's new National Education Policy highlights the need for education to reduce the focus on content and focus more on learning how to think critically, solve problems and innovation across disciplines to stay relevant in a rapidly changing job market.[16] This policy is heralding opportunities to innovate at state and national level through the introduction of programmes such as UPSHIFT and is also triggering novel inter-departmental partner-ships between, for example departments of Education, Information Communication Technologies and Micro, Small and Medium Enterprises. Social innovation programmes are delivering across multiple objectives relating to education, enterprise development, intellectual property development and innovation skills. Previously, the focus of innovation opportunities had been largely on adults.

Case Study – Young Social Innovators in Ireland

Young Social Innovators (YSI) is a non-profit organisation that has been a pioneer of social innovation education in the Republic of Ireland since 2001. What began as a small pilot programme to explore social innovation as a mechanism for engaging, empowering and giving voice to young people is now a national organisation with a wide reach into the youth population and education system in Ireland.

Through its unique Social Innovation Learning Framework, values-based action programmes, educator training and events, YSI enables young people to grapple with difficult social issues and empowers them to come up with and implement new and innovative ideas for change. Each year, thousands of young people throughout Ireland are supported by trained and resourced educators to explore social issues that concern them and their communities and to work in teams to bring about positive social change. In this way, Young Social Innovators builds social capital and helps young people contribute to the creation of a fairer, more equal and sustainable world whilst developing key skills and competencies through their practical application.

Ireland's Transition Year option[17] for students in second-level schools provides a unique space within the education system for programmes like Young Social Innovators to find a home. Transition Year is an opportunity for teenagers to explore a wider range of subject interests, develop general, technical, social and academic skills, take part in work experience and engage in more diverse, practical and action-based learning without the pressure of exams. It supports young people to develop the tools and competencies needed to transition from the more dependent learning of the Junior Cycle to the more independent and self-directed learning required for Senior Cycle. Each school designs its own Transition Year Programme within a national set of guidelines, and it has been primarily within this space that Young Social Innovators has scaled and tested many of its approaches. While Young Social Innovators now offers social innovation education programmes at primary, lower secondary, and informal settings, it benefitted from the space provided by the Transition Year Programme in Ireland to test and develop its pedagogy which it now shares internationally.

Also key to Young Social Innovators success was early and on-going support from different government Departments. Social innovation and its benefits to young people and communities align to and support the delivery of policies spanning community, health, education, youth and more.

CONCLUDING THOUGHTS – PUT INNOVATION SKILLS AT THE CENTRE

These two case studies from very different contexts both highlight the importance of an enabling policy framework, albeit with the policy objectives being different in the two countries. In one there is a clear policy goal of integrating twenty-first century and innovation skills into the core curriculum; the other explicitly carves out a dedicated space (the transition year) to focus on different skills, experiences and opportunities. Teachers play a key role in both models – facilitating, supporting and enabling teams of young social innovators. The teachers themselves benefit from professional development, but without a more formal recognition within the curriculum this type of activity risks being purely additional workload for already stretched teachers.

The Skills Builder Partnership provides a clear focus on the skills requiring development. To enable society to benefit from young people with these skills it seems vital that these skills are moved to a central stage in the curriculum and that young people and teachers are provided with support to enable their development. These skills also need to feature more prominently in an assessment system which is currently focused on that which is easy to measure but at times less valuable.

In summary, young people are full of ideas, but often lack the access, skills and resources to make ideas happen. We need to work together to create a policy framework and wider enabling environment that will give every young person the skills, agency and opportunity to become active citizens who will shape (now and in the future) an ideas informed society.

REFERENCES

1. Gabriel, M., Ollard, J. and Wilkinson, N. (2018) Opportunity Lost: How Inventive Potential is Lost and what to do about it, Nesta.
2. Sawyer, S., Azzopardi, P., Wickremarathne, D. and Patton, G. (2018) The Age of Adolescence, Lancet.
3. Arain, M., Haque, M., Johal, L., Mathur, P., Ne,l W., Rais, A., Sandhu, R. and Sharma, S. (2013) Maturation of the Adolescent Brain. Neuropsychiatrtric Disease and Treatment.
4. Blakemore, S.J., Choudhury, S. (2006) Development of the adolescent brain: implications for executive function and social cognition, The Journal of Child Psychology and Psychiatry.
5. Blakemore, S.J. (2012) Development of the Social Brain in Adolescence, Journal of the Royal Society of Medicine.
6. Dept for Education (2022) Opportunity for All: Strong Schools with Great Teachers for Your Child, HM Government.
7. Dept for Education (2022) Education Inspection Framework, HM Government.
8. Dept for Education (2014) The National Curriculum in England: Key Stages 3 and 4 framework document, HM Government.
9. Dept for Education (2019) Guidance English Baccalaureate (EBacc), HM Government.
10. Spielman, A. (2017) HMCI's commentary: recent primary and secondary curriculum research, Ofsted.
11. Bakhshi, H., Downing, J., Osborne, M. and Schneider, P. (2017) The Future of Skills: Employment in 2030, Pearson and Nesta.
12. Skills Builder Partnership (2022) Trailblazers: Companies using essential skills to boost their recruitment, staff development and outreach, Skills Builder Partnership, available at https://www.skillsbuilder.org/universal-framework/listening.
13. Department for Business, Energy and Industrial Strategy (2021) UK Innovation Strategy, HM Government.
14. Department for Business, Energy and Industrial Strategy (2021) R&D People & Culture Strategy, HM Government.

15. Gabriel, M., Ollard, J. and Wilkinson, N. (2018) Opportunity Lost: How Inventive Potential is Lost and what to do about it, Nesta.

16. Ministry of Human Resource Development (2020), National Education Policy 2020, Government of India.

17. Dept of Education and Science (2005) Guidelines for Second Level Schools on the Implications of Section 9 (c) of the Education Act 1998, relating to students' access to appropriate guidance, Government Publications.

21

DEVELOPING IDEAS-INFORMED YOUNG CITIZENS

John Baumber

EQUIPPING YOUNG PEOPLE FOR A CHAOTIC WORLD

Schools have an important role in developing foundational attributes that encourages critical thinking, deep learning and an empathy and understanding of the society they live and will work in. However, in many jurisdictions we are far from this school culture and in some systems, they actually close minds and fail to stimulate curiosity and creativity.

We know that the minds of youngest of children are full of curiosity, and yet as they progress through the school years, this is reduced year by year as schools strive to achieve standardised outcome results in enlarged curriculums. However, the solutions do not lie just in the type of teaching, the assessment systems and curriculum which includes the development of personal and social and civic education programmes; it requires a whole school culture change.

Further, if we are to equip young people for this increasing chaotic and rapidly changing world, we need to ensure they can handle the 'mountains' of information. The big data statistics for 2023 are frightening:

- 90% of the world's data has been created in the last two years.[1]

- It is estimated that 1.7MB of data is created every second by every person on earth.[2]

- The average internet user spends 6 hours and 58 minutes per day online.[3]

- Each day Google processes 8.5 billion searches.[4]

Not only are we creating incredible amounts of information, but young people have unstructured access and as such need a whole new set of skills to be able to process this and turn it into verified valid knowledge. Those creativity skills we seek to enable, need to be based on knowledge and access to a wide range of processed ideas.

So, what part can educators play to create that positive ideas-informed society?

Chris Brown[5] identified four areas that define an ideas-informed society:

- Seeing the value in staying up to date.

- Actively and regularly keeping up to date.

Further he proposes that desirable effects accrue, namely:

- Citizens become more knowledgeable.

- They are better able to make optimal decisions to the benefit of others.

- They can align their perspectives to societal values of fairness and equality, as well as social and environmental justice.

EMPOWERING YOUNG CITIZENS

In this chapter, we will explore the concept of a knowledge-based curriculum, and how this might be interpreted in a narrow and limiting way in the creation of ideas and understanding. Knowledge is essential as the basis for young people to be creative and become problem solvers. Knowledge needs to sit alongside skills and although many schools will identify these in their curriculum intent, do we systematically develop them rather than just catalogue them.

There is a risk that these skills, and a personal and social education curriculum, will just be bolt-on requirements. Achieving our goals for young people requires a fundamental reframing of the curriculum structure and a whole school redesign. Ted Dintersmith and Sir Ken Robinson asked us 'What School Could Be' and joined a wide range of academic and practitioners calling for a radical overhaul of our school design.[6]

There are significant risks in not equipping all our young people to be able to synthesise, challenge and apply knowledge. Their view of the world is being shaped every day they are at school, and they need to enter the adult world informed, but able to discriminate and test information they receive. We would argue that many of the democratic challenges and rise of nationalist views within a number of western society populations arise by not having all the information to form considered ideas and opinions and being at the mercy of powerful media and influencers.

If young people are to leave formal education with their own informed idea about justice, fairness, citizenship and equity, their educational experience must have allowed opportunity for the application of knowledge and skill development. It must allow them to have the agency to shape the world around them, be able to build on their own passions and interests with a freedom to personalise their engagement and be able to build a sense of curiosity and experimentation. In these ways knowledge is embedded, and ideas tested. There are schools and curriculums that do this.

A KNOWLEDGE-BASED CURRICULUM?

In a speech in July 2021 Nick Gibb, UK Minister for Schools, said

> Since 2010, the reforms that we put in place have been driven by the idea that the transmission of rich subject knowledge should be the priority for schools.
>
> We replaced the 2007 National Curriculum because it was based on a series of general aptitudes with insufficient subject-based content. In its place we introduced a

> *National Curriculum which gives pupils a grounding in*
> *the best that has been thought and said.*[7]

He goes on to exemplify this with the lack of basic historical
knowledge university students have. He blamed the drive to teach
'historical skills' rather than historical knowledge as a key cause of
the problem quoting E. D. Hirsch (1996):[8]

> *Knowledge should be thought of as mental Velcro.*
> *People who have lots of subject-specific knowledge*
> *find that new knowledge 'sticks' to it, helping them*
> *commit the new information to long-term memory.*

It should be obvious that without knowledge it is hard to form
ideas and reach valid conclusions. Most adults have built up a
long-term memory of events and knowledge and experience that
they retrieve to solve new problems. Young people clearly have less
knowledge and less experience and therefore building
problem-solving programmes without a depth of knowledge can
only lead to trivial expositions and outcomes. It is obvious that
young people need to acquire knowledge and this needs to be
'sticky'. In other words, it needs to go into long term memory and
not be there just for that working moment. In addition, one should
not neglect to recognise that many young people hold a wide range
of knowledge and skill built from their own interests and this needs
to be incorporated and celebrated.

We know that to embed knowledge, students need to use it. Very
often they need to be motivated by a question or issue that stimulates a desire to research or develop knowledge and then understand the interplay of information to be able to form opinion.

What is a 'no-knowledge curriculum-there is not one?' What this
is, is a debate about balance. But it risks driving teachers to focus
simply on instructional didactic teaching which is often further
enhanced by the accountability framework and testing/assessment
regimes.

I will illustrate this by a personal story.

I went to a boys' grammar school in rural Lincolnshire, England
in the 1960s. As a 12-year-old the history curriculum for most of
the year was about The Pilgrimage of Grace. In Lincolnshire this

rising was a brief dissent of Roman Catholics against the establishment of the Church of England by Henry VIII and the dissolution of the monasteries set in motion by Thomas Cromwell's suggested plan of asserting the nation's religious autonomy and the king's supremacy over religious matters. Through the year the history teacher dictated a calendar of event day by day as the rising impacted on the area in 1536. At the end we were tested, and I remember the 89% score. I can tell you nothing about it now. I have not used anything from this learning episode since, but I did give up history at that point and never studied it again. Something I regret.

Had I been able to research documents and draw up my own story, had I been able to debate the issues and the validity of the documentation, had I been able to use the knowledge to apply to other issues, I probably would have remembered more. I would also have developed a range of skills for research, presentations and verification of truth that could then be applied to different contexts and episodes. I might have been able to develop a value set about social justice and fairness.

These are surely the fundamental building blocks about being an educated person. In Swedish they use expression *Bildning* when they describe the lifelong process by which the individual's view, understanding and interpretation of the world matures, deepens, and widens. The foundation for this is a combination of high-level thinking skills, self-knowledge and a strong driving force to learn and develop. The ability to describe, analyse and generalise – to detect patterns and be able to apply them in new situations – to see contexts, vary perspectives and connect knowledge from different fields is a crucial part of this foundation. In this way students develop knowledge about their learning process that, combined with curiosity and critical thinking, supports their will to learn. Students develops into an intellectually empowered and responsible individual who also understand the importance of people's interactions and interdependence. This requires self-knowledge, the ability to empathise and strong communication skills. We develop the students' ability to manage new situations, maintain a constructive attitude towards challenges, recognise opportunities, and dare to think in new ways – to be creative –and realize that 'life is what I make it' (Kunskapsskolan 2010).[9]

PERSONAL DEVELOPMENT

We surely want our young people to have a deep and sustained knowledge but one that they realise will need constant updating and review. We want them to know, develop a range of skills, but also have a range of learning habits that enables them to think, analyse, apply, debate, synthesise and question.

Building this curriculum imperative of personal skills and habits is complex and surrounded by many different approaches. High schools in particular are encouraged to set aside specific lesson time for Personal, Spiritual, Health and Citizenship Education (PSHCE) and whilst most schools have a set of personal learning skills that they try to embed into their lessons and curriculum. Inevitably, there are critical curriculum elements in this area, that schools must teach – sex and relationship education, health, and safety programmes. But outside these curriculum elements, practice is varied and often an expression of the school's stated values.

We are asked to 'prepare for an age where Artificial Intelligence, robots, and big data will fundamentally change the way we live, work, and relate to one another' (Fullan, 2017).[10]

So apart from traditional skills and knowledge young people need to develop capabilities such as complex problem solving, emotional intelligence and cognitive flexibility. To be successful, Fullan built on the work of the Partnership for Twenty-first-century Skills by adding Character Development and Citizenship to their previous 4 Cs – Creativity, Collaboration, Communication and Critical Thinking and Problem-Solving (Fig. 1).[11]

Kunskapsskolan who operate schools in a number of countries express these ideas differently. They have built a Future Skills Framework. You will recognise the similarity to Fig. 2.

However, these also reflect a call to action which reflects the OECD 2030 Learning Framework with its key goals of building agency and co-agency along with wellbeing. One other feature of Kunskapsskolan have built these skills into their teaching and learning framework. Tasks signpost opportunities to develop skills,

6C Global Competencies

Character

- Proactive stance toward life and learning to learn
- Grit, tenacity, perseverance and resilience
- Empathy, compassion and integrity in action

Citizenship

- A global perspective
- Commitment to human equity and well-being through empathy and compassion for diverse values and world views
- Genuine interest in human and environmental sustainability
- Solving ambiguous and complex problems in the real world to benefit citizens

Collaboration

- Working interdependently as a team
- Interpersonal and team-related skills
- Social, emotional, and intercultural skills
- Managing team dynamics and challenges

Communication

- Communication designed for audience and impact
- Message advocates a purpose and makes an impact
- Reflection to further develop and improve communication
- Voice and identity expressed to advance humanity

Creativity

- Economic and social entrepreneurialism
- Asking the right inquiry questions
- Pursuing and expressing novel ideas and solutions
- Leadership to turn ideas into action

Critical Thinking

- Evaluating information and arguments
- Making connections and identifying patterns
- Meaningful knowledge construction
- Experimenting, reflecting and taking action on ideas in the real world

Fig. 1. 6C Global Competencies (OECD).

Skills for the future

Learn to learn
Reflection
Strategy
Self-awareness

Cooperate
Communication
Team work
Management

Act globally
Openness
Change of perspective
Sustainability

Take action
Planning
Implementation
Responsibility

Be innovative
Curiosity
Creativity
Problem solving

Live digitally
Digital understanding
Digital use
Source criticism

Fig. 2. Kunskapsskolan's Future Skills Framework.

children work with their teachers to understand and practice these metacognitive strategies, and then through coaching build a portfolio of evidence to refine their skill level. This process has to be proactive.

The contention here is that unless you actually embed these attributes into the curriculum the chances are there will be little impact and poor skill development. Turning back to our discussion about an ideas-informed society, you can see how these skills, if effectively developed create a framework for discussion, agency, and action where

> *Young people can shape the world rather than being shaped by it. (OECD 2016)*[12]

But you can see that agency has to be predicated by knowledge and understanding if it is to be purposeful. Many young people have a real passion for justice and fairness as can be seen by their work supporting ideas from people like Greta Thunberg, but if it has to be more than protest and passion. If they are to be able to credibly argue their case, they have to know the detail and context. If we are building the foundations for an ideas-informed individual we have to balance Knowledge, Skills, Application and Agency.

REFRAMING THE CURRICULUM IMPERATIVE

Moving on from his work on multiple intelligences in 2007, Howard Gardner identified five minds for the future – the disciplined, the synthesising, the creating, the respectful and the ethical minds.[13] He is clear that these are what people will need to be able 'to thrive in the world in the eras to come'. These are not at variance with those who value the development of knowledge and understanding. In fact, 'the disciplined mind' is about mastery at least one specific discipline and its cognitive characteristics. It takes time to develop confidence and mastery – 10 years as Malcolm Gladwell suggested in 'Blink'. But this will then give a powerful reference for thinking and seeing meaning.[14]

But he then leads us to the *synthesising mind* which can pull together evidence to evaluate information objectively as one pulls from a wide range of sources to develop hypotheses to reach conclusions. Given the mushrooming amount of information available to everyone nowadays this is such an important skill. In his conclusion he builds a clear sense of what it would be like not to have these mindsets in the future. Without a synthesising mind for instance, you would be unable to make justifiable conclusions when overwhelmed with information of many types and source.

However, the OECD (2006) has argued for an overarching goal of adaptability – namely

> *...the ability to apply meaningfully learned knowledge and skills flexibly and creatively in different situations*[15]

rather than routinely completing subject based school tasks without any understanding of how this knowledge can be applied in other contexts or is interrelated to other issues.

School curricula in middle and high schools have continued to be subject driven. We know that the answer to the world's big issues involve the integration of ideas from a range of disciplines. If you take climate change for instance, in many schools we see it taught separately in Geography and Science. In fact, students need to consider not just the science, but technological solutions and options, the political dimension often driven by historical and developmental issues. If young people are to have the agency to shape their future, we sell them short if all we want is for them to know what causes the climatic change, or where it is impacting. An integrative approach will also test and modify their value position. Why should we be bothered by the differential impact of the increasing catastrophic aspects of climate change in the poorer parts of the world? What might our position be about refugees fleeing drought or flooding? What impact might this have on the political stability in those suffering communities and countries?

We know that if we draw on interest and passion, and that children can exceed their proximal zone of development to achieve more than they thought possible (Vygotsky, 1978).[16] Of course, there are established programmes and teaching and learning frameworks that take a different approach. The International Baccalaureate (IB) for instance is designed to develop well-rounded individuals who can respond to today's challenges with optimism and an open mind. In one of their booklets, it invites to teachers to consider if it is possible to create more experiences and opportunities that allow students to be genuine inquirers.

An ideas-informed society recognises that knowledge needs to be curated, explored, and validated. Building questioning minds would seem to be an essential prerequisite. And although some schools build the whole of their pedagogy in this direction – IB and Steiner for instance – in too many this work forms just one small part of their work and is often built around enthusiastic professionals rather than part of the whole school's way of working and being.

Let us explore some of the braver more holistic approaches.

EXAMPLES OF MORE HOLISTIC APPROACHES

Acton Academy[17] in Austin, Texas, was the starting point for what is now a network of over 60 micro schools. The school was founded by Jeff and Laura Sandefer and began with their family search for a school that would 'bring the light of curiosity burning brightly' in their own children's eyes, 'not just when they were young learners but throughout their childhood, teen years and far beyond'. Their story in 'Courage to Grow: How Acton Academy Turns Learning Upside Down' illustrates the passion they have for student agency and the belief that the work of teachers is to ask questions and then more questions (Sandefer, L. 2018).

Key elements include:

- Socratic Discussions and self-paced challenges that equip children to be curious independent lifelong learners.

- Hands-on Quests for Science, Entrepreneurship, and the Arts to prepare children for apprenticeships and real-world challenges.

- What they call 'The Hero's Journey', relational covenants and real-world consequences that transform difficult decisions into virtuous habits.

XP Schools[18] in the UK were built from the ideas of Ron Berger and the growth of Expeditionary Schools in the States in addition to ground-breaking work of Hi Tec High in San Diego. The curriculum is predominantly a set of cross disciplinary learning expeditions. These are standards-based projects that are specifically designed to make connections between, and across, subjects to encourage deep and purposeful learning experiences for our young people.

Learning is built so that students creatively curate the information they need so it can bring about social change. Their curriculum aims to empower students to question, challenge and empathise. There is a clear and resolute link between academic subjects, learning expeditions and the pursuit of character growth. As a consequence, the purpose of our learning is to make students discern and question, to be able to see through dishonesty and to strive to live their lives based on integrity, respect and with empathy for others.

Both these examples have many common features about the nature of teaching and learning and the agency they give to young people. We should not see any of them as permissive approaches but that they are driven by a moral purpose and belief in young people that they then map to a rigorous sequential map of learning. But the critical point here is that to be recognised as achieving more than more traditional schools in their context, they have redesigned what school can be. It is a matter of whole school design.

WHOLE SCHOOL DESIGN

Ensuring that we have a growing population for young people who can be informed, and can really become our future global citizens, has to be society's critical ambition. Despite a real focus on building a knowledge-based curriculum and real progress in schools to sequence their learning, we are still some way away from sustaining that objective. Young people cannot just be the recipients of knowledge and information, they have to active players and be motivated to learn and be given the opportunity to use and test their knowledge.

Fig. 3 illustrates the important elements that need to be in place.

Applying and Synthesising

It is easy to see how in seeking to have an informed society, we can focus teaching as instruction. There is no doubt that successful learning needs students to think. Daniel Willingham (2007)[19] described memory as the 'residue of thought'. Nuthall (1999)[20] reminded us that you have to encounter a complete set of

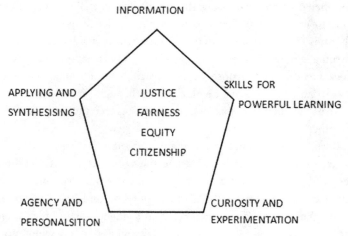

Source: Author.

Fig. 3. Essentials for Building Ideas Informed Students.

information about a concept at least three times to remember. We also know that we more readily process new information if it is linked in some way to something we know already.

But knowing something is different from understanding. This comes from being able to apply the new concept to a new situation and testing out one's comprehension.

Moreover, learning for some authentic relevant purpose encourages us to investigate information and develop knowledge that moves into our long-term memory.

Skills for Powerful Learning

We are exploring how we can create a cadre of school leavers who are ideas-informed and as such can use knowledge to inform, debate, discuss and make judgements. Developing this requires us to become powerful learners with a rich range of thinking skills. The pandemic has brought into sharp relief that learning is a collaborative activity. It allows us to test our ideas and build up a larger information base. These skills do not just happen, although inevitably we all have natural strengths in some of these areas. Schools need to systematically build opportunities into their plans and schedules so these can be developed through debates, planning, and prototyping.

Agency and Personalisation

These two words are now used regularly in education, but rarely do we give licence for them to truly happen. Yong Zhao (2018)[21] wants us to differentiate between personalisation and person-alisable education. He defines personalisable education as where students can be the agents of personalisation. It is carried out by the student under the guidance of the teacher. Personalisation in schools usually means just control over pace, timing and place not what is being learned.

The OECD wrote about agency as this:

> *In education systems that encourage student agency,*
> *learning involves not only instruction and evaluation*

*but also co-construction. Co-agency is when teachers
and students become co-creators in the teaching-and
learning process. The concept of co-agency recognises
that students, teachers, parents, and communities work
together to help students progress towards their shared
goals.*[12]

However, we choose to define agency and personalisation, if we
do not give trust to young people to explore, debate and make
decisions we miss an important step. We know how motivating
autonomy is to adults and young people. In a confident democratic
community, there should be the scope for everyone to explore the
full breadth of information and not just rely on the decisions and
interest of the purveyor. Christine Counsel (2018) wrote,

*Curriculum is all about power. Decisions about what
knowledge to teach are an exercise of power and therefore a weighty ethical responsibility. What we choose to
teach confers or denies power. To say that pupils
should learn 'the best that has been thought and said'
is never adequate. Start the conversation, and questions
abound: 'Whose knowledge?'*[22]

Curiosity and Experimentation

Here we can stretch the idea of an ideas-informed society. Given the
range of challenges facing humanity we should enlist all young
people in exploring new solutions. The challenge for those of us of
middle and older generation, is to keep stretching our thinking
'outside the box'. Our own paradigms, although powerful agents
for problem solving can also limit us as we will readily discount
things that do not fit into our knowledge and values systems.

Even very young children can come up with 'wacky ideas' that
no one had thought of before that with development can create new
ideas and solutions.

Knowledge is not fixed. Ideas can be reinterpreted.

As Sir Ken Robinson said,

> *Our only hope for the future is to adopt a new concep-*
> *tion of human ecology... Our education system has*
> *mined our minds in the way we have strip-mined the*
> *Earth for a particular commodity and for the future it*
> *will not serve us. We have to rethink the fundamental*
> *principles by which we are educating our children.*
>
> *Creativity is as important as literacy in education — but*
> *schools can educate the creativity out of people.*[23]

EQUITY

But finally, we have to address the lack of equity in education and its impact on an ideas informed society. In a fascinating book entitled Head, Hand and Heart, David Goodhart developed an argument about how we have become obsessed with valuing cognitive skill so highly as to denigrate those skilled for their artisan or caring ability. Even though in the UK we clapped through the pandemic for those who continued to keep our systems and hospitals going, emerging from the crisis they still receive significantly lower wages and to some lower esteem. Anyone who watches BBC's Repair Shop can only be amazed by the prodigious skills of those who take damaged and broken articles and renew them to former glories. They have skills many of us could only dream of.

But once that society has consistently undervalued through the last few decades.

Goodhart[24] categorises the population as anywheres and some-wheres. Anywheres are generally graduates, live further from their parents, and are more comfortable with openness, autonomy and novelty. They are more comfortable with social change and can probably fit in anywhere. A larger group are the somewheres, who are generally less well educated are more geographically fixed and feel more comfortable with the familiar and group attachments. It is always difficult to generalise, but mainstream political views tend to be dominated by modern political parties in the UK and USA with anywhere views. Although the values and world views of both groups are valid this divide helps us understand some the schisms and decisions in political decision making in the last decade.

I need to take care here as the author is definitely in the 'any-wheres' category, but are ideas and knowledge equally distributed across the population, so we reach the best of decisions? Or are large sections of the population alienated from political decision making? This works both ways. Lack of empathy and understanding of those most disadvantaged might impact negatively on the decisions taken by government. Children are not just influenced by schools but more especially by their families and their community.

This is a whole new subject for discussion, but I want to just relate this to children in our schools. If we add poverty to alienation, then we further limit access to information. Just take a few basic facts about education poverty:[25]

- Children who have lived in persistent poverty during their first seven years have cognitive development scores on average 20% below those of children who have never experienced poverty.

- It is estimated that 7.1 million do not have the literacy skills they need to read a newspaper or complete basic tasks such as filling in a job application.

- Research shows the deprivation that this brings puts them at significant risk from such things as crime and mental health issues.

- These can be traced back poor literacy skills in childhood. Children with poor skills at five are six times more likely to reach expected levels at 11 and the situation deteriorates though high school.

If we are serious about having an ideas-informed society, we have to deal with significant cohort who cannot access let alone analyse information or data. And this has to start in schools. It is much further than equality. It is about equity.

Much of the above discussion has been about the place of schools in ensuring people become well informed and are then active recipients of ideas. It would be wrong to assume that schools are the only place where learning can take place. There is a whole informal sector embracing families and communities that help young people form opinion and help them develop their values compass. Some of these are addressing the very equity issue mentioned above.

For instance, in Harlem in New York one such organisation Brotherhood Sister Sol[26] has been at the forefront of social justice, educating, organising and training to challenge inequity and champion opportunity for all. The impact of their work has been dramatic:

- Harlem's teenaged pregnancy rate is 15% – their members have a rate of less than 2%.

- In NYC, the general high school graduation rate of 70%; while the Schott Foundation found that the graduation rate of Black and Latino boys is 34%. Over 40% of Black men between the ages of 18–65 in New York City are unemployed.

- 90% of their alumni have graduated from high school, 95% either graduated from high school or earned their GED and 95% are working full time or enrolled in college whereas the similarly situated population in West Harlem, 18–25, has a 40% rate of either working full time or being enrolled in college.

IDEAS-INFORMED NOT KNOWLEDGE ACCUMULATION

In the introduction we defined what an ideas informed society might be and the benefits that might accrue. However further research showed that there appears to be a shift away from that ideal and factors such as the present economic challenge can focus minds on the immediate challenges rather than taking a more balanced view (Brown 2022).[5]

The future must ensure that those young people in education at the moment are better prepared and informed. The contention in the paper is that the present focus of the education system and the lack of equity, risks this ambition being undermined. Moreover, young people are at much greater risk than ever before from the influencers on social media. Ensuring truth validity of information has never been more challenging.

On a more optimistic note, there are many schools and communities that are providing a positive way forward. In particularly I would cite some recently published work by Dave Claricoates (2022) at Bosworth Academy: 'The School of the Fourth Way' 'Preparing Students for the Test of Life rather than a Life of Tests'. But I could add further to this title, warning of the risk of focusing too narrowly on the accumulation of knowledge.[27]

Ensuring our young people are ideas informed is not just about the accumulation of knowledge and it is certainly not about didactic instruction. It is about creating space for discussion and analysis. It is about building motivation and inculcating curiosity and experimentation.

Finally, we all respond best when we feel we have some investment in our own development and learning. Motivation comes from agency and doing things our way. In this way we are most likely to encourage young people to become knowledgeable and in so doing fight to ensure social justice and fairness.

But it is important to remember this is about a whole school culture and as such teacher actions and behaviours, the curriculum structures, and the place of the school in the wider community.

REFERENCES

1. U.S. Chamber of Commerce Foundation. https://www.uschamberfoundation.org/bhq/big-data-and-what-it-means Accessed on April 26, 2022.

2. McCain A (2023) 26 Stunning Big Data Statistics (Zippia).

3. Kemp S (2022) Digital 2022: Global Overview Report (Dataportal).

4. Mahsin M (2022) 10 Google Search Statistics you need to know in 2022. (Oberlo).

5. Brown, C and Luzmore, R and Groß Ophoff, J (2022) 'Facilitating the ideas-informed society: a systematic review', *Emerald Open Research*, *4*. p. 25.

6. Dintersmith T, (2018) What School Could Be. (Archer and Minion Pro).

7. Gibb N, (2021) The importance of a knowledge-rich curriculum Nick Gibb addresses a Social Market Foundation panel event.

8. Hirsch E.D (1996). https://philpapers.org/go.pl?id=HIRTSW&proxyId=&u=https%3A%2F%2Fbooks.google.com%2Fbooks%3Fid%3DGZucAAAAMAAJ%26printsec%3Dfront_cover (Doubleday).

9. Kunskapsskolan (2010) The KED Program. www.kunskapsskolan.com

10. Fullan M and Scott G(2014) New Pedagogies ofr Deep Learning (Collaborative Impact).

11. Partnership for 21st century Skills (2016) Framework for 21st Century Learning A unified vision for learning to ensure student success in a world where change is constant and learning never stops.

12. OECD (2016) Student Agency in Brief. https://www.oecd.org/education/2030-project/teaching-and-learning/learning/student-agency/in_brief_Student_Agency.pdf

13. Gardner H (2007) Five Minds for the Future (Harvard Business School Press).

14. Gladwell M (2006) Blink: The Power of Thinking Without Thinking (Penguin).

15. Halbert J and Kaser L (2006) Innovating the Pedagogical Core (OECD).

16. Vygotsky L S (1978) Mind in Society: The Development of Higher Psychological Processes (Harvard University Press).

17. Sandefer L (2018) Courage to Grow: How Acton Academy turns learning upside down. (Acton Academy).

18. ap Harri G & Sprakes A (2018) How We XP. https://xptrust.org/shop/

19. Willingham D T (2021) Why Students Don't Like School Jossey Bass.

20. Nuthall G. (1999) Learning How to Learn: The Evolution of Students' Minds through the Social Processes and Culture of the Classroom. *International Journal of Educational Research*, *31*, 139-256.

21. Zhao Y (2018) *Reach For Greatness*. (Corwin).

22. Counsel C (2018) Taking curriculum seriously (Impact).

23. Robinson K (2016) Do Schools Kill Creativity? (TED talk).

24. Goodhart D (2020) Head, Hand Heart. The struggle for Dignity and Status in the 21st Century (Allen Lane).

25. Child Poverty Action Group. The Effects of Poverty. https://cpag.org.uk/child-poverty/effects-poverty

26. The Brother hood Sister SOL. https://brotherhood-sistersol.org/

27. Bosworth Academy. Ed by Claricoates D (2022) The School of the Fourth Way: Preparing students for the test of life, not a life of tests.

22

THE FUTURE SKILLS SOCIETY NEEDS AND ITS CRITICAL IMPLICATIONS *

Jude Hillary

NEW SKILLS FOR A TRANSFORMED LABOUR MARKET

The global economy faces significant shifts in the coming decades. The growing adoption of new technologies in the workplace, alongside other factors, are predicted to disrupt the labour market in the future. These structural changes are likely to impact on both the nature of jobs available and the skills needed to do them. It is anticipated that skills such as creativity, critical thinking, teamwork, problem-solving and resilience – skills which complement the new technologies and other changes taking place – will become increasingly important in the labour market. This chapter explores what the implications of these changes might be and how they might make an important contribution to the emergence of an ideas-informed society in the future.

---

*This chapter draws heavily on two reports from *The Skills Imperative 2035: Essential Skills for Tomorrow's Workforce* research programme: (1) The Skills Imperative 2035: Occupational Outlook – Long-run employment prospects for the UK, Baseline Projections by Professor Rob Wilson et al. and (2) The Skills Imperative 2035: what does the literature tell us about essential skills most needed for work by Amanda Taylor et al.

THE SHOCKS AND MEGATRENDS THAT ARE SHAPING
THE UK LABOUR MARKET

In the later years of the last decade and early years of this, the UK had to face some significant disruptions ('shocks') that have had a widespread impact on the economy. These had a significant and immediate impact on the labour market which are expected to continue to be felt in the medium to long term. The first of these was the UK's withdrawal from the European Union (which was coined as Brexit). Following a UK-wide referendum in June 2016, in which there was a majority vote in favour of Brexit, the UK formally left on 31 January 2020. This departure caused the economy to contract, but forecasts suggest it will recover in the longer term, albeit with UK exports being markedly lower than they otherwise may have been had the country stayed in the European Union.[1]

Hot on the heels of Brexit, the second major shock which the UK faced was the worldwide COVID-19 pandemic. The virus, which began circulating in the UK in early 2020, had a huge impact on the way people lived and worked. Restrictions varied depending on the type of tasks and nature of work done by different occupations. Some sectors of the economy and occupations such as hospitality were affected by the restrictions more than others as they were not compatible with remote working. The impact of the virus, and lockdown measures introduced by the Government to avoid its spread, led to a sudden and sharp reduction in economic activity in nearly all sectors in the second quarter of 2020. Whilst a number of workers lost their jobs, this was not as many as might have been expected due to the Government's Coronavirus Job Retention (Furlough) Scheme. The pandemic has also accelerated some underlying trends in working practices, such as home working, as well as impacting many other areas such as greater online retailing, which are likely to continue into the future.

Most recently, in early 2022, as the world started to recover from the pandemic, the Russian government launched an invasion of Ukraine. This in part contributed to rapidly increasing energy prices and what has been described as a cost of living crisis. While these factors will undoubtedly have a significant impact on the short-term prospects for the British economy and labour market, they are not expected to affect the longer-term prospects for structural change.

In addition to these shocks, some structural changes, or *megatrends*, as they are sometimes called, have been identified that are expected to shape the world of work in the next decade and beyond. Firstly, the introduction of new technological advancements (digitisation, automation and artificial intelligence (AI)) into the labour market will continue to displace certain types of jobs or parts of jobs which are more routine. At the same time, these technological advancements are also likely to create new job opportunities as the technologies offer the prospect of developing new products and services.

The second relates to climate change and environmental issues. The global transition to a greener economy, with international pressures such as the 2015 Paris Agreement resulting in the government's ambitious target of reaching its 'net zero' carbon commitment by 2050, is expected to alter the occupational and skills composition of the UK labour market in the future.

Finally, demographic change is an important driver of the labour market. The composition of the workforce is changing considerably. The main drivers are the ageing population and an increasing percentage of females in work. The UK adult population is also expected to grow more slowly in the next decade compared to the 10 years to 2020.[2] This is partly driven by lagged effects of Brexit and the COVID-19 pandemic, which resulted in a large number of people (the majority of whom were of working age) leaving the UK, who are unlikely to return.

HOW WILL THESE MEGATRENDS AFFECT THE FUTURE LABOUR MARKET?

The next question to consider is what implications these megatrends will have on the economy. Government, employers, educationalists and other stakeholders need insights about what might happen in future so they can plan and prepare. Waiting for changes to happen before reacting is a recipe for disaster, as there is a real risk that the current skills mismatch in the UK will be further exacerbated. In turn, this may lead to underemployment and unemployment, along with enduring social and economic problems.

Predicting the future with great precision and certainty is impossible. However, it is nonetheless possible to draw on existing trends, linked to a coherent view of the prospects for the economy, to produce detailed quantitative projections. These can provide a sound foundation for thinking about how the economy and labour market may respond to both recent short-term shocks, as well as the longer-term drivers of change in the patterns of demand and supply of skills.

Emerging evidence is available from a strategic research programme entitled *The Skills Imperative 2035: Essential Skills for Tomorrow's Workforce*, which is being led by the National Foundation for Educational Research (NFER).[3] This is producing a robust data-driven understanding of the future skills needs in 2035, shining a new light on this pressing issue and the challenges which may lay ahead.

What do these projections say about how the labour market is changing? In summary, what we see is that the economy is changing slowly, but steadily and inexorably in favour of service sector jobs. By 2035, the structure of the labour market will have changed substantially. These changes will favour higher-skilled occupations and better-qualified workers. This picture is consistent across the range of future labour market scenarios considered by the study.

We will now look in more detail at these forecasts and the most important changes identified.

1. *A continuation of the journey towards a service sector economy*

Overall, there are expected to be 2.6 million new jobs in the UK labour market by 2035. At broad sectoral level,[4] the profile of change is expected to follow previous trends, with a further shift from jobs in manufacturing towards those with a service orientation. The sectors with the strongest growth rates are in the business and other services sector with over a million net new jobs between 2020 and 2035. This is followed by the non-market services sector (which is dominated by health and education), which is projected to grow by 835,000 net new jobs over the period. Conversely, employment in manufacturing is projected to decrease; its share of total UK employment falling from

7.5% in 2020 to 6.2% in 2035, continuing the long-term downward trajectory that has been seen in recent decades. This is driven by both increasing competition from overseas manufacturers and the UK continuing to move towards a services-oriented economy.

Drilling down further, the industries within the main sectors of the economy with largest absolute employment growth are generally all service industries. This includes health, food and beverage services, social work, education and residential care, which are projected to have strong employment growth between 2020 and 2035. Health, in particular, is expected to increase by 360,000 jobs. In contrast, the industries with the largest projected employment declines are focussed mainly in manufacturing. These include metal products, repair and installation, rubber and plastic, and other transport equipment, to name a few.

2. *Growth in higher and lower skilled occupations*

The forecasts also allow us to examine what impact these megatrends will have on employment by occupational groups. Here we find that the trends are expected to continue to favour highly-skilled, white collar, non-manual jobs. Most of the new jobs created by 2035 will be in professional and associate professional occupations, mainly due to a considerable rise for health and social care associate professionals. Interestingly, there will also be a significant employment increase for some less skilled groups such as customer service occupations, where jobs are less easily automated. However, it is expected that traditional manual/blue-collar occupations such as skilled metal, electrical and electronic trades, skilled construction and building trades (among others) will continue declining. Employment for both higher and lower skilled occupations is therefore projected to grow, but with some hollowing out in the middle of the jobs market.

It is within these occupational breakdowns that it is possible to see glimpses of the impact of technology and greater focus on green initiatives, with a shift from lower skilled to higher skilled occupations. One widely anticipated feature of greater use of technology in the labour market is job destruction and indeed the projections indicate that millions of jobs could be replaced by technology. These are generally in lower skilled jobs such as those in administrative and secretarial and skilled trades occupations, which are forecast to experience a negative net change in jobs. However, there are expected to be many new opportunities too, with new jobs created to manage the introduction and then to maintain the new technologies and green initiatives. The projections assume these will broadly offset the jobs being displaced. However, it is the higher skilled professional and associate professional occupations which are projected to see the fastest growth. Science, research, engineering and technology professionals and health and social care associate professionals, in particular, are expected to experience the largest net increases in job openings between 2020 and 2035.

3. *An increasingly qualified workforce*

More young people are forecast to stay in education longer and acquire more/higher level qualifications.[5] The percentage of economically active people aged 16+ who have a postgraduate degree level qualification or equivalent is projected to increase from around 14% in 2020 to 24% in 2035. More than half will have an undergraduate qualification or higher by 2035, compared to less than half in 2020. At the same time, the share of people who are economically active in the UK who are unqualified will continue to fall and is expected to represent only a small minority (less than 2.5%) of the workforce by 2035.

At the same time, the demand for skills, as measured by the numbers employed (satisfied demand) in higher level occupations, and the numbers employed holding higher level qualifications, is also projected to rise. The extent to which this is due to increases in demand as opposed to the supply side changes is a point of contention. However, what can be seen is that there is a clear pattern of a rise in the number of highly qualified people (economically active population with a high formal qualification), as well as increasing employment levels for the highest qualified workers.

THE GROWING IMPORTANCE OF SKILLS IN THE FUTURE WORKFORCE

It is not just the structure of the labour market that is projected to change in future. The megatrends will also have implications for the nature of the future jobs that are available, and the skills needed to do them. While knowledge and qualifications will continue to be important, it is anticipated that skills which complement the newer technologies adopted in the labour market in future will also be critical.

What skills are expected to become more important as technology becomes more embedded in the world of work? The literature review carried out as part of The Skills Imperative 2035 research programme identified a range of essential employment skills, which were categorised into 4 groups:

i. Analytical/creative skills – which include problem-solving, decision-making, critical thinking, analysis and innovation/creativity

ii. Interpersonal skills – which include communication and collaboration

iii. Self-management skills – which include self-motivation/learning orientation, flexibility/adaptability and resilience/optimism

iv. Emotional intelligence skills – which include empathy/social perceptiveness.

Of course, these are skills we are already familiar with. Many workers already have some or all of them. The key point is that these skills are expected to be needed more widely across the labour market in future and at a higher level of skill than currently. This has important implications for investing in skills for Government, employers and of course workers themselves – as around two-thirds of the 2035 workforce are already in the labour market. It also has implications for the education system, which has a role to play in helping future generations of pupils develop these essential employment skills, which they will need to successfully access jobs and thrive in the labour market of the future.

WHAT ARE THE CONSEQUENCES FOR AN IDEAS-INFORMED SOCIETY?

The anticipated changes outlined earlier in this chapter point to a shifting workforce with an increasing number of skilled white collar jobs at the expense of more traditional, semi-skilled blue collar jobs. This means that employers of the future will need a better qualified and more skilled workforce to fill the jobs that will be available.

Reassuringly, in terms of an increasing qualified workforce, the projections show that this demand will be met in part by young people with higher levels of education and knowledge joining the labour market between now and 2035, replacing older workers who will leave during this timescale, who are generally less qualified. This bodes well in terms of the needs of the future workforce, but also as it is a prerequisite for becoming an ideas-informed society, as more highly qualified people generally are trained to think, question and critically appraise situations and sources.

What then of skills? It is not just those whose jobs are being displaced by technology who will have to upskill or reskill to able to find new work. The majority of workers in the workforce will need to invest in upgrading their skills so that they can meet the needs of employers and fill the jobs that will be available. However, with technology being more prevalent in the workforce and replacing routine manual tasks, the nature of the skills needed is expected to change. What employers will need is workers who can add value to what the technology can already deliver. In other words, skills such as problem solving, critical thinking, analysis, innovation/creativity, empathy and social perceptiveness – skills which humans are able to perform better than technology in the foreseeable future – will all become increasingly important. But as well as complementing technology, these are also exactly the type of skills which are likely to help an ideas-informed society to take hold and flourish.

So taking the human skills needed together with the likelihood of an increasingly well qualified workforce, workers of the future are likely to use these skills not only in their jobs, but also in assessing the world around them. For example, by being more empathetic and socially aware, future workers are likely to question the status quo. They are also likely to want to turn their attention to thinking critically about the problems that exist in society and trying to identify new solutions.

In summary, the changes which are expected to happen to the labour market as it becomes more technology driven are also consistent with what will be needed to bring about an ideas-informed society and to help this flourish. The challenge for the Government, for employers, educationists, workers and wider society is how we prepare for this, so we are ready and able to reap the rewards.

REFERENCES

1. https://obr.uk/docs/dlm_uploads/CCS1021486854-001_OBR-EF
    O-October-2021_CS_Web-Accessible_v2.pdf
    https://www.bankofengland.co.uk/-/media/boe/files/monetary-
    policy-report/2019/november/monetary-policy-report-november-
    2019.pdf
    https://ukandeu.ac.uk/wp-content/uploads/2019/10/The-econom
    ic-impact-of-Boris-Johnsons-Brexit-proposals.pdf
2. Based on Office for National Statistics projections, but with adjusted migration assumptions. See https://www.nfer.ac.uk/me dia/5085/working_paper_2a_baseline-report.pdf, section 2.2.2, for more detail.
3. https://www.nfer.ac.uk/key-topics-expertise/education-to-emp loyment/the-skills-imperative-2035/publications/
4. Based on the Standard Industrial Classification – The six broad sectors are primary sector and utilities; manufacturing; construction; trade, accommodation and transport; business and other services; and non-market services. The services in the non-market sector are predominantly provided by the public sector and other non-market producers. They are dominated by health and education, which are mainly provided by the public sector.
5. See https://www.nfer.ac.uk/media/5085/working_paper_2a_base line-report.pdf

23

EDUCATION POLICY FOR A NEW
AGE OF ENLIGHTENMENT

Raphael Wilkins

CONSCIOUSNESS – SEEING WITH FRESH EYES

The current potential for a world of ideas, technically enabled through instant access to information and intensive interaction through social media, bears comparison with the eighteenth-century 'Age of Enlightenment'. Then, a concern for the pursuit of knowledge obtained by reason and the senses was directed towards human happiness, liberty, tolerance, the separation of church and state and growth of constitutional government. Now, concerns are for equalities and diversity, regard for stewardship of the natural world, democratisation and secularisation. There are parallels of mood, aspiration and apparent opportunity. In reality,[1] the hopes of enlightenment and romanticism in the late eighteenth century soon became derailed by industrialisation in the nineteenth century. What now prevents a new age of enlightenment from gaining traction? What would have to be done differently to allow the breeze of progress?

In the eighteenth century wider access to knowledge shifted the balance of power sufficiently to at least change the terms of debate. Now, access to data seems not to have improved the power and autonomy of the individual in relation to the state, since the state and its agencies have themselves used those technologies to achieve unprecedented levels of surveillance and soft-power control.

This chapter is about policy, which is essentially concerned with the norms, values and assumptions within which governments pursue their objectives. Some of those may be explicit and ideological, and some may be passive: the effect of not re-examining decisions taken a long time ago.

The concept of 'consciousness' is quite helpful in relation to passive policies. The term originated in Marxist writings but is not owned by any ideology and need not be confined to perceptions of oppression and struggle. It can be applied to seeing with fresh eyes what is going on in a situation and why it is a problem, which is always the first step towards a solution. The first half of this chapter identifies features of the English education policy scene that are problematical for an ideas-informed society; the second half explores potential solutions.

CENTRALISATION OF CONTROL

The school system set up after the Second World War, set out in the 1944 Education Act, was a deliberate reaction to the fight against fascism in Europe: to make sure that the political indoctrination of children could never happen in England. Checks and balances were built into the system at every level, separating the roles of education professionals and elected politicians.[2] At school level, every set of articles of government delegated to the headteacher 'the internal conduct, curriculum and discipline of the school', an interesting comparator to the so-called school autonomy of later periods.

For 20 years, central governments allowed education to develop as an essentially local service within a loose and permissive national framework. From the mid-1960s onwards, Labour governments in particular saw a need to develop national education policies in support of social and economic agendas. The Thatcher government in the 1980s did so more strongly, initially getting around the constitutional niceties by giving the (then) Department for Employment a growing range of education functions. The Blair government turned central control into an art form.

Only rarely will a national government cede powers its predecessor enjoyed, so it is a given that the minutiae of children's education are under the control of national politicians and agencies directly accountable to them. That would have been dismissed as impossible when today's old educationists were young.

THE STRAITJACKET OF MULTI-LAYERED, 'IRREVERSIBLE' REFORMS

Another very significant factor is that successive governments laid new policies on top of old ones without regard for inherent contradictions. That is because a number of important policy changes have come to be regarded, across a broad political spectrum, as being in practice irreversible. The following are some examples.

COMPREHENSIVE REORGANISATION

The post-war school structure included the separation of school pupils at the secondary phase according to their ability and aptitudes. This 'sheep and goats' distinction took nominally tripartite, but in practice bipartite, form in which the most academically able 25% of 11-year-olds went to grammar schools and the rest to 'secondary modern' schools. Two decades into this experience (i.e. by the mid-1960s) it was widely considered that the secondary modern schools occupied inferior buildings, had the least qualified teachers, limited aspirations and exacerbated social divisions. Comprehensive secondary education would address those problems: championed by a Labour government, no subsequent government has seriously considered reversing the change at national level. A consequence is to rule out of debate any suggestion that some young people might benefit from a different curriculum offered in a different learning environment.

MARKET FORCES IN SCHOOL ADMISSIONS AND FUNDING

The next apparently irreversible change occurred during the Thatcher government between the mid-1980s and the mid-1990s.

Then, the governing party behaved in a partisan or sectarian mode, definitely not 'One Nation Conservatism'. Market forces were introduced into school admissions and funding, with the overt intention to create 'winner' and 'loser' schools, and in the knowledge that this could result in some communities ending up with only 'loser' schools. Schools were set in competition with each other, which in practice meant making themselves attractive to aspirational families: that remains the case.

THE NATIONAL CURRICULUM

At the same time, the Thatcher government introduced a National Curriculum which bore a marked resemblance to the traditional grammar school curriculum. From that time forward, the practical, creative and expressive elements of the curriculum have been squeezed.

THE BLAIR GOVERNMENT'S 'DELIVEROLOGY'

The Blair government, which began in 1997, kept in place the market forces, curriculum and regular testing which it inherited, and superimposed on all that its own distinctive approach. This was the outcome of a creative intellectual collaboration between Michael Barber, an adviser to government, and Vicki Phillips, a highly successful American school district superintendent, who, I would add, was a dynamic, visionary and inspiring person. The two of them worked away quietly, before Blair was elected, on the tactics which would be employed, notwithstanding England's very different constitutional checks and balances, to run England's school system pretty much as if it was a US school district, especially through more intensive use of ICT, measurement and monitoring. The conceptual underpinning of the Barber-Phillips model involved five fusions: equity with diversity, pressure with support, constant innovation with sustained implementation, changing behaviour so as to change beliefs, and central direction with frontline empowerment.[3]

From many examples of how the Blair regime exercised command and control, two are illustrative. The National Literacy Strategy involved van-loads of government-produced highly prescriptive teaching materials arriving at primary schools, which re-cast teachers as trainers presenting lessons designed by others. Secondly, the requirement that every new headteacher must hold the National Professional Qualification for Headship, the content and delivery of which were controlled by government, ensured that every school would be led by someone thoroughly exposed to New Labour's education mantras.

EXPANSION OF CHAINS OF TRUST SCHOOLS

Subsequent governments, up to the start of Rishi Sunak's premiership in October 2022, produced no new big ideas, confining themselves to marginal adjustments, except in relation to school governance. Conservative governments have continued to minimise the role of local government in schools, by greatly expanding academies and free schools. The preferred business model is trusts running chains of schools, often covering wide geographical areas. This can reduce the status of the headteacher to that of local branch manager, and can reduce the sense of ownership by local communities.

NOT A GOOD PLACE TO START FROM

The actions of successive governments, adding new layers of policy on top of old ones without regard to incoherences, and being too busy and impatient to reconsider fundamentals, have created a policy environment which is not very conducive to intellectual creativity. The overemphasis on academic education, lack of diversity in the forms and contexts of learning and diminished learner agency promote standardisation and marginalise innovative free-thinkers. Weak engagement with local communities and cultures and de-professionalisation of teaching inhibit much sense of grass-roots co-creation of the education process: instead, it is something imposed top-down. All of the checks and balances between central and local, between politicians and professionals, have been swept away.

WHAT WOULD A NEW AGE OF ENLIGHTENMENT LOOK LIKE?

Eaton[4] summarised Rousseau's *Emile*, which typified enlightenment thinking about learning, in which self-esteem and learner agency were prerequisites; in which formal learning needed to run alongside practical learning and engagement in the life of the community. Eaton argued that of the eight types of intelligence identified by the 'thinker about thinking', Howard Gardner,[5] only two, linguistic and logico-mathematical, were significantly supported by formal learning. Colin Brock,[6] an expert on global education issues, distinguished the settings of formal learning from the rest of civil society within which the majority of learning occurs informally, and argued that problems in many countries were exacerbated by a disconnection of formal learning from learners' lives and communities.

Calls for reform have been going on for a long time. Nearly two decades ago, Alexander and Potter[7] wrote that 'we are in the middle of a battle of ideas about schools' caused by demographic and technological change, and by increased discretionary time. They asked whether education is just a consumer product for individual benefit, or whether it builds society, and if the latter, is that to be prescribed by the state or created by communities? They noted that education can lead to new ideas and new confidence in people to stand up for themselves. More recently, the emergent purposes of schools have been creatively encapsulated by Hannon and Peterson,[8] as being to enable young people to thrive at global, societal, interpersonal and intrapersonal levels.

The Times set up an education commission, which reported in June 2022.[9] Its 12-point plan included more investment in early years education and better identification of special educational needs, new higher education campuses, a changed inspection regime and a 15-year strategy. It recommended 'career academies' with technical and vocational sixth forms, and a 'British Baccalaureate'.

At the time of writing, the new Sunak government seems set to take up the 'British Baccalaureate' proposal.[10] Of course the actual, real International Baccalaureate, as well as being independent of government, requires distinctive approaches to pedagogy that are as much the point of the thing as breadth of subjects examined. Tackling curricular imbalance post-16 may be a challenge if earlier phases remain unchanged.

NEED FOR A NEW STATEMENT OF SHARED PURPOSE

Way back in history, methods of learning reflected widespread illiteracy and limited access to knowledge. The knowledge considered worthwhile was transmitted within the authority structure of official religion employed as social control ('Do as you are told or you will burn in hell. . .'), backed up by savage hierarchical powers ('. . . and in the meantime you will be flogged'). The skills and attitudes inculcated prepared people for their predetermined stations in life, in a society assumed to be largely static and homogeneous. That set of norms was still pretty much intact when schooling became universal in the late nineteenth and early twentieth centuries, and has been gradually losing power and traction ever since. Rightly so, but without being replaced by any modern and acceptable shared set of norms about the purpose of the school system. Historically, heresy was not tolerated, but an ideas-informed society absolutely depends on making space for 'heretics'.

In 1944, the aim of the curriculum, reaffirmed in all subsequent major legislation, was that it should 'promote the spiritual, moral, mental and physical development of pupils at school, and of society'. Those words have not been debated in modern times: they require careful updating to reflect cultural diversity, earlier maturation, the importance of learner agency and tolerance of vibrant pluralism.

Now, there is easy and unlimited access to vast amounts of knowledge. Young people pick up the majority of what they know, and many skills, through the informal and self-directed learning they do. Formally structured schooling is important but it is only part of the picture. Schools will continue to exist as institutions because their childcare function is essential to a developed economy, rather than because the pattern of learning they provide could not be achieved in other ways. The essential contribution of the teaching profession in guiding and supporting learning, and tailoring structured pathways of progression, does not have to be forever linked to the image of rooms with rows of desks.

Society is both diverse, and predominantly secular, and is much less inclined to accept authority unquestioningly. People in positions of responsibility have to earn respect; when they don't, their shortcomings are likely to be captured on social media. Now, more than ever, education depends on the consent and engagement of the learner. Some schools have replaced the heading 'School Rules' with 'Shared Expectations', which is unconvincing unless the students have had meaningful involvement in their formation. There is no longer any clear and broadly-shared answer to a student's question, 'Why should I?' This reflects the long-term absence of serious debate about the place, purpose and ownership of public education.

VARIED SETTINGS FOR LEARNING

Traditionally, say 40 years ago, a form of segregation occurred at age 16, when some young people entered their school sixth-forms while others left to go to further education colleges. Becoming a sixth-former implied signing up for a normative/moral[11] commitment to the school as an organisation: to its ethos and traditions (however imaginary they might be), its gilded honours boards and gowned staff, being a role model for younger students, accepting praefectorial responsibility. By contrast, the further education college offered a purely remunerative/calculative environment for obtaining skills, which could be achieved through a range of patterns of attendance. These historic caricatures have modern application. Then, the split was mainly by academic ability and social class. Now, diverse cultures and personalities justify different learning environments allowing different patterns of engagement. Because modern young people are more mature and sophisticated, those options should open up at age 14 rather than 16.

These thoughts point towards Key Stage 4 evolving into a network of varied and flexible learning opportunities, drawing on the full range of expertise and specialised facilities available in a locality, navigated with supportive guidance and mentoring. Competition between schools would give ground to a concern for the achievement of whole populations.

RELEVANCE OF LEARNING TO LIFE AND COMMUNITY

Learner agency is central to education, enabling people to make informed choices, cultivating the link between the learning that people do and their capacity to address the issues in their lives, now and in the future. Two factors support that. First, there must be a perceived connection in the learner's mind between the school curriculum and the matters that trouble them in their life outside the classroom. Second, there must not be dissonance in the learner's mind between the culture of the school as an institution, and the culture of their home and community. A new level of significance and priority should be given to the quality of relationships between schools and the communities they serve.

WHO OWNS AND DEFINES THE FUTURE?

Current education policies say to young people, 'We who are in charge understand the future, and what you need to succeed in it'. An emerging world of ideas requires a different message: 'We do not know the future, it belongs to you. We want to enable you to create a better future than we can currently envision'.

NEW VOICES AT THE TABLE

If discussion is to lead to a new 15-year strategy for education, then it needs to include some different voices to open up more radical visions. First, from special education, where multi-professional teams devise effective programmes for young people whose learning challenges are significant. They have been out of the spotlight and largely exempt from the bombardment of political initiatives: havens for curriculum development and innovative pedagogy. Reason enough for being at the table; a reminder that everyone is special. Then voices who understand out-of-school learning: youth workers and staff who organise education otherwise than at school, and further education experts on work-related learning. People from local authorities who understand the issues of challenging neighbourhoods. These voices would counterbalance those of the provider interests, the custodians of the status quo.

Will Emile get to learn about life by running through a meadow? Not likely, and he would be tracked by his smartphone. Nor can worthwhile education reform be imposed top-down. It requires a strong additional impetus from bottom-up and middle-out, as existing institutions and local organisations find the will to explore new approaches. True autonomy to enrich a world of ideas has to be taken, not given.

NOTES

1. Lawton, D. and Gordon, P. (2002) *A history of Western educational ideas*, London: Woburn Press.
2. Alexander, W. (1954) *Education in England: the national system, how it works*, London: Newnes.
3. Barber, M. and Phillips, V. (2000) *Fusion: how to unleash irreversible change - lessons for the future of system-wide school reform*, Hong Kong: Chinese University of Hong Kong Press.
4. Eaton, J. (2010) 'Rousseau revisited: formal and personal education', in Coates, M. (Ed) *Shaping a new educational landscape*, London: Continuum.
5. Gardner, H. (1993) *Frames of mind*, London: Fontana.
6. Brock, C. (2011) *Education as a global concern*, London: Continuum.

7. Alexander, T. and Potter, J. (Eds) (2005) *Education for a change*, London: Routledge Falmer.

8. Hannon, V. and Peterson, A. (2021) *Thrive: the purpose of schools in a changing world*, Cambridge: Cambridge University Press.

9. *The Times*, 15 June 2022, pp 12–13.

10. *The Times*, 27 October 2022, p 1.

11. The terminology in this paragraph refers to the 'congruent compliance structures' of Etzioni, A. (1961) *A comparative analysis of complex organisations*, New York: Free Press.

24

IDEAS IN ACTION: CRITICALLY REFLECTIVE PRACTICE

Neil Thompson

INTRODUCTION

This chapter explores the concepts of critically reflective practice and theorising practice as foundations for integrating ideas into professional practice of various kinds. The basic premises are that (i) ideas are of little value unless they are put to use; (ii) the traditional idea of 'applying theory to practice' is unhelpful and misleading; and (iii) ideas need to be used *critically*.

We begin by considering the significance of critically reflective practice as a foundation for making use of ideas in action. This is followed by a discussion of theorising practice as a more appropriate way of conceptualising the relationship between ideas and actions. Finally, we explore some obstacles to making theory-practice links.

CRITICALLY REFLECTIVE PRACTICE

The work of Donald Schön and others around reflective practice has proven to be very influential in shaping the relationship between ideas and their use in practice across the caring professions and management fields.[1] What has emerged from the earlier work on this subject has been an emphasis on *critical* reflection.

The basic principle underpinning reflective practice is the creation of thinking space in order to ensure that our actions are rooted in relevant knowledge and values, rather than simply based on habit, routine, guesswork or simply copying others. Ideas are therefore at the heart of reflective practice. Without ideas we would not have the tools we need for reflecting and for making sense of the situations we encounter, whether in our personal lives or in our work.

However, for clear, productive and effective thinking, we need to be prepared to review those ideas and not allow them to become unquestioned dogma – an open epistemic order to use Rid's phrase.[2] This is where the notion of *critically* reflective practice comes into the picture.

Thompson and Thompson[3] discuss the significance of what they refer to as critical depth and breadth. The former refers to the need to look beneath the surface and question taken-for-granted assumptions. The latter refers to adopting a more sociologically informed holistic approach to incorporate an understanding of power relations and the potential for discrimination and oppression. The basic argument is that, without such a doubly critical perspective, reflective practice can omit consideration of some vitally important aspects of the situation, resulting in ideas being inappropriately channelled.

Without critical depth, problems with, or the limitations of, ideas are likely to go unnoticed. Ideas that are adopted unquestioningly become dogma and, as such, can distort our perceptions of reality. This can then lead to conflict between groups who have each adopted their own dogmatic positions and are not open to their assumptions being questioned. Consideration of conflict, whether interpersonal or on the wider socio-political stage, soon highlights the role of entrenched positions.

A dogmatic approach will also block the development of ideas. If we are not prepared to make the ideas we use open to question, the scope for developing those ideas, building on them and connecting them with other important ideas becomes severely restricted. So, while ideas are the building blocks of understanding, without critical depth, our understanding becomes static and unnecessarily limited.

Critical depth is therefore needed as a basis for learning and the development of a fuller understanding of the situations we encounter in our lives. This relates to everyone but has particular resonance for members of the people professions, by which I mean those occupations where success depends on being able to engage productively with people (for example, the caring professions and management across all sectors). People, their problems and their potential are all complex, and so a sophisticated understanding of various aspects of human psychology and the social context in which the human drama plays out is required to achieve the best results.

Holism Rather Than Atomism

Without critical breadth, there is a danger that our focus will be too narrow, that our perspective will not take account of significant aspects of the wider context. The technical term for this is 'atomism', the tendency to limit our attention to individual factors. The danger here is that we base our actions on a very limited understanding of the situation. For example, we may regard an aggressive reaction as a characteristic of the individual without considering the circumstances that will have prompted that reaction.

The opposite of atomism, then, is 'holism' which means adopting a holistic perspective, one that looks at the bigger picture. Intellectually, this means conceptualising psychological ideas within a wider socio-political context – that is, one that takes account of both social and political factors.

In terms of social factors, in an earlier work,[4] I have characterised these in terms of what I call the SPIDER model – that is, social:

- *Structures* This includes class, race/ethnicity, gender, language group, religion and so on.

- *Processes* These can be positive, such as socialisation, or negative, such as discrimination and marginalisation.

- *Institutions* By this I mean the 'building blocks' of society, such as the family, the law, the education system and so on.

- *Discourses* These are well-established frameworks of meaning, sets of ideas that can prove very influential.

- *Expectations* Socialisation instils in us sets of expectations around behaviour, emotional responses and so on.

- *Relations* This includes interpersonal interactions as well as relations between and across groups of people.

This framework helps us to appreciate the complexity of the social context, bearing in mind that these different elements do not operate in isolation – they will be constantly interacting and influencing one another.

In relation to political factors, these can be understood both narrowly in the sense of party politics and more broadly in terms of power relations and the ways in which these shape people's lives (for good or ill) in many ways.

Critical breadth is therefore important to ensure that our ideas reach beyond the individual level and take account of the wider picture. For example, a failure to consider the potential impact of racism on a black person may contribute to a far from adequate understanding of that person's life experience. A white manager who adopts a 'colour blind' approach by leaving racism out of the picture may be oblivious to discrimination that is going on. In this way, they can be understood as part of the problem, rather than part of the solution in relation to equality, diversity and inclusion.[5]

In practical terms, holism involves making sure that our reflection does not limit itself to individual factors. For example, in terms of health and well-being in the workplace, Costello[6] makes the important point that the key factors need to be understood within the wider context; otherwise, stress will be perceived in misleading reductionist terms:

> ...*people who experience stress at work are seen as weak, having some character flaw or lacking backbone. Thinking of stress in this way is inappropriate and potentially dangerous. It forces the issue underground*

for some, and promotes a culture of shame in others
that gets in the way of people either asking for help, or
taking time off to get better.

Wellbeing Interventions Continuum

It is for this reason that my own work on this subject introduces the idea of the wellbeing interventions continuum.[7] This involves recognising that an individual's experience of health and wellbeing will depend to a large extent on the team context, given that the quality of teamwork can be a significant help or a significant hindrance when it comes to promoting employee wellness. In turn, the team context needs to be recognised as depending to a large extent on the wider organisational context, especially in terms of its culture.[8]

Finally, the organisational circumstances owe much to the wider societal context in which the world of work has been changing significantly in a number of ways.[9] Wellbeing initiatives that fail to recognise this continuum and continue to focus narrowly on individual factors are therefore likely to have limited positive impact and can actually make the situation worse by placing additional pressures on the individual(s) concerned who come to be seen as the *locus* of the problem (rather than the *focus* of a much broader multidimensional set of problematic factors).

An example of the dangers of atomism is readily to be found in relation to the concept of resilience. An atomistic approach to resilience that presents it as simply a character trait has the disempowering effect of conceiving people's struggles with adversity as a personal failing, as some form of 'resilience deficit'. This can contribute to a vicious circle in which people who are already struggling with their life pressures are then made to feel that it is their own fault – the highly significant wider organisational and sociopolitical factors are disregarded.[10]

Cox and Thompson[11] explain the situation in the following terms:

Much of the existing literature gives the impression that resilience is 'within' the individual, part of their personality or 'nature', as if it forms part of the essence of who they are. This is unhelpful for (at least) two reasons:

1. It lays a foundation for a judgemental approach in which individuals can be rated in terms of how resilient (or otherwise) they are, as if resilience were simply a personality trait, rather than a complex, multidimensional phenomenon. It makes it easy for individuals who struggle with resilience to be criticised, without taking account of the full picture of the circumstances.

2. Failing to take account of wider factors can distort the picture and thereby fail to address important elements of the situation. For example, in a culture where women are expected to be submissive, efforts to bounce back from adversity that require a degree of assertiveness may require that the women concerned go against their culture, a step that could in itself have adverse consequences.

What I hope is now clear is that critically reflective practice, as conceived in terms of both critical depth and critical breadth, offers an important foundation for the effective use of ideas in action. Neglecting either critical depth or critical breadth leaves us in a highly problematic situation that can hold back progress in both intellectual and practical terms.

THEORISING PRACTICE

As an extension of critically reflective practice, my own work[12] argues the case for 'theorising practice'. This is as an alternative to the traditional approach of 'applying theory to practice' which begins by focussing on theory. Theorising practice, by contrast, involves beginning with the concrete practice situation and then drawing on the relevant theory base to identify what ideas can best inform how we move forward. My training work with managers and practitioners about this has generated considerable enthusiasm for this more helpful way of understanding the relationship between ideas and actions. Several such participants have told me that seeing the relationship between theory and practice in this way has lifted a considerable burden off their shoulders following years of trying unsuccessfully to fit the square peg of theory into the round hole of practice.

A theorising practice approach presents the relationship between theory and practice in vertical, rather than horizontal terms – that is, practice is seen to be *underpinned* by theory. Fig. 1 illustrates this.

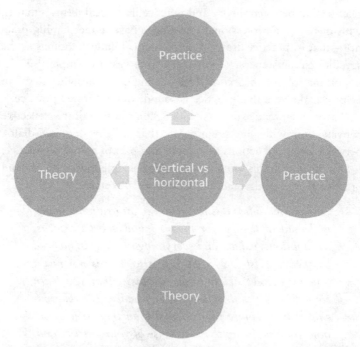

Fig. 1. A Vertical vs Horizontal Model of the Relationship Between Theory and Practice.

Traditionally, theory and practice are seen as being located in separate spaces, theory in the world of the academy and practice in the world of day-to-day professional endeavours (a horizontal relationship – on the same plane but in different locations). Unfortunately, this has the tendency to reinforce a separation between the two, rather than to integrate them. It increases the risk of students, as they move on from the academic world, leaving behind much of their professional knowledge and becoming more open to cultural influences in the employing organisation they subsequently join (usually a mixture of helpful 'practice wisdom' and not so helpful unwise unquestioned assumptions and bad habits). This problem is characterised by the comment heard by many a new graduate employee across many settings: 'Forget that college nonsense, you are in the real world now'.

By contrast, a theorising practice approach conceives of the relationship between theory and practice in vertical terms – that is, with theory (the professional knowledge base) underpinning practice – that is, practice drawing on theoretical understandings as the specific circumstances require. This serves to emphasise the important role of theoretical ideas as important insights that can help to make sure that practice is sound, well-informed practice.

Theorising practice fits well with Schön's notion of the 'reflective conversation with the situation' – that is, the ongoing dialog between ideas and actions that goes on as part of reflective practice. It also fits with Fish's work on the relationship between theory and practice.[13] As Handscomb and Cockburn[14] explain:

> 'No action, unless it is the action of an irrational being, is devoid of theory, for theory involves beliefs, ideas, assumptions, values, and everything we do is influenced by theory' (Fish, 1995, p. 57). Also, this is not just a 'one-way street' relationship – that is, that you learn some theory and then apply it to practice. The relationship is much more fundamental than that. It is about how you use theory to make sense of your practice and, indeed, as Fish powerfully explains, how as an individual you develop your own theory from practice.

The concept of 'making sense of practice' is a very important one, given the role of meaning making and narratives in human experience.[15] Although most, if not all, organisations provide policies, guidelines, procedures and protocols, these are, in a sense, a map of the territory. They do not provide enough information to exclude the need for some degree of judgement and weighing up of the circumstances. Such judgements will, of course, rely on ideas, either implicitly or explicitly. Where the ideas are being used explicitly – that is, knowingly – they are capable of being questioned (to check for error or flawed logic), developed over time and learnt from. By contrast, where ideas are being used implicitly, they are not open to question (they have the status of dogma), and so errors or flawed logic can slip below the radar and create significant difficulties; they will be static, in the sense that they will not develop over time; and they offer no basis for learning.

The idea that theory is not something that is 'applied' to practice, but rather is a set of insights that can help us make sense of the situations that arise in practice, is therefore one that has considerable value.

OBSTACLES TO USING IDEAS IN ACTION

There are many ways in which the theorising of practice can be prevented from happening. Here I want focus on two in particular.

High Pressure and the Need for More Reflection

First, there is the issue of work overload. Work pressures have been rising for some time now, with stress featuring more and more as an aspect of working life.[16] This is a large part of the reason why there is so much emphasis these days on investing in health and wellbeing in the workplace. More and more organisations are beginning to take seriously the harm that stress can do (to the individual and to the organisation) and the need to pay close attention to employee wellness challenges.[17] Where employees are constantly rushing to meet deadlines and keep their heads above water, they will be facing a major temptation to simply 'press on' in an effort to get the job done and not leave time or space for reflection and learning. This, of course, is a common pathway to burnout.

Thompson and Thompson[18] make the important point that being under a high level of pressure should be seen not as a reason for dispensing with reflective practice, but all the more reason for drawing on it. The busier we are, the more reflective we need to be in order to ensure that we are (i) using our limited time to the best effect; (ii) not allowing the pressure to push us into rash decisions or actions that we may later regret; and (iii) using our knowledge and experience to guide us in coming up with strategies for dealing with the high level of pressure (that is, a proactive approach, rather than a reactive one).

Where this lesson is not learned and a 'heads down, get on with it' approach is adopted, there is a very serious danger that a major disconnect between the individual's knowledge base and their actions will arise, potentially resulting in very unwise or counter-productive forms of practice. Similarly, such a non-reflective approach can result in values issues not being considered, poten-tially resulting in unethical or even illegal actions.[19]

Cultural Obstacles

Second, an organisation's culture can serve as an obstacle to the-orising practice. From my training and consultancy work, I have discerned three cultural approaches to learning:

- *A learning culture* This is where learning is supported, valued and nurtured. The personal and professional growth and development of individuals are seen as assets and therefore very much to be encouraged. It is where workforce development plans are integrated into the organisation's overall strategy and strategic vision and where learning is understood to involve more than just training provision.

- *A non-learning culture* This relates to organisations that think of learning in very narrow terms – for example, simply in terms of meeting minimum statutory training requirements. There is unlikely to be any integration of workforce development plans and activities within the wider organisational strategy. Learning is reduced to training which then becomes largely a box-ticking exercise.

- *An anti-learning culture* This where learning is actively discouraged, as if it is some sort of threat. Such cultures are characterised by comments along the lines of: 'If you've got time to think, then you haven't got enough work to do'. People who are keen to learn may actually be ridiculed. Cultures of this kind usually have a very low level of morale (which is partly a contributory factor and partly a consequence).

Both non-learning and anti-learning cultures can be significant obstacles to theorising practice in particular and reflective practice in general, anti-learning cultures especially so. Where these barriers exist, leaders are faced with a major challenge, in so far as the harm that can arise from practices based on the use of uncritical routines and ill-considered knee-jerk responses can be immense in terms of:

- Unwise or even dangerous decision making that can lead to complaints or litigation;

- The lack of return on human resource investment in terms of the failure to promote learning, development and improvement;

- Lower levels of job satisfaction and morale that can have adverse consequences in terms of staff retention; and

- Reputational damage as a result of adverse publicity (formal or informal).

The need for people in leadership positions to give careful thought to the development of critically reflective practice should therefore be quite clear.

CONCLUSION – MAKING USE OF IDEAS IN ACTION

The recognition of the value of reflective practice is reflected in the extent of related literature over the years (the journal *Reflective Practice* has been publishing for over 20 years). More recently, this has been supplemented by texts that highlight the importance of *critical* reflection – that is, reflection that includes a strong element critical analysis.[20] As part of this development, my own work has highlighted in particular the need to rethink the relationship between theory and practice, to replace the traditional idea of applying theory to practice with that of 'theorising practice'.

This is proposed as a more realistic and effective way of making use of ideas in action. However, we have recognised that there are obstacles to theorising practice as a basis for critically reflective practice in those organisations that overload their employees to the point of stress, tolerate a culture that does not value learning and development or both. In such circumstances, leaders are faced with major challenges in terms of organisational culture if they are to get the benefit of work practices that are rooted in professional insights and careful thought, rather than being based on habit, routine, guesswork or copying others.

REFERENCES

1. Schön, D. A. (1983) The Reflective Practitioner: How Professionals Think in Action, New York, Basic Books.
   Rolfe, G., Jasper, M. and Freshwater, D. (eds) (2011) Critical Reflection in Practice: Generating Knowledge for Care, 2nd edn, Basingstoke, Palgrave Macmillan.
2. Rid, T. (2018) Active Measures: The Secret History of Disinformation and Political Warfare, London, Profile Books.
3. Thompson, S. and Thompson, N. (2023) The Critically Reflective Practitioner, 3rd edn, London, Bloomsbury.
4. Thompson, N. (2017) Applied Sociology, New York, Routledge.
5. Thompson, N. (2021) Anti-discriminatory Practice, 7th edn, London, Bloomsbury.
6. Costello, J. (2020) Workplace Wellbeing: A Relational Approach, London, Routledge.
7. Thompson, N. (2021) 'Promoting Employee Wellness – Making it a Reality', Leadership Issues in Social Care, 3 (4), pp. 2–24.
8. Schein, E. H. (2017) Organizational Culture and Leadership, 5th edn, Chichester, Wiley.
9. Cheese. P. (2021) The New World of Work: Shaping a Future that Helps People, Organizations and Our Societies to Thrive, London, Kogan Page.

10. Costello, J. (2020) Workplace Wellbeing: A Relational Approach, London, Routledge.
    Thompson, N. (2019) The Managing Stress Practice Manual, Wrexham, Avenue Media Solutions.
11. Cox, G. R. and Thompson, N. (2020) 'Making Sense of Resilience', in Thompson and Cox (eds) Promoting Resilience: Responding to Adversity, Vulnerability and Loss, New York, Routledge, pp. 5–24.
12. Thompson, N. (2017) Theorizing Practice, 2nd edn, London, Bloomsbury.
13. Fish, D. (1995) Quality Mentoring for Student Teachers: A Principled Approach to Practice, London, David Fulton.
14. Handscomb, G. and Cockburn, A. (2012) Setting Out in Cockburn, A. and Handscomb, G. (eds) Teaching Children 3–11: A Student's Guide. 3rd edn, London, Sage.
15. Payne, M. (2006) Narrative Therapy, London, Sage.
16. Jaffe, S. (2021) Work Won't Love You Back: How Devotion to Our Jobs Keeps Us Exploited, Exhausted and Alone, London, Hurst & Co.
17. Bevan, S. and Cooper, C. L. (2022) The Healthy Workforce: Enhancing Wellbeing and Productivity in the Workers of the Future, Bingley, Emerald Publishing Limited.
18. Thompson, S. and Thompson, N. (2023) The Critically Reflective Practitioner, 3rd edn, London, Bloomsbury.
19. Moss, B. and Thompson, N. (2020) The Values-based Practice Manual, Wrexham, Avenue Media Solutions.
20. Thompson, N. and Pascal, J. (2012) 'Developing Critically Reflective Practice', Reflective Practice 13 (2), pp. 311–325
    White, S., Fook, J. and Gardner, F. (eds) (2006). Critical Reflection in Health and Social Care, Maidenhead, Open University Press/McGraw-Hill Education.

25

TURNING SCHOOLS INSIDE OUT – COMMUNITY CURRICULUM MAKING

David Leat, Alison Whelan, Ulrike Thomas, Carolynn Kerr and Ruth Webb

INTROVERTED SCHOOLS AND UNTAPPED TALENT

In theory schools in England have curriculum freedom, but in practice few use that freedom. Many are risk averse and will pivot to the latest emphasis in policy, Ofsted inspection framework or consultant advice. Most recently traditional subject teaching, cognitive load theory, knowledge retrieval and evidence of progress in books are among the trends to have grabbed attention. Government is the arbiter of the curriculum ideas and anything not favoured or called into doubt in some way, perhaps spuriously, is anathema. Creative ideas are choked off by the desire to play safe. Schools need to be brave to explore ideas that better serve young people in the 21st century.

As part of a teacher training course lecture each year, one of us asks trainee teachers to indicate whether they think the current school system in England does provide an adequate education for the early C21st and in particular regarding the context of climate change, online dangers, mental health, inequality and poverty. On average about 75% of these new entrants to the profession indicate that they don't and only 10% are confident that it does. This reflects the common critique that schools are exam factories,

constrained by neoliberal market ideology in which competition
'drives up' standards. One consequence has been a narrowing of the
curriculum, to the detriment of the arts, practical subjects and the
humanities, thus failing many from disadvantaged backgrounds
and those who do not swim in academic waters.

A competing trend internationally is a curriculum shift towards
competences, for example in New Zealand and also in Scotland,
where the Curriculum for Excellence[1] is centred on four capabilities
(a synonym for competences): Successful Learners, Confident
Individuals, Responsible Citizens and Effective Contributors. Sadly,
despite teachers' best efforts, the wider talents and human capability of young people in the UK (and especially England) remain
largely untapped. Worryingly, the focus on exam results, often
leads to pupils who do not readily conform to this model being
ejected from the system. Data shows that the total of students
excluded from school rises annually. 5,740 children and young
people were permanently excluded in England in 2009–2010 and
by 2018–2019 the number had reached 7,894 (a 38% rise) (DfE,
2011, 2020).[2] A further indication of the collateral damage is the
number of young people with mental health issues.[3] The managerialism in schools also has profound negative effects on teachers'
well-being and commitment (Skinner et al., 2021).[4] We believe that
schools need to turn themselves outward (inside-out) to their local
and wider communities as sources of inspiration and support in
curriculum development for human flourishing.

THE BIG IDEA

Many people are familiar with the African proverb that 'it takes a
village to raise a child'. There is a profound viewpoint here, which
reflects the idea that it is the responsibility of everyone to raise the
next generation of children. If the future is to be 'better' than the
past or the present, then it requires as much human resource and
wisdom as we can muster to educate young people so that they
enjoy 'good lives' without detriment to others. Well-planned,
project-based learning (PBL) developed with community partners,
using community resources and drawing on community issues can

provide both service to the community and meaning to the students. This ambition draws on a number of traditions including the village colleges movement in Cambridgeshire (Hopkins, 2020),[5] place-based learning (Facer & Thomas, 2012),[6] service learning (Celio et al., 2011),[7] and the Community Funds of Knowledge model (Gonzalez et al., 2006).[8] This is a progressive step in the combatting of the issues of teacher alienation, student engagement, exclusion and well-being, and the development of a wider array of talent in young people. It also gives serious muscle to the outcomes indicated in the Personal Development section of the Ofsted framework, such as knowing how to keep physically and mentally healthy, and be responsible and active citizens. These outcomes cannot be 'instructed', they depend in part on the experiential nature of PBL.

SOCIAL JUSTICE ARGUMENTS

Current educational policy does put emphasis on cultural capital, but it has a myopic view of what constitutes such capital, conceiving it as subject knowledge only, that knowledge being distilled by communities of scholars in well-established disciplines – the best which has been thought and said in the world. The case being made here is that cultural capital needs to be drawn more widely, to take in 'going places, meeting people and doing and making things' (Leat et al., 2020).[9] Why would young people value the natural environment and its benefits if they have never had the chance to visit inspiring places? How will they become good citizens unless they have the chance of serving their community?

TWO EXAMPLES FROM THE LITERATURE

A good example of what can be achieved comes from Australia[10] where the Australian School Innovation in Science, Technology and Mathematics (ASISTM) initiative, involves partnerships between schools, community and industry organisations in developing local curriculum projects. The projects faced up to social, ethical and personal dimensions to real world issues. They were co-planned between teachers and associate partners from universities, public agencies or companies to improve student experience and provide service to the community or partners. The authors describe some teachers as wanting to open the school to the community and vice versa, as explained in this description of linked projects in one area:

> BioTech Units at Serendip Sanctuary: *The BioTech project in this Geelong satellite area was devised in response to a felt need to strengthen the community engagement of youth in the local schools. The cluster of schools agreed to develop a four-year plan with sustainability as the theme whilst allowing diversity amongst the schools in their curriculum development within this agreed theme. Meg, the coordinator, managed a complex web of initiatives involving visiting scientists and other community members, environmental projects, excursion programs and project-based learning initiatives.*

In England, the work of the RSA[11] on Area Based Curriculum provides some valuable pointers on emergent benefits and potential barriers. The RSA are long-time advocates of localism, democracy and human capability. In Peterborough the RSA engaged with five schools in the Peterborough area for two years helping them to partner with local organisations. The RSA team supported curriculum development with a focus on learning about a place, by a place and for a place, with benefits to include the following:

- Access to local expertise and resources to support learning;

- Access to local sites for learning;

- Shared ownership with local stakeholders of the learning going on in schools;

- Positive contact for students with adults from a range of sectors and backgrounds.

The evaluation showed that most of the benefits were realised with many pupils being more engaged, enjoying learning outside the classroom and knowing more about (and valuing) the Peterborough area. However, for some schools the project was seen as a choice between the standards agenda and a wider curriculum and indeed the secondary school seemed to turn its back on the initiative as classroom teachers were difficult to contact by the local partners.

A SCHOOL CASE

Valley Gardens Middle School (Years 5-8) is in Whitley Bay in North-East England. In 2019 the bold decision was made to embed PBL as part of our curriculum in an attempt to contextualise learning in the twenty-first century and avoid the erosion of the curriculum that threatens some arts based and practical subjects. PBL therefore also supports the wider moral aims of a cohesive curriculum with benefits including widening pupil experience, developing critical skills, strengthening community links, engaging with outside learning partners and agencies and thus extending the wider cultural capital on offer to our children. The added advantage is being able to further embed the core school values of Kindness, Resilience and Respect as a thread that runs through all the projects.

PBL is timetabled on Monday afternoon on Week 2 of the 10-day timetable for all year groups. There are three projects in each year group which the children access on a carousel. Pupil consultation happens every year, asking the children what they would like to include in the projects and that isn't covered in the curriculum. Projects are developed, adapted or extended as a result. PBL therefore reflects the concerns and interests of our children. They are aware of environmental issues and interested in their social, political and cultural surroundings, and as a result the projects cover personal issues such as self-image, finance, locality, global warming and climate change. We also use our extensive school grounds and benefit from trips to nearby locations: our cluster schools, Newcastle University, Whitley Bay and Tynemouth, North Shields Quayside, local museums and art galleries. All the trips focus on gathering information that is used in the final project or as a location for the showpiece that is the final project.

CLIMATE CHANGE PROJECT

Providing opportunities for the pupils to be heard was key to establishing our Climate Change PBL project which was initiated with Year 8. We were aware, through an active Eco-Club and pupil voice surveys, that climate change is a topic of great concern and the project would allow discussion with peers and staff, giving them confidence to raise such issues and therefore some ownership of the curriculum. With an emphasis on a solution focused mindset, we arrived at several pertinent questions.

- What action can we as pupils take and how can we encourage others to take similar action?

- What solutions are there?

- How can we manage and adapt our way of life?

- How can we express our views and concerns?

Project leaders quickly realised that such questions could not be answered without the support of additional expertise from our local community and it emerged that many groups and organisations were willing to offer support when asked - to coin a colloquial expression, 'shy bairns get nowt'! Immediately, the North Tyneside local authority offered support and guidance to the school and were genuinely excited to hear about our project as the pupils' questions dovetailed with the authority's action plan to become carbon neutral by 2030. They provided us with a bespoke video which included an introduction by a local councillor, followed by the Sustainability Team outlining their mission to achieve net zero, providing specific information about our local area and data about our school's energy use. They were always quick to answer specific questions about data, technology and terminology. In addition, an existing partnership with scientists and engineers from Newcastle University was extended to design and create practical solutions in school. Plans were made for a launch event at the university to further enthuse the pupils and highlight higher education opportunities and careers in the STEM sector. Unfortunately, COVID-19 restrictions meant that this had to be postponed but post-COVID-19 we are planning a showcase at Newcastle University with an invited audience of 'dignitaries' and parents.

A voluntary wildlife conservation group, The Friends of the Brierdene, provided a guided tour of a local Site of Special Scientific Interest (SSSI) explaining how climate change is mitigated through their conservation measures such as planting a range of species to improve biodiversity, conserving water, recycling items and plant management. Pupils expressed interest in joining this group and some now support it during their own time, volunteering to plan, plant and be involved in clearing and clean-up operations. We were also able to work with Cap-a-Pie Theatre Company to express, through drama, the thoughts, feelings and ideas from the pupils.

Involvement with the local community quickly snowballed as the climate change project developed. The involvement of external visitors and off-site visits brought deeper engagement and interest, and pupils looked forward to the sessions with obvious enthusiasm. The pupils are very positive about the PBL experience and a few comments below indicate a very wide range of benefits:

> When we did an amazing and fun beach clean with all the groups that were doing the Eco Project and I really enjoyed it!!

> We learn about other subjects...that aren't in the curriculum.

> You build teamwork and character building in PBL.

> [I enjoyed] learning how to work with people and different skills to what we learn in normal lessons.

> [We learned] being really resilient to help us give our opinion on things.

WHAT WE HAVE LEARNT

The Climate Change project was a learning curve for us, building as it did on existing provision. The opportunity to work with such diverse partners gave a new depth and breadth to the project. The drama aspect gave the children a voice to express concerns over the issues that affect them. The engineering element gave the opportunity to look for practical engineering solutions such as wind turbines and solar powered appliances, while the eco aspect allowed focus on specific areas of the school ground that could be developed, reducing our carbon footprint. In retrospect, we were overly ambitious with outcomes with the constraints we had on time, both for planning and the sessions, and also because of COVID-19 restrictions which were a limiting factor. Because of the number of outside agencies, we would have benefited from more planning time. Nonetheless, the results of the projects were still impressive

- an area of the school was transformed through planting of hedges through work with The Tree Council;

- a short protest drama-documentary was created which the children planned and performed, giving them a creative opportunity to voice their concerns about global warming;

- the children gained engineering insights into the value of sustainable energy and ways we could utilise this in school.

We recognise that PBL poses a challenge to staff in finding external community expertise to enhance the experience in school, but once we start to make links, we find that individuals, groups and organisations have all been willing and extremely keen to work with us. They are able to use our school community as an opportunity to showcase their purpose, and in many cases, inspire the pupils to consider following in their footsteps. Following our visit to the local conservation area, two local environmental volunteers were keen to support our Year 8 PBL students in the planting of a hedgerow on the school grounds, using free whips provided by The Tree Council. Arrangements have already been made for them to return and extend the hedgerow when our next batch of free whips arrive, this time from The Woodland Trust.

The Climate Change Project is still being developed to give it greater practical relevance and we have recently heard that our application to the Royal Society for further funds has been successful. Future plans include pupil visits to our local feeder primary schools for the pupils to demonstrate their learning to a younger audience, thereby encouraging the wider community to consider their carbon footprint and suggest changes in mindset and behaviour.

The advantage of having specific time for PBL is that it releases staff from the constraints of a content-laden national curriculum in which schools are encouraged to funnel pupils into academic subjects which are unsuitable for some and do not allow them to develop all their talents. In PBL the community involvement encourages the development of community links and involvement to give a real-life context. This in turn widens pupils' experience, contextualises the learning and develops critical skills rather than judging on Age Related Expectations (ARE) or Grade 1–9 assessment.

As we develop our PBL expertise we are increasingly able to integrate more National Curriculum subject knowledge into our projects, but equally links made through PBL filter into the wider curriculum. For example, in Year 8 Geography, pupils start the year with a topic on Climate Change, where they explore causes and impact. In PBL, the Climate Change project explores possible creative solutions, so pupils work in a solution focused mindset. We have also discovered a further crossover within English where speeches of Greta Thunberg are now used as a basis for exploring persuasive speech. The closely linked Sustainability Project is also closely woven into our science curriculum as it was led by our Head of Science who then utilised the extended depth and breadth of knowledge and understanding of the children. It becomes a symbiotic relationship which improves the provision of both PBL and the more traditional curriculum. This will take time and is an unexpected benefit which we hadn't planned for, but fully appreciate. As a result, the wider cultural capital of our pupils is extended and the skills-based focus of PBL becomes formalised in a curriculum setting.

CONCLUSION

The Climate Change project at VGMS is a clear example of the processes and benefits of turning a school 'inside-out' and appreciating the local and wider community as partners in the education

of young people. Although there is some adjustment needed, this
does not mean that subject knowledge is being sacrificed – instead it
is given meaning through context and experience which promises
much deeper learning. The whole person and their full capabilities
benefit from education being a community endeavour in which
young people can indeed 'Go Places, Meet People and Do and
Make Things' – at least for part of their curriculum. Through such
an approach young people are far more likely to develop the agency
not only to be active citizens, but also to be open minded and
outward looking in their personal and social lives.

REFERENCES

1. Scotland's Curriculum for Excellence. https://scotlandscurri-
   culum.scot/.
2. DfE. (2011). Permanent and fixed period exclusions from
   schools and exclusion appeals in England, 2009/2010 (SFR
   17/2011). London: DfE; DfE. (2020). Permanent and
   fixed-period exclusions in England: 2018 to 2019. London:
   DfE.
3. NHS (2022). Mental Health Services Monthly Statistics, Final
   March, Provisional April 2022 - NHS Digital Downloaded
   August 3rd 2022.
4. Skinner, Barbara, Gerard Leavey, and Despina Rothi. 'Managerialism and teacher professional identity: Impact on
   well-being among teachers in the UK'. *Educational Review* 73,
   no. 1 (2021): 1–16.
5. Hopkins, Neil. 'Creating sites of community education and
   democracy: Henry Morris and the Cambridgeshire village
   colleges. A reflection 90 years on from their inception'. *British
   Educational Research Journal* 46, no. 5 (2020): 1099–1110.
6. Facer, Keri, and Louise Thomas. 'Towards an area-based
   curriculum? Creating space for the city in schools'. *International Journal of Educational Research* 55 (2012): 16–25.
7. Celio, Christine I., Joseph Durlak, and Allison Dymnicki. 'A
   meta-analysis of the impact of service-learning on students'.
   Journal of Experiential Education 34, no. 2 (2011): 164–181.

8. González, Norma, Luis C. Moll, and Cathy Amanti, eds. *Funds of knowledge: Theorizing practices in households, communities, and classrooms.* Routledge, 2006.

9. Leat, D., U. Thomas and A. Whelan (2021). Curriculum-embedded Project Based Learning – with real world connections, Newcastle University.

10. Tytler, R., D. Symington and C. Smith 'A curriculum innovation framework for science, technology and mathematics education'. *Research in Science Education* 41, no. 1 (2011): 19–38.

11. Thomas, L. 'Learning about, by and for Peterborough'. (2012). https://www.thersa.org/action-and-research/rsa-projects/creative-learning-anddevelopment-folder/area-based-curriculum/.

26

THE CASE FOR PLACE: HOW WE CAN IMPROVE OUR IDEAS ABOUT 'PLACE' IN EDUCATION POLICYMAKING

Will Millard

PLACE MATTERS!

Ideas Matter. Place Matters

In an ideal world these two sentences, above – banal to the point of truism – would barely need saying. Yet, alas, the world is not ideal and the ways in which ideas about place shape policymaking leaves much to be desired.

This is not for want of political interest or airtime. Indeed, that policy should be 'place-based' has become something of an axiom in political discourse, shaping agendas such as the Big Society and Levelling Up.[1] However, despite the proliferation of place-based policy, wealth and opportunities across the country remain starkly unequal, suggesting these policies have so far been ineffective. But should we throw the baby out with the bathwater, and ditch place-based policymaking altogether?

Absolutely not, and especially not in relation to education policy. In her book, *Leadership of Place*, the academic Kathryn Riley explains why a sense of 'place' – 'where we are from; the place where we live; the place where we would like to be'[2] – is so fundamental to children and young people:

> *[Place] refers to particular localities and to the knowl-*
> *edge that shapes young people's views about who they*
> *are in relation to those localities. The everyday activ-*
> *ities, experiences and cultural practices in their neigh-*
> *bourhood influence how young people see themselves*
> *as being valued in the wider world.[3]*

While measuring the impact of 'place' is not straightforward for a host of conceptual and practical reasons (complexity that is explored in depth elsewhere),[4] high quality studies indicate that where a young person grows up has a demonstrable impact on their school outcomes.[5] In this chapter I argue that evolving our ideas about place has a fundamental role to play in developing better policy.

I am indebted to Dr Sam Baars, whose careful thought and research on this topic has sharpened my own thinking on the matter.[6]

A BRIEF AND INCOMPLETE HISTORY OF PLACE-BASED POLICY MAKING IN EDUCATION

The Not-So-New Normal

Place-based education policy is nothing new. Such policy generally seeks to:

- understand how policy issues are experienced in different places and

- design policies to increase their effectiveness in local contexts.[7]

As Michael Barber explores in his history of late-nineteenth and early-twentieth-century education policy in England, the 1870 Education Act established over 2,500 school boards to provide elementary schools where churches were not already providing them.[8] Then, the 1902 Education Act shifted responsibility from the school boards to 318 multi-purpose local authorities, who began paying teachers' salaries and maintaining schools' premises. Although education remained riddled with arguments about the role of the church in the provision of education, and many schools' dire disrepair, the Acts of 1870 and 1902 represented a shifting of nominal responsibility for education to the local level. For over a century after the 1902 Act, it was the norm in England for education to be centrally funded and delivered by local authorities.

Lupton argues this approach was implicitly 'place-blind', seeking to provide children with the same standard of education no matter where in the country they lived.[9]

History Repeating Itself?

From time to time, central government has also made use of additional schemes to target specific locations to tackle place-based inequalities in educational outcomes. For example:

- *Education Priority Areas* (EPAs) were initiated in 1968. Local authorities identified their most disadvantaged communities, and the policy funnelled additional funding into these areas for buildings, teachers and resources. How local authorities defined 'disadvantage' was up to them. One of the more sophisticated measures – the 'Education Priority Indices' developed by the Inner London Education Authority – was based on pupil-level measures such as eligibility for free meals and area-level measures such as class composition and overcrowding.[10]

- *Education Action Zones* (EAZs) were introduced 30 years later in 1998 by another Labour government. EAZs sought to build partnerships between local stakeholders – local authorities, schools, colleges, businesses, parents and community groups – and attract investment from the private sector. EAZs were established in 'areas of relative disadvantage ... where educational performance is well below average',[11] and the partnerships could adapt the National Curriculum and teachers' pay and conditions.

- *Excellence in Cities* (EiC) launched in the Spring 1999 and saw 'disadvantaged' secondary schools in 'deprived urban areas' in

25 local authorities draw up partnership plans to take steps to improve outcomes for gifted and talented pupils, provide greater to support (such as learning mentors) for pupils struggling with learning, and improving access to and use of ICT.[12]

- In 2009, through *Inspiring Communities*, partnerships in 15 'deprived' neighbourhoods received funding to deliver activities that would 'encourage realistic aspirations' among young people, their families and communities. The programme targeted neighbourhoods 'where low aspirations and narrow horizons would typically obstruct children and young people from realising their full potential'.[13]

- *Opportunity Areas* (OAs), announced in 2016, sought to give pupils in social mobility 'cold spots' 'the best start in life'.[14] A local partnership comprising the local authority, schools, colleges, universities, businesses and charities set individual strategic goals. However, most OAs had goals in common around raising poor pupils' attainment and improving teaching and school leadership.

- *Education Investment Areas* (EIAs) were launched in 2022. These 55 'left behind' 'cold spots' 'where school outcomes are the weakest' will 'target investment, support and action that help children from all backgrounds and areas to succeed at the very highest levels'.[15] These areas contain 'struggling' schools, and the policy offers schools retention payments to help them retain teachers in high-priority subjects. Areas will also be prioritised for new schools.

HOW PREVAILING IDEAS OF 'PLACE' INHIBIT POLICY

The brief overview provided, above, captures two of the prevailing ways in which education policy has tended to conceptualise 'place'. One frames local need in terms of the broad (and negative) labels 'deprived', 'disadvantaged', 'left behind', 'cold spot' and so on. The other singles out particular locations such as 'coastal', 'the North', 'rural' or 'inner city'.

Labels like 'disadvantaged' lack nuance and gloss over the fact that disadvantage comes in many different guises. In London, many young people grow up in poor families and, therefore, face material disadvantage. However, they have other advantages lots of their peers outside London don't: world famous cultural institutions on their doorstep; higher performing schools on average; a 24-hour transport system. The disadvantage faced by a young person growing up in poverty in Cornwall is very different in its nature: young people are less likely to attend a high performing school and will likely need their own car to reach one of the county's beautiful beaches.

Likewise, labels such as 'rural' or 'urban' also underestimate how different young people's experiences may be of growing up in these locations. Growing up in the centre of Grimsby will feel different to growing up in southern Birmingham, for example, yet the term 'urban' lumps these two locations into the same bracket. Growing up in the 'coastal town' of Salcombe, where millionaires drive Range Rovers to pick up oat milk from an organic deli, will yield a different set of experiences to growing up in Folkestone.

Many children and young people living in 'deprived' areas do not face material disadvantage, while many children living in more affluent places face significant barriers to success. Applying such broad labels to places means missing many pupils and families who might in theory benefit from targeted support. This is an 'ecological fallacy': we wrongly assume individuals' characteristics can be inferred from the sorts of places in which they live.

Additionally, *how* an area contributes to educational disadvantage is often 'weakly articulated' by policy.[16] As Baars highlights, while place-based education policies often utilise robust means by which to identify areas in which to target interventions, they are invariably responsive to poor pupil outcomes, rather than the factors causing these outcomes:

> ...*targeting discrete locations takes emphasis away from the shared challenges these areas have in common. This in turn makes it harder to recognise the coordinated national policies that would be most effective in tackling them.*[17]

Over-reliance on these non-specific labels means that place-based policy in education therefore tends to be limited in one of three ways:

1. Sometimes it's too vague. Broad, non-specific labels such as 'deprived' and 'disadvantaged' capture a wide variety of contexts, and many of these do not actually harbour poor outcomes.

2. Sometimes it homes in on specific areas where outcomes are poor on average (such as coastal towns) without identifying the factors in these areas that contribute to these outcomes.

3. It is deficit-focused. Talking about 'disadvantage' and 'deprivation' can help to highlight social, cultural and economic inequities. However, these labels don't reveal anything about local assets that could be leveraged to address these inequities. Historically, and as the examples above show, this has led to the locally implemented one-size-fits-all responses designed by central ministries rather than local stakeholders.

HOW CAN WE IMPROVE IDEAS AND POLICY RELATING TO PLACE?

An alternative approach is to identify area 'types'. This involves identifying 'qualitatively distinct clusters of area'[18] with one or more shared characteristics. While some of the data sources used to identify these areas may be the same as those for the approaches described, above, area types move beyond simplistic descriptions of places being 'deprived', 'disadvantaged', 'rural', 'coastal' or 'inner city'.

This approach acknowledges that young people's outcomes are just that: outcomes. These outcomes are not the defining characteristic of the area itself. Area types are constructed on the basis of characteristics of the areas themselves, making it possible to identify some of the structural, cultural and economic conditions shaping young people's experiences.

Two criticisms can be levelled at this approach. One is that while local factors influence young people's lives, these do not exist in isolation of wider (regional, national and international) social and economic policies. Another is that grouping areas by type recreates the problem this approach seeks to redress, i.e. it imposes an external classification on somewhere and, in the process, skims over characteristics that make it different to other, similarly-classified places.

My belief is that while these critiques are valid, grouping areas into types could nonetheless help to move the dial in how we think about 'place'. This in turn could address some of the fundamental flaws that currently permeate education policy. Furthermore, it would flip how we currently think about place on its head by encouraging us to think more in terms of context and inputs than outcomes.

AREA 'TYPES' IN PRACTICE

'Place Is a Foundation Stone for Social and Social Interactions'[19]

As Lupton highlights, places are both physical and social spaces.[20] A sizeable body of research describes the mechanisms by which area effects are realised.[21–23] These include:

- Institutional resources, such as the presence of amenities

- Norms, traditions and customs

- Perceptions about how a place is seen by people living there and by others.

Baars' research demonstrates how conducting analyses based on area types highlights significant differences in aspirations, school effectiveness and pupil attainment between 'cosmopolitan' inner city areas that are ethnically mixed, and ethnically homogenous 'hard pressed' neighbourhoods on the outskirts of urban areas.[24]

The OCSI's Community Needs Index is another interesting model, focusing on the social and cultural factors that can contribute to poorer life outcomes in communities. The Index covers 19 indicators across three domains:[25]

1. Civic assets – the presence or absence of key community, civic, educational and cultural assets in and in close proximity to the area

2. Connectedness – connectivity to key services, digital infrastructure, isolation and strength of the local jobs market

3. Engaged communities – civic, third sector and community participation of the local population and barriers to participation and engagement.

Using the Index, OCSI has then identified areas that could be defined as 'left-behind'. These areas have high levels of deprivation and socio-economic challenge, and lack community and civic assets, infrastructure and investment. I like this research because it usefully targets areas in need of additional support, but it also identifies some of the causes that have contributed to the areas' struggles.[26]

I have been involved in research in Buckinghamshire that sought to understand the factors shaping young people's trajectories through its education system.[27] This research shows how glibly describing Buckinghamshire as 'leafy' or 'affluent' does little to explain the stark differences in outcomes for different groups of young people. Rather, by understanding some of the different ways in which young people interact with their surrounding neighbourhoods, we were able to generate a series of targeted recommendations about how opportunities for marginalised young people could be improved.[28]

NEXT STEPS

The ideas that underpin place-based policymaking focus too much on the effect – deprivation, disadvantage – and not enough on the underlying causes of educational (and wider social and economic) inequality.

Historically, policy has sought to identify the areas where young people's outcomes seem most perilous. This is well-intentioned and permits the targeting of resources to areas that are most – to use the nom de rigueur – 'left behind'. Yet there are some clear and relatively straightforward ways in which we can improve how ideas about 'place' inform policy. A useful evolution would be to improve our understanding of the mechanisms that sit behind observed outcomes. This would enable us to design responses that address cause rather than effect.

By improving our ideas about 'place' we can improve our ideas about policy.

REFERENCES

1. Of course, historians will argue about the extent to which these agendas have represented genuine, well-intentioned attempts to make policy more responsive to local communities, or platitudes for justifying government decisions that were never seriously intended to do this.
2. Riley, K. (2013) *Leadership of Place: Stories from Schools in the US, UK and South Africa*, London: Bloomsbury.
3. Ibid, p. 18.
4. Lupton, R. (2016) Re-Thinking Values and Schooling in White Working Class Neighbourhoods. In C. Timmerman, N. Clycq, M. McAndrew, B. Alhassane, L. Braeckmans and S. Mels (Eds.), *Youth in Education: The Necessity of Valuing Ethnocultural Diversity*, pp. 233 – 248, Abingdon: Routledge.
5. Webber, R. J. and Butler, T. (2007) Classifying Pupils by Where They Live: How Well Does This Predict Variations in Their GCSE Results? *Urban Studies*, 44(7). Available at: https://www.researchgate.net/publication/32887508_Classifying_Pupils_by_Where_They_Live_How_Well_Does_This_Predict_Variations_in_Their_GCSE_Results.
6. Baars, S. (2021) 'Area-based Inequalities and the New Frontiers in Education Policy', In L. Menzies and S. Baars (Eds.), *Young People on the Margins: Priorities for Action in Education and Youth*, London: Routledge.
7. Policy Lab Blog (2022) 'What Can Innovation Bring to Place-Based Policymaking?' Available at: https://openpolicy.blog.gov.uk/2022/09/28/what-can-innovation-bring-to-place-based-policymaking/.

8. Barber, M. (1994) *The Making of the 1944 Education Act*, London: Cassell.

9. Lupton, R. (2009) 'Area-Based Initiatives in English Education: What Place for Place and Space?' In C. Raffo, A. Dyson, H. Gunter, D. Hall, L. Jones and A. Kalambouka (Eds.), *Education and Poverty in Affluent Countries*, New York: Routledge.

10. Sammons, P., Kysel, F. and Mortimore, P. (1983) 'Educational Priority Indices: A New Perspective', *British Educational Research Journal*, 9, 25 – 40.

11. TES (1998) 'Everything You Need to Know about Education Action Zones'. Available at: https://www.tes.com/magazine/archive/everything-you-need-know-about-education-action-zones.

12. Kendall, L., O'Donnell, L., Golden, S., Ridley, K., Machin, S., Rutt, S., McNally, S., Schagen Costas Meghir, I., Stoney, S., Morris, M., West, A. and Noden, P. (2005) Excellence in Cities the National Evaluation of a Policy to Raise Standards in Urban Schools 2000–2003 – Research Report RR675A, Nottingham: DfES Publications. Available at: https://webarchive.nationalarchives.gov.uk/ukgwa/20130401151715/http://www.education.gov.uk/publications/eOrderingDownload/RR675a.pdf.

13. Communities and Local Government (2011) *Inspiring Communities Customer Insight Research Report*. Available at: https://assets.publishing.service.gov.uk/government/uploads/system/uploads/attachment_data/file/6324/19234914.pdf.

14. GOV.UK (2016) Opportunity Areas, *The Education Hub Blog*. Available at: https://educationhub.blog.gov.uk/2016/10/04/opportunity-areas/.

15. GOV.UK (2022) 'Package to Transform Education and Opportunities for Most Disadvantaged', GOV.UK Press Release. Available at: https://www.gov.uk/government/news/package-to-transform-education-and-opportunities-for-most-disadvantaged.

16. Lupton, R. (2010) Area-Based Initiatives in English Education: What Place for Place and Space? In C. Raffo, A. Dyson, H. Gunter, D. Hall, L. Jones, and A. Kalambouka (Eds.), *Poverty and Education in Affluent Countries*. London: Routledge, pp. 111 – 123.

17. Baars, 2021, p. 78.

18. Baars, 2021.

19. Riley, K. (2013) *Leadership of Place: Stories from Schools in the US, UK and South Africa*, London: Bloomsbury, p. 22.

20. Lupton, R. (2003) "Neighbourhood Effects': Can We Measure Them and Does It Matter?' – CASEpaper 73, CORE/LSE. Available at: https://core.ac.uk/reader/93880.

21. Baars, 2021.

22. Galster, G. C. (2011) 'The Mechanism(s) of Neighbourhood Effects: Theory, Evidence, and Policy Implications', *Neighbourhood Effects Research: New Perspectives*, 23 – 56.

23. Sampson, R. J., Morenoff, J. D. and Gannon-Rowley, T. (2002) 'Assessing "Neighborhood Effects": Social Processes and New Directions in Research', *Annual Review of Sociology*, 28, 443 – 47.

24. sambaars.com (2013) Counter-Deprivational Outcomes. Available at: https://sambaars.com/counter-deprivational-outcomes/.

25. OCSI (2022) 'Left-behind' Areas. Available at: https://ocsi.uk/left-behind-areas/.

26. OCSI (2020) *Left Behind Areas 2020 – Interim Set: Summary Data Set*, OCSI Website. Available at: https://ocsi.uk/wp-content/uploads/2020/12/Left-Behind-Areas-IMD-2019-REVISED-SLIDE-DECK-with-revised-unemployment-slide-Read-Only-copy.pdf.

27. The Centre for Education and Youth (2021) Supporting Youth Transitions in Buckinghamshire: Interim Report. Available at: https://cfey.org/reports/2021/06/supporting-youth-transitions-in-buckinghamshire-interim-report/.

28. Huband-Thompson, B., Baars, S. and Millard, W. (2022) Supporting Marginalised 16- to 25-Year-Olds in Buckinghamshire: Analysis and Recommendations – The Centre for Education and Youth. Available at: https://cfey.org/wp-content/uploads/2022/03/Rothschild-analysis-and-recommendations-v8-final-report.pdf.

INDEX

348   Index

Printed in the USA
CPSIA information can be obtained
at www.ICGtesting.com
JSHW010209300823
47527JS00002B/11